ANARCHISM IS NOT ENOUGH

A NARCHISM

is not enough

~

Laura Riding

Edited and with an Introduction
by Lisa Samuels

UNIVERSITY OF CALIFORNIA PRESS
Berkeley   Los Angeles   London

University of California Press
Berkeley and Los Angeles, California

University of California Press, Ltd.
London, England

First California paperback printing, 2001

First edition published by Jonathan Cape, 1928.
Reprinted by arrangement with Laura (Riding) Jackson
Board of Literary Management.

Additional materials © 2001 by the
Regents of the University of California

Library of Congress Cataloging-in-Publication Data

Riding, Laura, 1901–
    Anarchism is not enough / Laura Riding ; edited and with an
introduction by Lisa Samuels.
      p. cm.
    Includes bibliographical references.
    ISBN 0-520-21394-7 (pbk. : alk. paper)
    I. Samuels, Lisa.   II. Title.
    PS3519.A363A7 2001
    809—dc21

                          99-20038
                          CIP

Printed in the United States of America

09 08 07 06 05 04 03 02 01
9 8 7 6 5 4 3 2 1

The paper used in this publication meets the minimum
requirements of ANSI/NISO Z39.48-1992 (R 1997)
(*Permanence of Paper*). ∞

CONTENTS

Acknowledgments   vii

A Note on the Text   ix

Creating Criticism: An Introduction to
   Anarchism Is Not Enough   xi

Laura Riding: A Chronology   1

THE MYTH   9

LANGUAGE AND LAZINESS   13

THIS PHILOSOPHY   15

WHAT IS A POEM?   16

A COMPLICATED PROBLEM   19

ALL LITERATURE   20

MR. DOODLE-DOODLE-DOO   22

AN IMPORTANT DISTINCTION   25

THE CORPUS   27

POETRY AND MUSIC   32

POETRY AND PAINTING   37

POETRY AND DREAMS   39

JOCASTA   41

HOW CAME IT ABOUT?   133

HUNGRY TO HEAR   136

IN A CAFÉ   138

FRAGMENT OF AN UNFINISHED NOVEL   142

WILLIAM AND DAISY: FRAGMENT OF A
    FINISHED NOVEL   150

AN ANONYMOUS BOOK   152

THE DAMNED THING   187

LETTER OF ABDICATION   209

Notes on the Text   225

Appendix I. Three Commentaries on
    Anarchism Is Not Enough   253

Appendix II. Author to Critic: Laura (Riding) Jackson
    on "Anarchism Is Not Enough"   261

Selected Bibliography of Works by Laura Riding   268

Selected Critical Bibliography   272

ACKNOWLEDGMENTS

I am grateful to the staff of the Division of Rare and Manuscript Collections, Carl A. Kroch Library, Cornell University — and especially Lorna Knight and Margaret Nichols — for their assistance in locating materials relevant to *Anarchism Is Not Enough*. I also thank the Laura (Riding) Jackson Board of Literary Management for encouraging this project and providing access to some of her unpublished remarks. Barrett Watten was an early supporter, James Tyler a genial contact, and Alan Golding gave the introduction a helpful last-minute reading. My deepest gratitude goes to Alan J. Clark, Elizabeth Friedmann, John Nolan, and Jerome McGann for their generous and useful responses to my work on this edition, and to Linda Norton for her faith in and dedication to this project.

A NOTE ON THE TEXT

Anarchism Is Not Enough was originally published in 1928, by Jonathan Cape in London and Doubleday Doran in America. The original manuscript materials were lost in the flight from Majorca in 1936, when those escaping the encroaching Spanish civil war were permitted only one suitcase apiece. (Riding) Jackson's few extant comments on *Anarchism Is Not Enough* consist of private responses to a dissertation about her work, remarks in some private letters, and twelve handwritten pages in the Laura (Riding) Jackson and Schuyler B. Jackson Collection, housed in the Division of Rare and Manuscript Collections, Carl A. Kroch Library, Cornell University. A transcript of these latter pages and edited excerpts from private remarks are included as appendices to this edition.

CREATING CRITICISM

An Introduction to *Anarchism Is Not Enough*

Death is the sanction of everything the storyteller can tell. He has borrowed his authority from death.

Walter Benjamin

The poem is at last between two persons instead of two pages. In all modesty, I confess that it may be the death of literature as we know it.

Frank O'Hara

DESIGNED WASTE

Anarchism Is Not Enough is a manifesto against systematized thinking, a difficult book by a famously "difficult" writer. The scope of its critical imagination makes it the most radical work of Laura Riding's early period. This period begins in 1923 with her first published poem, intensifies in late 1925, when she left America for Europe and Robert Graves, and ends in 1939, when she returned to America. Soon thereafter she renounced any further writing of poetry, married Schuyler Jackson, and published almost nothing for a quarter of a century.

Published when Riding was twenty-seven, *Anarchism* is a kind of early *biographia literaria*. It begins with "The Myth," a defiant genesis tale that depicts poetry as a contrary baby who overthrows the socializing dictates of adulthood. The eleven subsequent pieces move through half-explained attitudes toward music, painting, collective literary consciousness, and the nature of language and poetry, as though Riding is turning over various cards of literary belief. Then comes a fully fashioned critical essay, "Jocasta," in which Riding questions the purposes of canon-making, representationalist fiction, and professionalized literary traditions and argues for the primacy of what she calls the "individual-unreal." After setting out her critical principles in the first thirteen pieces, the book moves into eight final pieces that enact these compellingly strange beliefs. These last pieces engage problems of identity – personal, authorial, and textual – by way of various narrative, familial, and sexual points of view. The book ends with a "Letter of Abdication," a triumphant declaration of its inevitable "failure."

Anarchism's iconoclasm and variety, its swings between intense authority and intensely felt self-exposure, are unique in Riding's early critical work. Two texts she wrote with Graves, *A Survey of Modernist Poetry* (1927) and *A Pamphlet Against Anthologies*

(1928), present more normative approaches to criticism. The *Survey* provided William Empson with some of the close-reading tools he developed in his highly successful *Seven Types of Ambiguity* (1930).[1] Riding's *Contemporaries and Snobs* (1928) shares *Anarchism*'s antipathy toward critical systematizing and literary professionalism, but it is more single-minded, with no creative sketches enacting its beliefs. *Anarchism* might be thought of as the culminant dream of these other critical texts, a fuller realization of their antisystematic mandates.

Of course, an introduction such as this must do some of the very contextualizing that *Anarchism* wants to question, and of course *Anarchism* can be historically situated: it is an important example of unconventional modernist criticism, a criticism which insists on eclectic and subjective processes. Some well-known texts belong to this category of modernism — much of Ezra Pound's *ABC of Reading* (1934) and *Guide to Kulchur* (1938), for example — but it is an unorganized "tradition" by its very nature. It extends into a twentieth-century body of work we might call the Other Criticism, including William Carlos Williams' *The Embodiment of Knowledge* (1930), Georges Bataille's *Inner Experience* (1943), Charles Olson's *Call Me Ishmael* (1947), Louis Zukofsky's *Bottom: On Shakespeare* (1963), Angela Carter's *The Sadeian Woman* (1978), Charles Bernstein's *Content's Dream* (1986), and Susan Howe's *My Emily Dickinson* (1989). All of these texts are self-conscious, at times quasi-mystical, about literary commentary, and all believe that attentive individuals (not just credentialed specialists) have the right to address literary and cultural experience. The language in these works shifts from prosaic to poetic, from critical to personal, refusing to be held to stable definitions. Such shifts are principled features of the landscape of creative criticism: like *Anarchism*, these are critical works by creative writers. Tellingly, while each of these texts can (albeit with difficulty) be individually described, the absence of a common project leaves us little choice other than to group them together as "Other." Individuality *is* their project.

Also tellingly — given that the aforementioned texts are mostly left out of the dominant stories of literary studies — this Other criticism recalls some of the "lost" modernist critics invoked in "Jocasta." Wyndham Lewis, Roger Fry, and Oswald Spengler are at a tertiary level of our literary history, behind T. S. Eliot and I. A. Richards, behind Ezra Pound and even Ludwig Wittgenstein. The "losing" critical side of Lewis and Spengler is characterized by three commitments: to authoritative subjectivity (including the pursuit of value judgments), to interdisciplinarity, and to imagining the critic as a social thinker with the right – even the duty – to address all educated individuals in society, not just those involved in literary pursuits. Although she disagrees with the methods and conclusions of these two lost modernists, and although *Anarchism* is very different from the books they produced, Riding nevertheless takes her cue from their concerns, particularly those of Lewis.

This context bears on Riding's relative non-presence in stories of modernism and on her particular relevance today. It is commonly agreed that from the ascendency of New Criticism until about the 1980s Anglo-American literary studies largely pursued a neo-classical and specialized approach to professional fields and methods. Consider for example one book Riding criticizes in *Anarchism*: Richards' *Principles of Literary Criticism* (1925), which, with intelligence and humor, promulgates methods for "understanding literature." Richards continuously asserts divisions and subdivisions in literary value and popularity, relying on the understandability of critical and aesthetic terms and working to link "the commonplaces of criticism to a systematic exposition of psychology" (3). Limiting the spheres of discussion, Richards crafts a book that succeeds on its own "systematic" terms.

Though many critical texts continue to be written within such scholarly and interpretive limits, in roughly the past fifteen years literary criticism has increased its interdisciplinary commitments. Writers now have more license to explore multiple perspectives: self-conscious subjectivity, for example, has renewed breathing room, and cultural studies validates access to a wide field of commodity and comment. We are giving ourselves more permission to act as human perceivers in a world that contains many different forms of artistic and expressive production.[2] This inclusive scope is reminiscent of the world of Riding's "lost" modernists. In books such as *Time and Western Man* and *The Art of Being Ruled*, Wyndham Lewis ranges from Russian ballet to the Bergsonian time-mind to Gertrude Stein to "God as Reality," exploring multiple disciplines in search of effective ways to think about art, language, philosophy, history, time (and the list continues).

Riding characteristically writes within this large provenance, in *Anarchism* and several other books of her early period, and notably in the major works of her later period, *The Telling* (1972) and *Rational Meaning: A New Foundation for the Definition of Words* (1997). But *Anarchism*'s broad scope differs in a crucial way because its language and analysis are oriented to the *unknown*. Poetry and human beings are "true" for Riding insofar as they are permanently incommensurate with, always on the

other side of, what we might say about them. The
model *Anarchism* provides for our interdisciplinary
age is partly one of generative indeterminacy, a
script for further process. It combines Surrealist
unknowability (though it doesn't mention the Surrealists[3]) with modernist authority (though not in
order to establish a *system* of thought). It proposes
that criticism can be "commentarial rather than
systematic," a discourse of thinking rather than a
record of thoughts, and (as Riding says poetry
should be) "an incentive not to response but to
initiative" (*Anarchism*, 114).

As this interest in the active reader indicates,
Riding wants to provoke individualized human self-
consciousness. In a 1974 critique of a dissertation
about her work, she wrote that *Anarchism* "is concerned with the placing of poetry, the poet, and,
centrally & most importantly, the nature of the person who seeks to treat of main things of being, in
thought & expression from a position of self-
reliance as against reliance upon definitions of
things delivered from socially constructed or philosophically systematized frames of authority."[4] Riding's "self-reliance" echoes Emerson and situates
her book in a tradition of American idealism, setting it apart from the context that led Wyndham
Lewis, the critic to whom Riding most often re-
sponds in *Anarchism*, to fascism. Indeed, the title

itself argues a turn against any such systems: "Anarchism is not enough" because anarchism operates in reaction to the structures of (social and political) reality and so remains within their systematizing orbits. Such "anarchism" is like the Romantic resistance to classicism, or the experimental resistance to tradition: these are reactions to "real," historically instantiated systems rather than self-reliant explorations of "main things of being."

Riding believes that poetry, poetic language, and the fullest human potential can only be achieved in a space *Anarchism* calls the "unbecoming" or, more often, the "individual-unreal." She resists common modernist binaries (classicism/romanticism, abstraction/experience) in favor of this "unreal," which is a kind of synthetic shadow, an invisible syllogistic avatar, of those binaries. Riding insists that poetry has no truck with the real: it is not a cultural artifact. As *Anarchism* puts it, "[a] poem is made out of nothing by a nobody — made out of a socially non-existent element in language" (34). Poetry is unique among human activities because it turns language — the prime tool of cultural meaning and understanding — inside out. It takes language through the reflexive looking glass into uncapturable meaning and a saving inutility. In the critical work of *Anarchism*, as well as in *Contemporaries and Snobs*, Riding protests the conversion

xviii

of the poetic *event* into the poem-urn, of poetic knowing into interpretive system, and of the reader into a consumer in search of an aesthetic delivery system. Poetry needs to be kept out of what she later called "wisdom-professions" if it is to retain its value as an asocial force.

It may seem at first paradoxical, given its non-productive character, that the "individual-unreal" is the place of highest seriousness for Riding. It is the sense of incommensurable self-awareness that human beings possess, the "consciousness of consciousness" (27) distinct from constructed socio-economic identities. It gestures toward the gift of mortality, toward the ultimate "uselessness" of individuals, and therefore toward the perfect *means* of their existence. Poetry, more than any other human creation, can engage this "unreal" as long as it is written within the realm of expenditure, or what Riding calls "designed waste." The true poetic word is an unreal thing made by an unreal individual, serving no tradition of reality. And poetry is a realm for engaging with unknowables, not an historical accumulation of improving points of view. As Riding remarks in *Contemporaries and Snobs*, "No one seems to realize that the destruction of poetry as a tradition would not destroy poetry itself" (141–42).

This remark can of course be read as a rejection

of Eliot's "Tradition and the Individual Talent," and indeed in *Anarchism* Eliot is made to exemplify the "collective-real," a category in which the superior group holds the talented individual firmly within ordering histories of tradition. Virginia Woolf's *To the Lighthouse* is Riding's most extensive example of a second category, the "individual-real." Woolf's book "individualizes the simple reality of nature" (46), presenting the destiny of human beings, however interestingly, as a matter of biological psychology. In Riding's judgment, Lewis is also an individual-realist, insofar as he writes as a citizen in touch with cultural and political world-improvement, but he has some access to the crucial category of the "individual-unreal."

Riding believes that poetry can be saved only if it is written within this imaginative zone, where the writer is neither a superior being nor a member of an organized intellectual community. She sees Eliot and Woolf as exemplary participants in *reality*, either (group) political or (individual) aesthetic; Riding, by contrast, goes in search of various *unrealities*. The way to disrupt the process we now call "the marginalization of poetry" is to embrace this "unreal" realm. To this end, her odd rhetorics and neologisms are not used in the service of logical argument. True to their unreal aims, they slip and alter, and after *Anarchism* she never again refers to the "individual-unreal." In this regard she may be thought of as carrying out the imaginative project of the Romantics rather than the critical project of the major Modernists. She is always personal and always looking for unfoldings of what the self cannot quite conceive. Her novelties are in the service of human and linguistic identity, not critical or aesthetic certainty. Her prose, then, is "critical" in its urgency; but it is imaginative in its reasoning, and Riding knows the latter combination to be impossible.

Like the Romantics — or like the Blakean and Byronic strain of Romanticism — Riding pays the price of invoking a project of impossibility. The informed utopianism of British Romanticism meets the capitalistic idealism of American Romanticism and leads her to a triumphant embrace of "designed waste." Poetry is a "vacuum," a "nothing," the closest we can come in language, our keenest intellectual medium, to *Anarchism*'s ideal. Since "vacuum" and "nothing" are not *destinations*, this ideal is unreachable, as Riding readily admits. An important early passage embraces "failure" as a necessary starting point, a key part of the book's operational machinery:

> The only productive design is designed waste.
> Designed creation results in nothing but the
> destruction of the designer: it is impossible to

add to what is; all is and is made. Energy that
attempts to make in the sense of making a
numerical increase in the sum of made things is
spitefully returned to itself unused. It is a would-
be happy-ness ending in unanticipated and disordered unhappiness. Energy that is aware of the
impossibility of positive construction devotes itself
to an ordered using-up and waste of itself: to an
anticipated unhappiness which, because it has
design, foreknowledge, is the nearest approach to
happiness. Undesigned unhappiness and designed
happiness both mean anarchism. (*Anarchism Is Not
Enough*, 18–19)

Against such anarchisms poetry offers designed
unhappiness, since only in reaching for such failure can we achieve positive "impossibility." Poetry
is "idle, sterile, narrow, destroying," and "[t]his is
what recommends it" (36). Georges Bataille gets at
a similar idea some years later with his notion of
"expenditure" in a "general economy,"[5] and in our
time Kathy Acker has acted out the paradox of
creative waste with even more distraught urgency
than Riding.

Riding's vision of designed waste anticipates what
has become a poetic strength, a way to rescue poetry from its supposed irrelevance. That this way
has developed mostly through figures like Bataille
and attendant Continental theorists speaks volumes

about the frequent inattention of Anglo-American scholarship to some of its own strange poetics. *Anarchism* can help to fill a significant gap in our literary and cultural theory. Riding's effort to save poetry from a Western preoccupation with utility and tradition persisted for another ten years, up until the appearance of her *Collected Poems* in 1938. By 1941 she had renounced the further writing of poetry because it "adumbrated a potentiality that was not developable *within it*" (*Poems* [1980], 3) — because it promised, in other words, a salvation she felt it could not deliver. She turned almost exclusively to her growing concern, articulated at length in *Rational Meaning*, with saving the knowledge of the entire (English) language. Which is to say that she turned from one difficult project to an even larger and more general set of difficulties.

SOCIAL DISAPPEARANCE

Although Riding can be seen as a neglected ancestor (and a less politically troubling one than Lewis) of later interdisciplinary and poststructuralist writers, *Anarchism* never lets us forget its (avowedly) asocial ideals. And though we might associate Riding's work with a radical literary constructivism, she resists the demystifying impulses of much current criticism. She claims that the "accidental quality of reality" (104) is properly secondary, subject to the deliberate and deliberating qualities of the poetic mind. Here at the end of history, she claimed, human beings have access to an *unnatural* state of consciousness that must be cultivated through the unreal features of language. In the spirit of her empowered and apocalyptic hopes, she sometimes called herself Lilith Outcome.[6]

Riding meant her vision of achieved human agency to change the world. In an important way, and as she herself recognized, *Anarchism* takes seriously Lewis's improvement projects in *The Art of Being Ruled* (1926) and *Time and Western Man* (1927). But Riding's vision is not political. She set aside Lewis' civil solutions, and his paranoias, in favor of an imaginative actualization of human beings. In *The Covenant of Literal Morality* (1938), the implacably idealist and anti-political pamphlet she oversaw ten years later on the eve of the Second World War, Riding calls on individuals to follow what might be thought of as a beneficent Nietzscheanism, to be their best selves. The hope of *The Covenant* is that each person will be "morally conscious," and that independent thought and personal responsibility will make the world one that could not dream of war.[7] In *Anarchism*, too, Riding wants to stop the real-world-making groupthink that results in difference and conflict. Anarchism is not enough because anarchism operates with reference to reality-functions, distracting the individual from the unreal world.

For Riding, it is crucial to resist such distractions, to overcome our past connections with nature and history, not only to regain poetry as a force separate from socialized art, but also to interrupt what she saw as the fatalistic Darwinism of the historical sense. As a writer most active between the twentieth century's biggest wars, Riding wanted to escape the dictates of history. She judged that history and the "time-sense" had ended in the same period when Lewis was asserting that "the Great War and the wars that are now threatened are the result of the historic mind" (*Time and Western Man*, 275).[8] And "nature" was no help: Riding resists nature because of its (lonely) individual and (oppressive) group dictates. Human agency need not be subject to any past orders. People, she insists, are "product[s] of the refined disintegration of nature by time," part of "conscious, contradictory nature" rather than "unconscious, consistent nature." She tries to set us straight in this summary passage from "Jocasta":

> Self is poetic self. Nature, mathematical life, is
> the become, the eternally grown-up; History,
> logical life, is the becoming, the eternally
> childish.
>
> The time advocate, whom I shall call the

philosopher, does not see, or is afraid to see, that
the become and the becoming are both mutually
illusory Worlds of reality: that they are self-created
refutations of individuality to which the individual
succumbs from imperfection. He forgets, that is,
that the individual is an *unbecoming* and that the
categories "becoming" and "become" are really a
derivation from him, a historical reconstruction.
Unbecoming is the movement away from reality,
the becoming unreal. What is called the become
is therefore really the starting point of the unbecoming. What is called the becoming is therefore
really a hypothetical opposition to the unbecoming. . . . [Both try to trap the unreal individual by]
making Nature suggest History. This is done by
reading into Nature a necessity and inventing for
the species man, a digression from Nature, an analogical Darwinistic Nature. The necessity of Nature
is then called Causality, the necessity of History,
Destiny. (73–74)

Riding argues that the group mind tries to prevent
the individual — "a digression from Nature" — from
realizing its unreality, its "unbecoming," its unnat-
uralness. The group mind does this by making history analogous to nature, trying to make social
institutions seem inevitable. But once out of nature, Riding says, we should never take our bodily
forms as *either* natural *or* civil things, be they aes-

thetic civilities or otherwise. She can be seen as reacting against both Eliot's literary contextualizing
and the evolutionary valuations following out of
Darwin. She is also rejecting Spengler's claim that
"*Nature* and *History* are the opposite extreme terms
of man's range of possibilities" (*Decline* I, 94). Riding wants to forestall the increasing division of intellectual and artistic life into organizations based
on historical and natural fact — a division whose *re-
ductio ad absurdum*, that history is a temporal analog
of nature, she challenges here.

One way to stop such destructive analogies is to
keep changing the language, to imagine it as "unbecoming." Riding's resistance to a settled vocabulary is related to one of her primary criticisms of
Lewis: "Mr. Lewis feels obliged to organize his unorganized view of wrong, which cancels the potency of his rightness, which is only valid so long
as it is unorganized (that is, commentarial instead
of systematic). So he becomes ... the advocate of
a vocabulary" (*Anarchism*, 42). Advocating a vocabulary, in Riding's view, encourages not only system-
building but also (as contemporary critics might
put it) a narrow subject-position; both in turn can
indeed lead to the ravages of fascism. As Vincent
Sherry writes in his study of Pound and Lewis,
"the radical particularity of the Image underwrites
the autonomy of the Self, a kind of heroic individ-

uality. Antistatist and libertarian as this sign may be, it may serve the designs of the tyrannical, self-authorizing ego" (46).

It is important to see that Riding wants to avoid such a "self-authorizing ego" in *Anarchism*.[9] She resists a stable vocabulary because the truest, poetic use of words unwrites the social self in favor of the "unreal" self. As she puts it: "[w]ords in their pure use, which I assume to be their poetic use, are denials rather than affirmations of reality. The word *hat*, say, does not create a real hat; it isolates some element in the real hat which is not hat, which is unreal, the hat's self" (98–99). These sentences may sound like twentieth-century Platonism, but however ideal it might be, Riding's concept of "self" is not metaphysical.[10] She wants to make language the material key to a dialogue of unreality, in which "the hat's self" is summoned by the languaged human self that speaks it. Riding's self-in-language "denies reality" rather than making up a world within or "behind" reality because it is not *one*self, nor the "hat's self," but the self itself that she wants to sing. A truly creative production is "discharged from the individual, it is self; not *his* self, but self" (97). Indeed, "so thoroughly 'unselfish' is the character of the unreal self that its just conclusion is a sort of social disappearance" (75). Together, the self of poetic words and the self of human beings can scour away their status as "means" and achieve their status as "ends."

A seeming paradox of her belief in "social disappearance" is that Riding wants the creative act to generate other creative acts. A real poem is "a model, to the reader, of constructive dissociation: an incentive not to response but to initiative" (114). But what it initiates is *unreality*. Riding's impulse is thus radically democratic – though it refuses organized social consequences – and dialectical, however critically essentialist or philosophically Heideggerian it might appear. Her world-changing impulses begin with the individual and move to other individuals through the medium of human language acts. A *Times Literary Supplement* reviewer of *Contemporaries and Snobs* saw (with evident delight) that Riding wanted to rejoin the work and the human being.[11]

In addition to modeling interdisciplinary and eclectic criticism, then, Riding provides a text for recuperating authorial and readerly humanities. Self-reference is the foremost aspect of the "individual-unreal," and the unreal self "is without value. It is more than anarchistic; it does not treat individually with values; it supersedes them" (78). She calls on people to remain grounded in their unique identities, as in this passage from "In a Café":

I, who am neither sluttish nor genteel, like this place because it has brown curtains of a shade I do not like. Everything, even my position, which is not against the wall, is unsatisfactory and pleasing: the men coming too hurriedly, the women too comfortably from the lavatories, which are in an unnecessarily prominent position – all this is disgusting; it puts me in a sordid good-humour. This attitude I find to be the only way in which I can defy my own intelligence. Otherwise I should become barbaric and be a modern artist and intelligently mind everything, or I should become civilized and be a Christian Scientist and intelligently mind nothing. Plainly the only problem is to avoid that love of lost identity which drives so many clever people to hold difficult points of view – by *difficult* I mean big, hungry, religious points of view which absorb their personality. (138–39)

Riding insists on a *personalism* that accesses the unreal and refuses to be assimilable to psychological, natural, historical, or group projects. In advocating human agency, Riding is not promoting self-absorption or self-satisfaction, what she calls in *Epilogue* "the suicidalism of mere consciousness" (I, 16). Neither is she promoting practical individualism as it is often understood in America (as antisocial "rugged individualism" or socio-economic

self-promotion). Her version of individual authority is an absolute spiritual imperative, compared to
which the more common Western ideology of personal liberty is a temporal shadow. Riding wants
each person to process the inexplicable continually and so to arrive at a condition (rather than a
conclusion) that can access truth. Given such a
goal, Riding's "social disappearance" most certainly has social consequences.

HUMAN CRITICISM

Riding's rigorous personalism is not an abstract
proposition. She was adamant about using language according to her beliefs and not exactly
gentle with contemporaries who failed to do the
same. *Anarchism* was not the only work in which she
launched provocative attacks against the literary
scene she had joined, after a fashion, after returning with Graves from Egypt to London in 1926.
Many writers in London countenanced their adul-
terous relationship, befriending her as his literary
partner and providing many publishing opportunities for her work. Instead of demonstrating her
gratitude, Riding wrote as she pleased about other
critical and literary projects. Along the way she
(and Graves) offended many, including Virginia
Woolf, whose Hogarth Press had published two
books of Riding's poetry.

Graves joined Riding in the project of literary and critical independence. As he wrote to Eliot in 1927, in an exchange of severe letters which ended their correspondence until 1946: "I have recently come to the point of always saying exactly what I mean in matters concerning poetry: and expect reciprocal activity on the part of those to whom my views are distasteful. When, as will shortly happen, I have no literary friends left, this will provide a natural and graceful end to my literary career. Miss Riding is as little interested in her literary career as I am in mine" (*In Broken Images*, 177). Ironically, the independence so prized by Graves and Riding was funded in large part by Graves's success with popular writing — his biography of T. E. Lawrence and his error-ridden farewell to the past, *Goodbye to All That* (1929), written as Riding recovered from her suicide attempt and published on the eve of their departure for France and then (on Gertrude Stein's recommendation) the Spanish island of Majorca.

Riding is neither the first nor the last writer to refuse gratitude and success. Her severity about individual and literary relationships is the strangely principled result of a special intransigence about language and intelligence. She might well have sympathized with the protagonist of "In a Café," who wanted what was "unsatisfactory and pleasing" in order to "defy [her] own intelligence." Certainly, she never let herself or her compatriots get comfortable, nor did she want other writers or critics "comfortably" to situate her work. As the dust jacket on Doubleday's edition of *Anarchism* declares, "Here is cold and concentrated acid from an individual who refuses to be absorbed." Part of the reason for Riding's exclusion from the general stories of modernism may have been that she was never willing to relinquish the right to interpret her writing.[12] Pursuing the role of poet and critic as a strident and oppositional force was another way of writing this book under the sign of failure. Riding presages contemporary women writers like Veronica Forrest-Thomson, Kathy Acker, and Carla Harryman:[13] the goal is to *speak up*, to make human *attention* the central event of the literary act. Simply to condemn as lapses in critical intelligence the outrageous remarks Riding sometimes makes in *Anarchism* is to miss the provocative purpose and self-acknowledged failings of the book. Riding is not interested in the conventionally moral *good*. She wants to demonstrate what she believes to be *true*.

The remarks that prove most offensive occur within Riding's investigations of identity. These investigations take place in three important, and often contradictory, arenas. First, Riding wants to renounce her own cultural and gender distinc-

tions — specifically, Jewish heritage and female biology — in order to be able to speak to her idea of
the individual-unreal. Second, and paradoxically,
Riding feels that women are in a superior position, largely because their relatively nonpublic, un-
empowered status has given them unique access to
realms of the individual-unreal. Third, and subjec-
tively, she uses extreme statements to express her
position as time-ending "Queen" (see her "Letter
of Abdication") and oppositional female modernist,
one whose will and self-possession outweigh any
external authority. In these contradictions and
concerns Riding is echoed most closely by another
relatively neglected and hard-to-label modernist
writer, Mina Loy.[14]

In a typical example of Riding's provocative critical maneuvers, "The Damned Thing" uses genital
discourse to reject the culture's focus on gendered
and sexual *difference*. She writes, for example, that
"[a]ctive Lesbianism is a form of sexual derangement resulting from the female's mistaken effort
to become sexually equivalent to the male: passive
Lesbianism is a romantic substitution of the feminine branch for the masculine branch in the
forced absence of the latter" (191), and that "feminism is an unnatural preoccupation in woman with
her sexual self" (192). Riding's comments about
homosexuality and feminism are less interesting in

themselves than in what they reveal about the privilege of alienation. She refuses to be sentimental about difference. She believes that women have the opportunity — just eight years after having finally achieved suffrage in America (and ten years after limited female suffrage in the United Kingdom) — to profit from their marginalized status and to stop thinking about it *as such*. For similar reasons, she conflates the fact of homosexuality with the fact of its repressed status, condemning the first in order to criticize the way repression directs attention to homosexual difference.

"The Damned Thing" also rejects professional preoccupation with difference, especially as pursued in psychoanalytic criticism. Riding was no prude, but she deplores the modernist obsession with Freudian sexual psychology and anthropological voyeurism. Particularly in the context of a whole library of books overwhelmed with new talk about sexual deviance and cultural variety (see especially her references to Havelock Ellis, Lewis, and Spengler), even Riding's most troubling remarks are comparatively *enlightened*. Sex, Riding wants to say, is not such a big deal; our preoccupation with it keeps us from reaping the real benefits of newly liberal views of gender and sexuality. It keeps us from seeing ourselves as human beings with *shared* concerns about identity and language use.

The problem of "otherness" recurs in "An Unfinished Novel," in which the character of the daughter seeks to understand the strange speechless sexuality she has inherited from her mother. The problem here is of "the human form, of which my mother being half Jew and perhaps a dash negro, was an exotic and irresistible example" (147). How to reconcile this vaguely sexy story with Riding's censure of sexual preoccupation in "The Damned Thing"? Precisely in recognizing that the problem of sexuality in "An Unfinished Novel" is yet another result of too much attention to human differences. It presents the excitement of violable separateness as maddening and crippling: the sexed woman is exposed on the chamberpot in a voyeuristic nightmare. And she is powerless to come to any *language*, to speak (for) herself.

Problems of human difference and inequality come to a head toward the end of "An Anonymous Book," where dualism itself is attacked. The "Queen," whose imploring adamancy is a kind of noble caricature of Riding, sets aside orders of fascistic difference in favor of a total development of the logics of selves. The figure of the Christian publisher (sounding like Riding's view of Eliot or Lewis) says "[t]hose who think more powerfully than others will create order." The Queen (sounding like Riding) replies "[b]ut this would not be

real order, rather the disorder of a false order created by the most powerfully thinking individual or
individuals of the moment. This would be anarchism, and anarchism is not enough" (184). Such
a logic of identity presages what Riding wrote
much later in "The Sex Factor in Social Progress"
(1963): "[i]t is from dualism, precisely, that human nature needs saving. To be unitarian explicitly – women are that only implicitly, as they are –
is humanness fulfilled. By mutual initiative, recon-
ceiving all their being, their past, their present,
even God, men and women can make themselves
and one another humanly perfect" (*The Word
"Woman,"* 182).

Riding sets feminism, then, within her larger
critique of difference and dualism, asserting the
priority of an all-encompassing "unitarian" humanism. What we might call the general humanities of
Anarchism increasingly filled her prose writings. As
she wrote over sixty years later, "I am trying, here,
to function in the field of human criticism rather
than in that of literary criticism."[15] Much of current feminist criticism can be seen to share, in
some respects, Riding's desire for a "human criticism." Diane P. Freedman posits, for instance, that
"the critical is the autobiographical," and goes on
to quote Sandra Gilbert's contention that "most
feminist critics are engaged not just in women's

studies but in what we might call Life Studies" (190). Riding, too, insisted that her work be taken as a human whole, rejecting piecemeal criticism as an attempt to subdivide her own life study.[16] But despite the resonance of some feminist comments with some of her own beliefs, Riding objected to feminism as an increasingly institutionalized separation of female and male concerns. Riding was attentive to gender differences, and she held to the paradoxical notion — at least in the early part of her writing career — that women are in fact superior to men and shouldn't be caught up in what she saw as the reactive self-justification practiced in feminist writings. In the context of feminist studies, we could call her an anti-systematic, or antinomian, feminist. Her praise for women can be usefully understood with reference to the "unreal" spheres within which women have been (in her view) fortunate, rather than condemned, to live — in other words, with reference, once more, to the privilege of alienation.

Anarchism's rejecting mode is grounded in Riding's effort to eviscerate institutional apartheid. She wants to abolish everything that categorizes individuals and language: the placement of art and individuals in histories and groups, the promotion of authority structures for ensuring that the "best and wisest" rule, the separatisms of gender and sexuality, and the ideal of a "perfect" poetry that turns the poet into the superior keeper of the flame, transmuting human psychology and cultural mystery into "well-wrought urns."

SUBJECTIVE CORRELATIVES

One difficulty of Riding's rejecting modes is that she also makes important statements about literature. Emersonian self-reliance was not her only ideal; Whitmanesque contrariness was every bit as important.[17] She keeps on sounding like a critic who wants to convince us of a particular argument and then turning into a writer who willfully contradicts herself: "I have no philosophical or critical system to advance; I am interested in generalizations that mean something without instances, that are unreal, since they mean something by themselves" (*Anarchism*, 83). Such generalizations are "unreal" absolutes, both unrepeatable and unexportable.

At the same time, Riding lays out some important critical imperatives. For example, she objects to E. M. Forster's notion of characters as representative of human beings. She would never study literary characters as "People" (the title of a chapter in Forster's *Aspects of the Novel*). Characters operate within the liberating restrictions of language, not according to measurements of "reality." Riding insists elsewhere that "[i]n literature people must be measured as words are measured: for their truth, not for their humanistic vitality – for what they are ultimately, not historically" (*Epilogue* II, 2). Her position presages that of our contemporary William Gass, who argues that characters never leave their language and are not limited to representative subjects with proper names, in spite of the fact that virtually all theorists since Aristotle have imagined characters "as living outside language."[18]

Riding's view of character extends into a rejection of the whole representational field of literary realism. The individual-*real* claims that symbols correspond to things in the world; it "insist[s] on the authentic quality of the symbol," thus neutering the symbolic by way of crude analogy (*Anarchism*, 53). She prefers the "false," the linguistically hyperconstructed, to the representationally accurate depictions of life so valued by a critic like Richards. When she writes that "restraint, statistics, falsification, is [*sic*] more accurate than courage, reality, truth, and so truer" (182), Riding is getting at the desirable difficulty of writing ineffable experience rather than representational human "fact." Writing must be restrained and falsifying if it hopes to enact events that we recognize (but cannot, and should not, hope to duplicate) within our own images of thought. She wants to set up what we might call *subjective correlatives*, matrices of words that evoke for each person — writer and reader — an experience of the individual-unreal, the shared but never duplicable sense of a languaged self. The tripartite poetic language Riding promotes in *Anarchism* — that is, the use of "intrinsic," "applied," and "misapplied" senses of words (12) — can, she hopes, help construct such correlatives. Riding's verbal artifices are akin to the happy results of the perspective wars in painting, namely cubism and depictive freedom, insofar as they realize disrupted perspective as "truer" than realism.

Another way to imagine Riding's subjective correlatives is to compare them to the "ratio of fabrication" that de Certeau locates in the eerie worlds of Hieronymus Bosch: "[i]n a painting by Bosch, though one may not be able to explain 'what it means' (and for the very good reason that it attacks precisely that pretension, which nevertheless reappears endlessly), one can analyze how, according to what rules, it is produced. This replacement, too, is characteristic: the *ratio* of meaning is taken over by a *ratio* of fabrication" (60). Both de Certeau and Riding are suggesting something quite different from Eliot's "objective correlative," which seeks a literary equation for a *precise* set of feelings so that the reader will re-experience those feelings through a kind of metaphorical translation.[19] Riding's famous difficulty stems partly from the fact that her "correlatives" are not "objective" in Eliot's sense. Her poems, and much of *Anarchism*'s prose, are instead constructs for entering into events that are linguistically and epistemologically unstable. They cannot feel the same to all readers precisely because their language and syntax refuse fixed meaning-ratios. Riding's subjective correlatives are "ratios of fabrication," linguistic equations for the instability of thought and emotion. They make the reader experience that instability rather than indulging in the comfort of an "objective" human representation.

Why does she write this way? Riding wants her prose, like her poems, to force the reader to pay creative attention. She described the problem of readerly passivity in the preface to her 1938 *Collected Poems:* "readers have been encouraged to transfer their compulsion to the poet: the poet in turn serves as muse to them, inspires the reasons of poetry in them. And the result is that readers become mere instruments on whom the poet plays his fine tunes . . . instead of being equal companions in poetry" (411). She disapproves of Edgar Allan Poe (briefly in "What Is a Poem?" and at length in *Contemporaries and Snobs*) because of his admitted desire to thrill the mass of readers. As Poe writes in "The Philosophy of Composition," he wants to produce "an *effect*" on the reader, "a degree of excitement" that is "*universally* appreciable" (13–16). This goal is reprehensible, according to Riding; it is tantamount to frigging the reader's imagination (as Byron said of Keats' poetry). Riding wants authors and readers to be companions, in response to a situation very much like the disconnect that Roland Barthes describes forty-two years later in *S/Z*:

> Our literature is characterised by the pitiless divorce which the literary institution maintains between the producer of the text and its user, between its owner and customer, between its author and reader. The reader is thereby plunged into a kind of idleness – he is intransitive; he is, in short, *serious*: instead of functioning himself, instead of gaining access to the magic of the signifier, to the pleasure of writing, he is left with no more than the poor freedom either to accept or reject the text: reading is nothing more than a *referendum*. (4)

Riding is more and more resolute in refusing any split between author and reader in *Anarchism Is Not Enough*, which culminates in the direct address of her "Letter of Abdication." Her generative dialectic serves as a model for contemporary experimentalists like Harry Mathews, who writes in paths charted by her collection of metafictional short stories, *Progress of Stories* (1935).[20]

This dialectic also serves, however, as one reason for Riding's eventual repudiation of poetry. Though *Anarchism* promotes poetry as the highest human language, Riding soon concluded that it cannot be appropriately communicative and exact. Poetry cannot correlate; its artistic signifiers are too idiosyncratic. From the mid-1930s on — and particularly in *The Telling* and *Rational Meaning* — Riding turns to prose as the least specialized arena for language, the least *genre*-like, and thus the most effective for human communication and improvement.[21]

ILLUMINATING IGNORANCE

The issue of what Barthes calls "the magic of the signifier" was virtually forgotten in the twenty years after *Anarchism*. In his 1947 study of modernist criticism, *The Armed Vision*, Stanley Edgar Hyman limits the organizing ideologies of modernism to four, identified with their promoters — namely Darwin, Marx, Frazer, and Freud (6). Although none is explicitly engaged, we can extrapolate *Anarchism*'s reactions to each of these critical modes. Riding rejects the determinism of both Darwin (whom she mentions adjectivally) and Marx, eschews the obsessive categories of Freud, and opposes what she would see as the sentimentalizing and male-dominated mythologies of Frazer.

But what about language procedures? With his critical apparatus attuned almost exclusively to "literature," Hyman leaves out any mention of figures like Ferdinand de Saussure and Ludwig Wittgenstein, even though Saussure's work was certainly impossible to ignore, as is clear from C. K. Ogden and I. A. Richards' successful work, *The Meaning of Meaning* (1923). In effect, Riding reacts to Saussure by way of Ogden and Richards, who discuss problems of "the sign situation" akin to (and with reference to) those analyzed by Saussure. Structural linguistics was on its formidable way to prominence with the 1916 publication of the *Cours de linguistique générale*, and literary critics were aware of problems of morphology and syntax as well as of value judgments and literary movements. True to the modernist impulse to purify language, the question "what is literature?" was being debated alongside the question "what is language?" As (Riding) Jackson recalled in a 1974 commentary on *Anarchism*, "Language was not working. What was said hung between people, they took from what they said to one another something extracted from the words – not the words themselves, in their liveness of *meaning*."[22] While she hoped that poetry might solve this problem, Riding anticipated from her earliest writings its ultimate failure to do so. In *Anarchism*'s prose, as (Riding) Jackson also notes in 1974, she strove for what Emily Dickinson called "success in circuit": "I try to surround the truth that I am trying to enunciate by nearly surrounding it as nearly communicable: I don't try to surround it as entirety surroundable for complete statement because I am afraid that my terms of statement might be fed by readers back into the area of conceptual classification." Back, in other words, into systems.

If Riding's comment sounds like a recipe for failed logic, that's because it is. By any constructed logical measure, language is an imperfect sign system; by *Anarchism*'s measure, language is thus in a perfect position to write the "unreal" human. Riding wants here to solve "the problem of language" by writing within its defeats and inadequacies. Attacking the commodification of language, the "merchant-mindedness" of intellectual production, she writes that "[p]erfection is what is unbelievable, the joke" (15). Responding to the problem of scientistic systems, "Mr. Doodle-Doodle Doo" satirizes the impulse that gave rise to a mathematical approach to the study of linguistic meaning (producing such quantified adequacies as "Basic English"). And in her closing "Letter of Abdication" Riding acknowledges the impossible nature of her task: "The point of it is, I think, that we are all in an impossible position; which you handle by making less, myself more, impossible" (211). The direct address of this final piece is by turns magisterial and importunate, and its message recalls the epigraph from Benjamin at the beginning of this introduction. As Riding wrote later, in *Epilogue* III: "but if we give ourselves death – if we *think* death – then we acquire a self-redeeming aptitude for reality" (127). You must live as though you are "dead" and "invisible" if you want to be fully alive. You must write within the penumbra of language, in its "designed" imprecision, to achieve human clarity.

Because poetic language has nothing to do with utility or success, it provides a way to this design. Because it has no measurable *telos*, it is, for Riding, self-sufficient. In *Contemporaries and Snobs*, she challenges the subordination of poetry to the "social offices" of inspiriting message or compensatory pleasure:

> This common misapplication of poetry to supplementary offices is the result of a confusion between an intelligence that we may call concrete, because it regards everything as potentially comprehensible and measurable, and the poetic intelligence, which is an accurate sensation of the unknown, an inspired comprehension of the unknowable. . . . [T]he poetic intelligence [is] an illuminating ignorance in which everything is

more than certain, that is, absolute because
purely problematical. (19–20)

The only absolutes are uncertain absolutes. Riding's thought is a linguistic version of what science
is justly careful to call its "theories" (as opposed to
its facts). In the face of Henri Poincaré's "conven-
tionalism," she might say, we ought to be able to
see that language is only a teleological instrument
when we make it so.[23] It follows, for Riding, that
language is most itself when it is *not* trying to
measure the outside world. Poetic "theories" of
linguistic meaning are not "supplementary" but
central (however theoretical they might be), according to Riding. When she writes of a "language
of complete intelligence" (172), Riding is insisting
that words have quiddity. They are unnatural, dynamic *makings* by unnatural and "unreal" human
individuals.

The "illuminating ignorance" of the poetic intelligence sees the "unknowable" as the form of knowledge most worth pursuing. The unknown *always*
exists, so the pursuit must be continual. Riding
builds the rhetoric of this pursuit into such contrary sentences as "I will argue further against
what I am arguing for" (213). Uncomfortable
guards (this is also a way to understand the resistant difficulties of her poems) must be erected be-

tween ourselves and our confidence that we understand the world, and we should face the poetic "vacuum" as often as we can. Her vision of poetry as enlightened unknowing runs directly counter to Richards' more accepted claim, in *Science and Poetry*, that "[t]he business of the poet, as we have seen, is to give order and coherence, and so freedom, to a body of experience" (61).

For Riding, language does not gesture toward a described world. It is the core of human experience. Truth, always dynamic and theoretical, possesses words, always dialogic. (She articulates this view at length in *The Telling*.) Language is not a unitary tool whose purest use is in "clear" prose and whose other uses are inferior, diluted, or (in the case of "difficult" poetry) obscurantist. If nothing is more real for the human mind than language, language needs both its "concrete" and its "poetic" intelligence. But poetry is not a *solution* to a problem of knowledge. It is a constative utterance that aligns a shared moment: "truth is always laid out in an infinite number of circles tending to become, but never becoming, concentric – except occasionally in poetry" (*Anarchism*, 19). Truth must therefore live within poetic risk-taking, which, for *Anarchism*, always involves failure.

Riding's views of language, then, match her views of truth. Both are necessarily failed, self-contained, and unknowing, but at the same time neither can really "fail" us. Truths in poetic language are incommensurable expressions of the nature of human (un)knowing. In other words: in the pursuit of poetic truth, success and failure are the same thing. Riding states this view fairly explicitly in *Though Gently* (1930):

> Thinking of one thing you cannot help thinking
> of everything. What is expressionism, what is sur-
> realism, what is to make a picture? Truth is not
> one answer but every answer. To make a picture
> is to make a start: a start at the only thing there
> is to do, which is, of course, to think, which is,
> of course, to bring together: to start to bring
> together, therefore: therefore to bring together
> slowly what has already brought together. And so
> I might go on: not by way of saying what is to
> make a picture, or what is surrealism, or what
> is expressionism, but by way of saying what is
> everything, which is by way of telling the truth.
> Truth is not one answer or every answer but any
> answer. (21)

Truth is "every answer" and "any answer," a "thinking of everything." Poetry utters absolute uncertainties. And this impossible frontier of signification is what Riding is after: "the critical reality *failure* is offered to those who reject pseudo-realities of achievement" (*Epilogue* I, 61).

1

If her views of poetic language make Riding impatient with Ogden and Richards (and through them Saussure), she might have been more sympathetic to Wittgenstein, had his work been available to her in the 1920s and 30s. Like Wittgenstein, who claimed that "philosophy should be written only as poetry," Riding is involved in a continuous search for the means of truth (or what is the same thing, a search for the means of continuous truth). Also like Wittgenstein, Riding combines sober earnestness of purpose with mercurial and sometimes playful language.[24] The paradoxical status of the pursuit of truth and the writing of poetry as processes that lead necessarily to failure – since neither produces a static, perfected, final *object* – is noted in many nonstandard modernist critical texts.[25] When Riding imagines truth as a process and not an object, and when she disdains analogy as a false system of thinking, she is not only in the company of a language philosopher like Wittgenstein. She is also carrying forward some of Nietzsche's best projects.[26] One of the frustrations of *Anarchism* is that Riding does not explicitly engage with significant writers who share some of her views – Nietzsche, Gertrude Stein, William Carlos Williams, the surrealists. Despite their felt absence, *Anarchism* moves within comparable orbits of intensity.

NOTHING IS ENOUGH

Poetry appears as another absence here. Although it insists that poems can "occasionally" approach truth, *Anarchism* includes no poetry (apart from two lines misascribed to Lord Byron). One reason for this exclusion is Riding's desire to keep the realms of poetry and criticism separate at this point, to keep criticism from "speaking for" poetry.[27] (In fact, she never uses prose to explain her own interlaced poems as does Dante, for example.[28]) So it remains for us to ask what poetry results from her "individual-unreal," to see how we might fill in *Anarchism*'s absent poetic center.

Riding admired Gertrude Stein's poetry at the time, its willingness to experiment and "fail," though she later repudiated its simplicities.[29] As we have seen, Riding felt that "[p]erfection is what is unbelievable" and that poetry had come to bear "an unnatural burden of faultlessness" (*Contemporaries*, 144) due to increasing literary professionalism. But — despite her ability, in the late 1920s, to see the merits of Stein's poetic project — Riding more often declared that poetry must not succumb to the verbal immediacies that captivated Stein. It must push toward complex intellectual matrices of truth. Accordingly, Riding's poems are extremely and uncomfortably *awake*, full of difficult nouns and syntax and rarely given to lyric trance. They are meant to prick the reader to self-consciousness rather than to function as dream events (for writer *or* reader).

From the late 1920s on, Riding's subjective correlatives only intensify. Consider her final integrated poetry books, *Poet: A Lying Word* and *The Life of the Dead*, both published in 1933. Both books are highly structured, and each structuring device is simultaneously destabilized. *Poet: A Lying Word* begins in winter ("Shrewd Winter, and the Last: The Next Year Stands Still"), moves through the seasons to autumn, and ends with "Failure of Season." In this final part, Riding disassembles the poems — and thus, retrospectively, the book's first four sections — in various thematic and structural ways. This disassembly works to expose poetry's failure to report accurately, to "tell" aesthetically, the truth. *The Life of the Dead* goes further: it works on five interacting levels, whose collaborative multimedia operate to distance Riding and the reader from any originary lyric moment. As her prefatory "Explanation" reveals, Riding imagined illustrations, commissioned John Aldridge to draw them, hired R. J. Beedham to engrave them, wrote the book's ten poems in French, and finally "translated" them into English.

True to its multiple structure, *The Life of the Dead*

can be variously interpreted. One can imagine it as a satire of modernist writers and writing communities.[30] One can also see its structure achieve exponential reflexiveness. That is to say: the French talks to the English, the English answers the illustrations, the illustrations translate the French, and so on, in a continuous loop which does not allow any one element to "solve" the book's puzzle. Riding wants writing to have the self-value and built-in complexity that figures like Barthes and Derrida later claim for it. In this way she opposes her more famous contemporaries, namely F. R. Leavis, who wants language to synthesize textural richness and referentiality, and Richards, who wants words to be typewriter strikes against the ribbon of the self, unimportant except as we can determine their *effects*. Riding writes against both the treatment of linguistic works as unassailable bodies of *mots justes* and the notion that they involve subjective (writerly) expression and (readerly) reception.

In another move to disrupt authorial and readerly privacies, Riding renounces the distractions of the individual voice in *Poet: A Lying Word*, presaging Robert Grenier's famous "I HATE SPEECH" manifesto of 1971.[31] Riding's criticism of speech from the late 1920s to the mid-1930s is motivated by another rejection of difference and dualism.[32] If individuals are isolated by idiosyncracies of speech, they are cut off from the possibility of being understood and of understanding idiosyncratic others. If, however, people can be transmuted into bodies of words (on pages), they can join in a medium of sufficient identity, unimpeded by subjective vocal manifestations. Riding helped inspire Robert Duncan to fashion a poetic world inhabited by such linguistic bodies (consider for example his "woman in the shape of a sentence"[33]). Both writers imagine poems not as private records but as local habitations for sharing the linguistic intensities of the human condition. As Riding wrote in *Epilogue* II, "[b]ooks are by people; but literature is by people only as they are literature — as they exist in the world of words rather than in the world of people" (4).

Riding's later poetic works are forecast by her relatively gentle poetry books of the mid to late 1920s. *Love as Love, Death as Death* (the first Seizin Press production, published the same year as *Anarchism*) lacks the elaborate structuring devices of *The Life of the Dead*. But its individual poems continue the urgent style that won her the attention of the Fugitives, a style that prompted John Crowe Ransom to write that she "tries perhaps to put more into poetry than it will bear."[34] One exemplary poem from *Love as Love, Death as Death* demonstrates Riding's effort to enact the poetic "unreal"

desired by *Anarchism*. "Ode to the Triumph of Bodily Intelligence" strives to access the poetic "nothing" and to embrace its necessary failure, its own
"ruin":

> Season of nakedness not winter,
> Climate of the second moon,
> Bright absence of fleshliness, –
> Into this dreamt antithesis of death
> The bodily intelligence has come
> By wakening and death,
> By a full moon of nothingness
> Sees nothingness, is struck with ague,
> Stands in a great sweat.
>
> The zig-zag green of mountain firs,
> No less than rhetoric of the book turns plain.
> The flesh of engines withers
> Even as the flesh of arms.
> Flesh labours, thought keens,
> The brain is dumb with brute transparence.
> Little there is that is not blemish,
> Death, tired verse, bruised decoration,
> Except this period of ruin and brilliance,
> This fool's age, this hollow calculation.
>
> Here is where victory walks,
> Learned in desolation,
> Gifted with pain, love of decline,
> Hunger of waste and fresh corruption.
> And here it shivers and laments

Weeps over empty space, kisses the rased cities,
Hovers where sense has been,
In a ravished frame, and calls the pities.

Be blessed, passionate intelligence,
In this prime, that has uncovered
The fond geography of ghosts.
You are enchanted against ruin
By that you are but ruin
And nothing but ruin can love or know.

I include this poem because it was published in
the same year as *Anarchism* and serves as a small index of *Anarchism*'s poetic desires. I also choose it
because it is not included in any readily available
collection of Riding's poems, despite its characteristically complex syntax and absolutist rigor.

The "Ode" is a moving enactment of "designed
waste," of the paradoxical coexistence of success
and failure in *Anarchism*'s vision of poetry. The season is of "nakedness" because language is naked: it
does not wear the "kid gloves" that keep Lewis, according to Riding, from knowing his unreal self
(*Anarchism*, 131). The "bodily intelligence" embraces
both the sensate discourses that Lewis deplores
and the thinking discourse that is his only declared interest. Giving sensory facility to abstractions is the poem's way of embodying the human
in language. If language is abstract and humans

are material, one way of joining them is to make language's abstractions material so they can speak (for) the human.

The poem's difficulty also encourages this identity of self and language. The experience of resistance is stronger than the feeling of agreement, and the "Ode" resists normative syntax and clear identity. "You" are a "passionate intelligence," a desolate "victory" in an unreal season – both a human self and a poetic self. The awkward rhythm and syntax introduce temporal rifts between the physical act of reading and the interpretive act of understanding. This rift underscores Riding's rejection of the representationalism of literary language: the "bodily intelligence" sees "nothingness" and does not turn away. It is "enchanted against ruin" by being ruin; it achieves truth by achieving failure. The "calculation" and the "rased cities" of modernism both can and cannot be resisted by the form that begins and ends the poem, by the "bodily" or "passionate intelligence." The languaged self walks through the privilege of historical ruin. In effect, Riding provides an interpretation for this poem in *Anarchism*: "The poem dances the dance of reality, but with such perfect artificiality that the dance, from very perfection, cancels itself and leaves, as far as reality is concerned, Nothing. But as far as the poem is concerned, Nothing is a dancer walking the ruins; character, by the ascetic nature of its energy, surviving gesture" (120).

Through the "dream antithesis of death" the poetic consciousness arrives — where? At "nothingness." Which answers the question implicit in *Anarchism*'s title. If "anarchism is not enough," then what is? Riding tells us at the end of "Jocasta": "Nothing is enough" (132). This answer declares at least three things: no *thing* by itself is enough; no satisfaction is possible in the ongoing, desiring self; and our knowledge of the state of emptiness — of positive "nothing," of the poetic "vacuum" — suffices, is enough. In her "Ode," susceptibility to this "nothing" comes "by wakening and death" to "ruin," and only ruin can achieve love and knowledge. Only Nothing can be "a dancer walking the ruins."

Riding's poetic embrace of nothingness recalls Loy's poem "The Dead" and helps to make place for poems like John Ashbery's "These Lacustrine Cities."[35] Riding moves along a path very different from the lyrical one we might chart from Wordsworth to Yeats,[36] and very much like that chiseled by Blake. Blake's self-broken, universal-voiced poetry of power and failure often echoes in Riding's poems.[37] She too wrote within the paradox that the fall of poetry is also its salvation, so long as it recognizes its fallen state. As she prophesied in 1925 in her first published essay, the poetic risk is a worthy one: "By taking the universe apart [the new poet] will have reintegrated it with his own vitality; and it is this reintegrated universe that will in turn possess him and give him rest. If this voyage reveals a futility, it is a futility worth facing" (*First Awakenings*, 280). It is this futility that Riding faces in *Anarchism Is Not Enough*, arcing from myth to abdication and longing for us to follow her resolutely dissolving trajectory.

NOTES TO THE INTRODUCTION

1. Leaving out any mention of Riding's co-authorship, Empson included the following acknowledgment in the first version of *Seven Types of Ambiguity*: "I derive the method I am using from Mr. Robert Graves' analysis of a Shakespeare sonnet, 'The expense of spirit in a waste of shame', in *A Survey of Modernist Poetry*" (1930, v). An erratum-slip found in some copies of Empson's first edition corrects the *Survey*'s authorship to Riding and Graves. I. A. Richards later reported on Empson's work toward *Seven Types*: "At about his third visit he brought up the games of interpretation which Laura Riding and Robert Graves had been playing with the unpunctuated form of [the sonnet]" (in *Accent*, summer 1944; qtd. in Hyman, 263). In the second edition of *Seven*

Types (New York: New Directions, 1947), however, Empson abbreviates his acknowledgment even further, again leaving out any mention of Riding's coauthorship: "(I ought to say in passing that he [Robert Graves] is, so far as I know, the inventor of the method of analysis I was using here)" (xiv).

2. Consider the examples of Greil Marcus in *Lipstick Traces* (Cambridge: Harvard University Press, 1989) and Avital Ronell in *The Telephone Book: Technology — Schizophrenia — Electric Speech* (Lincoln: University of Nebraska Press, 1989). See also Barrett Watten's recent historical/political/cultural/personal project in *Bad History* (Berkeley: Atelos, 1998).

3. The premiere issue of *Epilogue* (1935) contains Riding's first published comment on (though not her first mention of) surrealism. The comment is general: in "The Cult of Failure," an "exchange" between Riding and Madeleine Vara (one of Riding's pseudonyms), she writes principally of Rimbaud, who is characterized as a (desirable) café. The café Rimbaud interacts with others around it, and with the street, and "the Surrealists are as it were exhaled by the street; they are the result of a sympathetic commingling of The Rimbaud with its associated signs. They lift up first, or physical, immediacy, farcically to final immediacy, with the object of enjoying the sensation of the fall from one to the other. Exaggerated honesty, wilful naïveté, anti-social impudence, defeatist satire — these are stock Surrealist articles" (62–63).

4. From (Riding) Jackson's "Comments on a study of my work – a draft, unpublished": TS transcript, Cornell University Library Division of Rare and Manuscript Collections #4608, Box 95, Fol. 741. Also see Appendix II in this edition.

5. See *L'experience intérieure* (Paris: Gallimard, 1943): "The general economy, in the first place, makes apparent that excesses of energy are produced, and that by definition these excesses cannot be utilized. The excessive energy can only be lost without the slightest aim, consequently without meaning" (233).

6. See *Experts Are Puzzled* (1930) and *Everybody's Letters* (1933). According to (Riding) Jackson's official biographer, Elizabeth Friedmann, Riding wrote in 1970 that she chose "Lilith" because it was "phonetically rather lovely" and she "liked it also for hailing from prehistoric storifying" (personal letter to the editor). In another letter (to Robert Sproat, January 1, 1970), Riding explained that she used the surname "Outcome" "with some joking pleasure in the choice, in which I both teased myself and paid myself the due of recognition of my *great* concern with the terms, the values, the finalities of comprehended experience, belonging to the out-*come* of this human existence."

7. In *The Covenant of Literal Morality*, Riding's rejection of publicly organized action is absolute: "We renounce the political way, and all contentious argument and rhetorical appeal to facts." "[M]orally conscious people" is what *The Covenant* demands: "a

confident, co-operative exercise of moral judgment by such a body – acting as private persons, not as a public society – is the only sure method for bettering the state of the world" (unpaginated).

Members of the First Protocol of this covenant had to agree to five "Preliminary Questions" before they could be privy to the protocol itself. The questions insist that "there is such a thing as essential morality, based upon truth and a love of what is good; as distinguished from relative morality, determined by conditions of time and place"; that "morally conscious people should now seek one another out ... and establish an intercommunication based on a common will to repudiate evil"; and that "as a morally resolved person it is your right and responsibility to work in this self-assured way for world order."

See also *The World and Ourselves* (1938), which lists inadequate "solutions" to world troubles and discards "any solution that has in any way been tried before" (476). Its closing "Resolutions" have much in common with the goals of *The Covenant*.

8. Or, as Riding puts it in *Epilogue*, "The nineteenth century was the last of the historical centuries; it extended into the twentieth century, as far as the Great War, which was the real end of history" (I, 23).

9. The human loss entailed in the misapplication of self-understanding was one of Riding's recurrent themes. As she wrote almost sixty years later, "The

energy of the human mind's innate aliveness to the general, in the substance of the encountering activity of consciousness, has been transferred to processes of self-preoccupation, which are incapable of employing it to ends of truth." See "Twentieth-Century Change in the Idea of Poetry, And of the Poet, And of the Human Being" in *Poetry Nation Review* 14.1 (1987), 73.

10. See Appendix II for (Riding) Jackson's denial of charges of Platonism in these lines from *Anarchism*.

11. The reviewer summarizes Riding's diagnosis that poets are serving merely the Zeitgeist, time and community, and observes that "Miss Riding's excellent remedy for all this is to make poetry again a humanity and the poem the expression of the individual, the person, the poet." See *The Times Literary Supplement*, April 5, 1928: 254.

12. Because we do not really want writers to interpret themselves, nor to refuse readers the right to interpret them. As Jo-Ann Wallace argues, "Riding represents the case of a writer who has been effectively *de*canonized because of her insistence upon being the ultimate referent of her own work and because of her refusal to cede either interpretive or descriptive authority over her own work." See "Laura Riding and the Politics of Decanonization," *American Literature*, Vol. 64, No. 1 (March 1992), 111–26. Wallace's essay does a good job of explaining Riding's chosen critical resistance to any form of self-interested predetermined ideological use. As Wallace summarizes,

"By insisting that her intention be made part of the historical record, Riding effectively undermined the *usefulness* of her texts to [new criticism, feminism, and deconstruction]. In doing so, she ensured (albeit unwittingly and certainly unwillingly) her effective decanonization while at the same time helping to expose the degree to which all critical approaches are (self-)interested. My own is obviously no exception" (120–21).

13. While Forrest-Thomson has the calmest voice of these three women writers, her critical and poetic projects were no less resistant – and clear-minded about their acceptance of failure – than those of Riding and Acker, or more recently Carla Harryman. Riding's 1929 suicide attempt (she threw herself out of a fourth-story window and endured a slow and near-miraculous recovery) expressed her access to intense anguish that Forrest-Thomson fell prey to in her own life. And see Harryman, *There Never Was a Rose without a Thorn* (San Francisco: City Lights, 1995).

14. See for example Loy's "Aphorisms on Futurism" and her "Feminist Manifesto," reprinted in *The Lost Lunar Baedeker*, edited by Roger Conover (New York: Farrar Straus Giroux, 1996), 149–56. Among women modernists, Loy's peculiar intellectual intransigence most often approaches Riding's – which is not to say that other forms of intransigence are lacking in this group: see Stein's insistent sensibility of immediated words, Else von Freytag-Loringhoven's

insistent passions, and Marianne Moore's insistent poetic and editorial rigor.

Though Moore never wrote publicly about Riding's work, in her brief review of *Fugitives: An Anthology of Verse* Moore deplored the "hydra-headed" and "insatiate" *thought* of the book's poetry, the way it was "relentless toward itself." See *The Complete Prose of Marianne Moore*, ed. Patricia C. Willis (New York: Penguin, 1986), 256. Alan J. Clark has located a private letter which Moore wrote to Bennett Cerf at Random House, however, in which she expressed admiration for Riding's *Collected Poems*: "My response as I read, is not perhaps what could usefully be quoted, but I . . . derive considerable courage from Laura Riding's self-determination, and the proof this collection gives that those who refuse to compromise or write what the public thinks it wants, are not obliged to back down" (December 6, 1938, Random House papers, Columbia University Library).

15. Laura (Riding) Jackson, "The Promise of Words," in *London Review of Books*, Vol. 17, No. 17, September 7, 1995, 23. The contributor's note says this excerpt is from a sequence of eleven essays in a previously unpublished work, "From a Notebook of Essays-in-Little."

16. See for example her reaction to Susan Sontag's choice of *Progress of Stories* as one of the "Neglected Books of the Twentieth Century" (*Antaeus* 20, winter 1976, 153–61): "Choosing a single work out of a

life production of size, and discarding the rest . . . is an especially self-flattering form of condescension, and also a conveniently self-protective evasion of critical responsibility" (157).

17. Riding refers to Whitman with affection and respect in her very first published essay: true poets must "press meaning upon life" with a "vigorous idealism"; "[t]hey will have the souls of children and the sense of men. Whitman more than any other was one of these." See "A Prophecy or a Plea" (1925) in *First Awakenings*, 278.

18. See "The Concept of Character in Fiction" (originally published in Gass's 1970 work *Fiction and The Figures of Life*), in *Essentials of the Theory of Fiction*, second edition, edited by Michael J. Hoffman and Patrick D. Murphy (Durham: Duke University Press, 1996). Gass continues: "Characters are those primary substances to which everything else is attached. . . . A symbol like the cross can be a character. An idea or a situation . . . , an obsessive thought, a decision (Zeno's, for example, to quit smoking), a passion, a memory, the weather, Gogol's overcoat – anything, indeed, which serves as a fixed point, like a stone in a stream or that soap in Bloom's pocket, functions as a character" (176–77).

19. As Eliot puts it in his 1919 essay "Hamlet and His Problems": "The only way of expressing emotion in the form of art is by finding an 'objective correlative'; in other words, a set of objects, a situation, a chain of events which shall be the formula of that

particular emotion; such that when the external facts, which must terminate in sensory experience, are given, the emotion is immediately evoked." See *Selected Essays, 1917–1932* (New York: Harcourt Brace, 1932), 124–25. Eliot is of course following Tolstoy's formula for art: "To evoke in oneself a sensation which one has experienced before, and having evoked it in oneself, to communicate this sensation in such a way that others may experience the same sensation." See *What Is Art?* (1897), section V.

20. Mathews wrote an excellent review essay on Riding's *Progress of Stories* (reprinted in 1982) for *The New York Review of Books*. "At the end of each [story]," he writes, "we cannot be sure of what has finally happened; and yet, while it is happening, there is no doubt about it. Each story is perfectly clear and perfectly inconclusive." See "Queen Story," reprinted in *Immeasurable Distances* (Venice, California: Lapis, 1991), 130.

   Mathews is not the only contemporary experimental writer to respond to Riding. "Language" poets also find her poetry of knowledge a sympathetic ancestor to their self-conscious cultural projects. See especially the work of Charles Bernstein, Carla Harryman, and Barrett Watten.

21. As Graves puts it in *Epilogue*, speaking for himself and his "fellow-poets": "[I]n the poetic material of the last three centuries, we felt, a gradual decrease in universality had taken place; so that more and more of our thought (poets' thought) had become

private, and hence speculative rather than poetic"
(III, 121). By the time of *Rational Meaning*, (Riding)
Jackson is more absolute: "Where language is converted into the mere instrument of an art, it loses
its virtue as the expressive instrument of humanity"
(23–24).

22. From Laura (Riding) Jackson, "Three Commentaries on *Anarchism Is Not Enough*" (1974). Transcribed
from the Laura (Riding) Jackson and Schuyler B.
Jackson Collection, Division of Rare and Manuscript Collections, Carl A. Kroch Library, Cornell
University, #4608, Box 94, Fol. 711. See Appendix I
in this edition.

23. In *La science et l'hypothese* (1902), Poincaré writes of
the "conventions" of Euclidean geometry: "*the axioms
of geometry . . . are only definitions in disguise.*" Quoted
in Sanford Schwartz, *The Matrix of Modernism: Pound,
Eliot, and Early Twentieth-century Thought.* (Princeton:
Princeton University Press, 1985), 15–16.

24. Riding would have disapproved of Wittgenstein's
analogy of language use with "games," possibly for
reasons akin to those advanced by Roy Harris. Harris has two main objections to the "games" analogy
(used by both Saussure and Wittgenstein): first,
games are not relevant to reality in the way that
language is (language *is* reality, insofar as it expli-
cates daily life); and second, neither Saussure nor
Wittgenstein dealt well with the matter of linguistic
change, and "how much variation is compatible with
the notion that the players are playing the same

game?" See *Language, Saussure, and Wittgenstein: How to Play Games with Words* (London: Croom Helm, 1988), 77–92.

25. Such as, for example, Gertrude Stein's praise for "outlaws" (that become "classics"). See her "Composition as Explanation" in *Selected Writings of Gertrude Stein*, edited by Carl Van Vechten (New York: Vintage, 1962), 512–23. Riding would certainly have seen this Stein essay, which was published in 1926 by Hogarth Press (London). See also William Carlos Williams' prologue to "Kora in Hell," reprinted in *Imaginations* (New York: New Directions, 1970): "By the brokenness of his composition the poet makes himself master of a certain weapon which he could possess himself of in no other way" (16).

26. See for example "On Truth and Lies in an Extra-Moral Sense" (1873), in which Nietzsche disdains analogy ("equating what is unequal") and the "worn out" dead metaphors of "truth." Reprinted in *The Portable Nietzsche*, edited by Walter Kaufmann (New York: Viking, 1954), 42–47.

Riding wrote critically of Nietzsche in the first issue of *Epilogue* (in an essay penned, she notes, "*before the Nazi revolution*"): "In other countries Nietzsche is always the watchword of adolescent virility. In Germany he persists as the unofficial prophet of human apotheosis" (96).

27. Ron Silliman articulates this problem of the critical tradition establishing itself as a necessary transla-

tion for poetry. Sounding like a Marxist version of Riding, he writes: "A history of literary *criticism* could be written, identifying its origins also within the poem, its exteriorizing serialization and the resolution of its subsequent crisis through state subsidy by its implantation into the university structure, a process of bureaucratization through which writing is transformed into the canon of Literature. Such a history would begin with a definition of the function of literary criticism as the separation of the self-consciousness of the activity of the poem from the poem itself." See *The New Sentence* (New York: Roof, 1977), 15.

28. In the *Convivio* and in *La Vita Nuova*. Some twentieth-century poets rendered prose interpretations of their poems as well, of course: two examples are William Empson, in his 1955 *Collected Poems*, and John Crowe Ransom, in the "Sixteen Poems in Eight Pairings" section of the third edition of his *Selected Poems*.

Riding's *Though Gently* does combine prose and poetry, but not programmatically. It reads as a kind of abstract and severe *Spring and All*. The inclusion of poetry in the 1930s *Epilogue* project is of a different order: *Epilogue* is a communal "work of general criticism" (as described in a note facing the title-page of *The World and Ourselves*), concerned with much else besides literature.

29. See especially her appreciation of Stein, "The New Barbarism, And Gertrude Stein," originally published in *transition* (1927) then reprinted, in variant

forms, in *A Survey of Modernist Poetry* and *Contemporaries and Snobs*. Riding wrote this piece in response to Eliot's attacking review of Stein.

Stein's *An Acquaintance with Description* was the second book printed by Riding and Graves' new Seizin Press, in 1929. In a letter to Hugh Ford in 1971, Riding wrote that "despite there being strong differences between Gertrude Stein's and [Riding's] own conceptions of the functions of language and 'the spiritual significances of humanness,' and an awareness in her of a destructive purpose in Gertrude Stein's use of words (to have language on the page and yet nothingness), she read into this wordplay a therapeutic intention and potential." See *Published in Paris: American and British Writers, Printers, and Publishers in Paris, 1920–1939* (New York: Macmillan, 1975), 389. Forty years earlier, Riding had written more harshly in *Epilogue* II about "'automatic' literature, consisting of records of experience without explanation – experience that cannot be explained because it is meaningless: fatal, helpless, convulsive reactions of consciousness. This literature confesses not merely limitation, but innate human stupidity. The best that can be said of Gertrude Stein is that she is the prophet of this literature. It has been her function to display truth as the unintelligible to the stupid" (16–17). Riding's earlier gentleness with Stein was presumably due to her admiration for Stein's attention to the power of *words*. It may also have been due to the friendship between the two women, which seems to have been at its peak from 1928 to 1930. See also (Riding) Jackson's essay "The Word-Play of Gertrude Stein," in *Critical Essays on Gertrude Stein*, ed. Michael J. Hoffman (Boston: G. K. Hall, 1986), 240–60.

30. As Jerome McGann does in *Black Riders*, 131–34.

31. See Robert Grenier, "On Speech." Reprinted in *In the American Tree*, edited by Ron Silliman (Orono: National Poetry Foundation, 1986), 496–97. Wyndham Lewis doesn't go so far, but he certainly finds speech weak next to the printed word: "Nothing you could *say* would ever be heard by anybody, whatever the value of your words. But . . . the *printed* word can still reach the mind, without having first to pass through an atmosphere shattered with cries" (*The Enemy* 2, xi–xii).

32. Compare for example her remarks about language and speech in *Epilogue* with her positive claims for the truthful possibilities of "the open ground of human speaking" in *The Telling*. In 1936 Riding wrote that the "purity" of English "is a consciousness of the impurities" of speech, and that "Speech has grammar, a convenience of sequence for words used in capricious living senses; language has relation – an internal grammar in which the living senses are reconciled" (*Epilogue* II, 111).

33. Duncan mentioned his interest in Riding's work more than once. The epigraph to his *Medieval Scenes* (1950) reads: "Upon the wall of her bed chamber, so the legend goes, the poetess Laura Riding had

inscribed in letters of gold: GOD IS A WOMAN."
(Riding) Jackson's biographer, Elizabeth Friedmann,
notes in personal correspondence with me that this
"legend" is indeed just that. Perhaps in reaction to
such legends, Riding made the following comment
in 1972: "I conceived of women . . . as agency of
the intrinsic unity-nature of being, and knew myself
as of the personality of woman – as of this identity:
and I endeavoured to make poems include ex-
pressly the sense of this as it was actively present in
me. But neither in nor out of my poems have I de-
graded my seriousness about the nature of woman,
and of poetry, with such goddess notioning as that
into which my thought in and out of my poems –
borrowed, as such things are called – has been mis-
shaped" (*Poems* [1980], 418).

34. Ransom wrote to Graves about Riding in September 1925: "She is a brilliant young woman, much
more so in her prose and conversation even than
in her verse. . . . She has had a remarkable career –
up from the slums, I think, much battered about as
a kid, and foreign (perhaps Polish Jew?) by birth.
English is not native to her, nor is the English tradition, greatly to her mortification. As a fact, she
cannot to save her life, as a general thing, achieve
her customary distinction in the regular verse
forms. And she tries perhaps to put more into poetry than it will bear." See Robert Graves, *In Broken
Images*, 162. As O'Prey notes (360), Riding was not
in fact born in the slums.

35. Ashbery names Riding as one of the three "writers who most formed my language as a poet" (the other two are "[t]he early Auden" and Wallace Stevens). See *The Poets of the New York School*, ed. John Bernard Myers (Philadelphia: Graduate School of Fine Arts, 1969), 29.

36. In the career-making position of editing the *Oxford Book of Modern Verse* in 1936, Yeats refused to carry the work of James Reeves, one of Riding's poetic followers. Yeats explains his view in a letter to Lady Dorothy Wellesley: "I wrote today to Laura Riding, with whom I carry on a slight correspondence, that her school was too thoughtful, reasonable & truthful, that poets were good liars who never forgot that the Muses were women who liked the embrace of gay warty lads. I wonder if she knows that warts are considered by the Irish peasantry a sign of sexual power?" See *Letters on Poetry from W. B. Yeats to Dorothy Wellesley* (1940), 69, as quoted in Mark Jacobs and Alan Clark, "The Question of Bias: Some Treatments of Laura (Riding) Jackson," *Hiroshima Studies in English Language and Literature*, Vol. 21 (1976), 4.

37. This echoing occurs not simply, nor perhaps most compellingly, in Riding's (comparatively) frequently cited poem "The Tiger" (see *Poems* [1980], 64–67). Blake's poetic visions, his belief in the "true man," his rejection of systematization and repression, and his emphatic, often awkward, ever-changing iteration of human and divine power and error, all have

echoes in Riding's energetic visions. *The Life of the Dead*, for example, is strongly reminiscent of Blake's prophetic works, particularly the *Four Zoas* and *The First Book of Urizen*. Compare for example the first poem in *The Life of the Dead* ("The Dry Heart") with *The First Book of Urizen*, chapter V, verses 7 and 8. Also compare Blake's named beings (Urizen, Los, and so on) with Riding's figures (Unidor, Romanzel, Mortjoy, and Amulette).

WORKS CITED

Barthes, Roland. *S/Z*. Tel Quel, 1970. Translated by Richard Miller. London: Cape, 1975.

de Certeau, Michel. *The Mystic Fable.* Vol. I: *The Sixteenth and Seventeenth Centuries.* Translated by Michael B. Smith. Chicago: University of Chicago Press, 1992.

Empson, William. *Seven Types of Ambiguity.* 1930; reprint, New York: New Directions, 1947.

Freedman, Diane P. "The Creatively Critical Voice." *"Turning the Century": Feminist Theory in the 1990s.* Edited by Glynis Carr. Lewisburg: Bucknell University Press, 1992.

Graves, Robert. *In Broken Images: Selected Letters of Robert Graves, 1914–1946.* Edited by Paul O'Prey. London: Hutchinson, 1982.

Hyman, Stanley Edgar. *The Armed Vision: A Study in the Methods of Modern Literary Criticism.* New York: Knopf, 1948.

Lewis, Wyndham. *The Art of Being Ruled.* 1926; reprint, Santa Rosa: Black Sparrow, 1989.

———. *Time and Western Man.* 1927; reprint, Boston: Beacon, 1957.

McGann, Jerome. *Black Riders: The Visible Language of Modernism.* Princeton: Princeton University Press, 1993.

Ogden, C. K., and I. A. Richards. *The Meaning of Meaning: A Study of the Influence of Language upon Thought and of the Science of Symbolism.* 1923; New York: Harcourt Brace, 1925.

Poe, Edgar Allan. "The Philosophy of Composition." 1846; reprint, in *Edgar Allan Poe: Essays and Reviews,* 13–25. New York: Library of America, 1984.

Richards, I. A. *Principles of Literary Criticism.* 1925; reprint, New York: Harcourt Brace, 1934.

———. *Science and Poetry.* 1926; reprint, London: Kegan Paul, 1935.

Riding, Laura. *Anarchism Is Not Enough.* London: Cape; New York: Doubleday, 1928.

———. *Collected Poems.* London: Cassell; New York: Random House, 1938.

———. *Contemporaries and Snobs.* New York: Doubleday Doran, 1928; reprint, St. Clair Shores: Scholarly Press, 1971.

———. *The Covenant of Literal Morality.* London: Seizin, 1938.

——— [as Laura (Riding) Jackson]. *First Awakenings: The Early Poems of Laura Riding.* Manchester: Carcanet; New York: Persea, 1992.

————. *The Poems of Laura Riding: A New Edition of the 1938 Collection*. Manchester: Carcanet; New York: Persea, 1980.

————. *Though Gently*. Deya: Seizin, 1930.

————. *The Word "Woman" and Other Related Writings*. Edited by Elizabeth Friedmann and Alan J. Clark. New York: Persea, 1993.

Riding, Laura, and Schuyler B. Jackson. *Rational Meaning: A New Foundation for the Definition of Words*. Edited by William Harmon. Introduction by Charles Bernstein. Charlottesville: University Press of Virginia, 1997.

Sherry, Vincent. *Ezra Pound, Wyndham Lewis, and Radical Modernism*. New York: Oxford University Press, 1993.

Spengler, Oswald. *The Decline of the West*. 2 vols. Translated by Charles Francis Atkinson. New York: Knopf, 1926.

LAURA RIDING
A Chronology

1901   January 16, born Laura Reichenthal in New York City.

   Raised in Manhattan and in Brooklyn where she attended Girls' High School. Her mother's parents were German Jewish and Dutch immigrants; her father was a Jewish immigrant from Galicia (Austro-Poland) who worked in tailoring and other trades and was active in socialist causes. She had a half-sister, Isabel, six years older than she. A brother, Robert, was born eight years after Laura.

1916   Renounces her father's political ambitions; they quarrel, and she moves in with Isabel.

1918   Leaves Brooklyn to attend Cornell University on scholarship.

1920   November: marries Louis Gottschalk, a history instructor at Cornell, and changes her name to Laura Riding Gottschalk.

1921   Spring: Laura finishes her junior year at Cornell.

   Autumn: the Gottschalks move to Urbana, Illinois, where Louis has a teaching position.

Laura takes courses at Urbana but never earns a degree.

1923 The Gottschalks move to Louisville, Kentucky, where Louis has a position in the history department at the University of Louisville.

The Fugitive magazine publishes Laura's poem "Dimensions."

1924 February: meets Allen Tate.
After spending the summer in Ithaca, Laura returns to Louisville in the fall and works on behalf of *The Fugitive*, raising funds.

November: Laura receives the Nashville Poetry Prize for the best poem published in *The Fugitive*. Visits Nashville to meet other members of the Fugitives.

December: hospitalized for myocarditis.

1925 May: marriage with Gottschalk dissolved.
Laura visits California for the summer then spends the fall in Greenwich Village, working for a publishing firm and socializing with Tate, Hart Crane, Kenneth Burke, and others.
December: leaves New York for England at the invitation of Robert Graves.

1926 January: accompanies Graves to Egypt, along with his wife Nancy Nicholson and their four children. Graves assumes a professorship at the University of Cairo.

June: they all return to London. Laura's first book of poems, *The Close Chaplet*, is published.

She soon drops her married name and calls herself Laura Riding.

September: Riding and Graves go alone to Vienna, where she begins work on *Contemporaries and Snobs*. The next three years are very productive for Riding and Graves, in both individual and collaborative work.

1927   January: Riding and Graves return to England.

May: they move in together and establish the Seizin Press. Their influential collaboration, *A Survey of Modernist Poetry*, is published by Heinemann.

1928   *Anarchism Is Not Enough*, and a collaborative book with Graves, *A Pamphlet Against Anthologies*, are published by Jonathan Cape. *Love as Love, Death as Death* (poems) is published by their Seizin Press.

1929   April: following personal crises among Riding, Graves, and Geoffrey Phibbs (an Irish writer who had joined their literary circle), Riding drinks poison and jumps out of a four-story window, sustaining severe spine damage. A near-full recovery follows.

October: Riding and Graves leave England for the Spanish island of Majorca, eventually settling in the village of Deya.

1930–36 Very productive and largely happy years for Riding and Graves. They carry out collaborative work, notably the three volumes of *Epilogue*

3

(1935–37), with a series of writers and artists who came to visit or live temporarily on Majorca. Riding's poetry books *Poems: A Joking Word*, *Twenty Poems Less*, and *Though Gently* appear in 1930. Her final integrated poetry books, *Poet: A Lying Word* and *The Life of the Dead*, are published in 1933, and her principal collection of short stories, *Progress of Stories*, is published in 1935.

1936   August: Riding and Graves flee Majorca and the Spanish civil war. For the next three years they live mostly in England but also in Switzerland and France.

1939   April: Riding returns to America for the first time since 1925. Graves accompanies her but returns to England in August. They never meet again. Also in April, Riding meets Schuyler B. Jackson, a New Jersey-born poetry editor for *Time* magazine who had written a positive review of Riding's *Collected Poems*. Riding stays with Jackson, his wife, and their four children on their Pennsylvania farm. By autumn, Riding and Jackson are living together, alternately in New York and in Pennsylvania.

1941   June: Riding marries Jackson. Around this time, Riding renounces the further writing of poetry. Apart from a 1942 piece on synonymy (written with Jackson) and an 1962 introduction to a radio broadcast, Riding publishes no new work between 1939 and 1963.

4

CHRONOLOGY

1943   February: Riding visits California to see her
        mother and brother for the first time in almost
        twenty years. Moves with Jackson to Wabasso,
        Florida. There they establish and run a fruit
        shipping business until 1950. They also work
        for decades on a dictionary project that devel-
        ops into *Rational Meaning*.

1968   July: death of Schuyler Jackson.

1970   *Selected Poems, in Five Sets*, is published in
        England.

1972   Publishes *The Telling*, a prose treatment of "the
        Personal Basis of Truth," under the name Laura
        (Riding) Jackson.

1968–1991   From Wabasso, (Riding) Jackson becomes
        active again in the publishing and literary
        world, writing hundreds of letters over the years
        to scholars and other writers. In 1975, *Chelsea*
        devotes an issue (35) to her work, and in 1982,
        The Dial Press issues an expanded edition of
        Progress of Stories. In 1973, the Guggenheim
        Foundation assists her with grant money for
        Rational Meaning; in 1979, the National Endow-
        ment for the Arts awards her a fellowship to
        write her memoirs (titled *Praeterita*, and still
        unpublished).

1991   Awarded the Bollingen Prize for poetry.
        September 2: (Riding) Jackson dies. Her ashes
        are buried in Wabasso.

5

ANARCHISM IS NOT ENOUGH

THE MYTH

WHEN the baby is born there is no place to put it: it is born, it will in time die, therefore there is no sense in enlarging the world by so many miles and minutes for its accommodation. A temporary scaffolding is set up for it, an altar to ephemerality – a permanent altar to ephemerality. This altar is the Myth. The object of the Myth is to give happiness: to help the baby pretend that what is ephemeral is permanent. It does not matter if in the course of time he discovers that all is ephemeral: so long as he can go on pretending that it is permanent he is happy.

As it is not one baby but all babies which are laid upon this altar, it becomes the religious duty of each to keep on pretending for the sake of all the others, not for himself. Gradually, when the baby grows and learns why he has been placed on the altar, he finds that he is not particularly interested in carrying on the pretence, that happiness and unhappiness are merely an irregular succession and grouping of moments in him between his birth and his death.

9

Yet he continues to support the Myth for others' sake, and others continue to support it for his. The stronger grows the inward conviction of the futility of the Myth, the stronger grows the outward unity and form of the Myth. It becomes the universal sense of duty, the ethics of abstract neighbourliness. It is the repository for whatever one does without knowing why; it makes itself the why. Once given this function through universal misunderstanding, it persists in its reality with the perseverance of a ghost and continues to demand sacrifices. It is indifferent what form or system is given to it from this period to that, so long as it be given *a* form and *a* system by which it may absorb and digest every possible activity; and the grown-up babies satisfy it by presenting their offerings as systematized parts of a systematized whole.

The Myth may collapse as a social whole; yet it continues by its own memory of itself to impose itself as an æsthetic whole. Even in this day, when the social and historical collapse of the Myth is commonly recognised, we find poets and critics with an acute sense of time devoting pious ceremonies to the æsthetic vitality of the Myth, from a haunting sense of duty which they call classicism. So this antiquated belief in truth goes on, and we continue to live. The Myth is the art of living. Plato's censorship of poets in the interests of the young sprang from a realization of the fact that poetry is in opposition to the truth of the Myth: I do not think he objected to poetry for the old, since they were nearly through with living.

Painting, sculpture, music, architecture, religion, philosophy, history and science – these are essentially of the Myth. They have technique, growth, tradition, universal significance (truth); and there is also a poetry of the Myth, made by analogy into a mythological activity. Mythological activities glorify the sense of duty, force on the individual a mathematical exaggeration of his responsibilities.

Poetry (praise be to babyhood) is essentially not of the Myth. It is all the truth it knows, that is, it knows nothing. It is the art of not living. It has no system, harmony, form, public significance or sense of duty. It is what happens when the baby crawls off the altar and is 'Resolv'd to be a very contrary fellow' – resolved not to pretend, learn to talk or versify. Whatever language it uses it makes up as it goes and immediately forgets. Every time it opens its mouth it has to start all over again. This is why it remains a baby and dies (praise be to babyhood) a baby. In the art of not living one is not ephemerally permanent but permanently ephemeral.

ல

Because most people are not sufficiently employed in themselves, they run about loose, hungering for employment, and satisfy themselves in various supererogatory occupations. The easiest of these occupations, which have all to do with making things already made, is the making of people: it is called the art of friendship. So one finds oneself surrounded with numbers of artificial selves contesting the authenticity of the original self; which, forced to become a competitive self, ceases to be the original self, is, like all the others, a creation. The person, too, becomes a friend of himself. *He* no longer exists.

∽

Words have three historical levels. They may be true words, that is, of an intrinsic sense; they may be logical words, that is, of an applied sense; or they may be poetical words, of a misapplied sense, untrue and illogical in themselves, but of supposed suggestive power. The most the poet can now do is to take every word he uses through each of these levels, giving it the combined depth of all three, forcing it beyond itself to a death of sense where it is at least safe from the perjuries either of society or poetry.

LANGUAGE AND
LAZINESS

LANGUAGE is a form of laziness; the word is a compromise between what it is possible to express and what it is not possible to express. That is, expression itself is a form of laziness. The cause of expression is incomplete powers of understanding and communication: unevenly distributed intelligence. Language does not attempt to affect this distribution; it accepts the inequality and makes possible a mathematical intercourse between the degrees of intelligence occurring in an average range. The degrees of intelligence at each extreme are thus naturally neglected: and yet they are obviously the most important.

Prose is the mathematics of expression. The word is a numerical convenience in which the known and the unknown are brought together to act as the meeting-place of the one who knows and the one who does not know. The prose word accomplishes no redistribution of intelligence; it merely declares the inequality, and so even as expression it has no reality, it is an empty cipher.

Poetry is an attempt to make language do more than express; to make it work; to redistribute intelligence by means of the word. If it succeeds in this the problem of communication disappears. It does not treat this problem as a matter of mathematical distribution of intelligence between an abstract known and unknown represented in a concrete knower and not-knower. The distribution must take place, if at all, within the intelligence itself. Prose evades this problem by making slovenly equations which always seem successful because, being inexact, they conceal inexactness. Poetry always faces, and generally meets with, failure. But even if it fails, it is at least at the heart of the difficulty, which it treats not as a difficulty of minds but of mind.

THIS PHILOSOPHY

THIS philosophy, this merchant-mindedness: how much have we here? what sum? And of what profit? Somewhere, in the factories of reality, all this has been produced which now floods the market of wisdom, awaiting its price-ticket. What is science? yard-measure and scale to philosophy, expert-accountant, bank clerk. What is poetry? miserable, ill-fed, underpaid, ununionized labourer, pleased to oblige, grateful for work, flattering himself that poverty makes him an aristocrat.

∽

Only what is comic is perfect: it is outside of reality, which is a self-defeating, serious striving to be outside of reality, to be perfect. Reality cannot escape from reality because it is made of belief, and capable only of belief. Perfection is what is unbelievable, the joke.

WHAT IS A POEM?

In the old romanticism the poem was an uncommon effect of common experience on the poet. All interest in the poem centred in this mysterious capacity of the poet for overfeeling, for being overaffected. In Poe the old romanticism ended and the new romanticism began. That is, the interest was broadened to include the reader: the end of the poem was pushed ahead a stage, from the poet to the reader. The uncommon effect of experience on the poet became merely incidental to the uncommon effect which he might have on the reader. Mystery was replaced by science; inspiration by psychology. In the first the poet flattered himself and was flattered by others because he had singular reactions to experience; in the second the object of flattery makes himself expert in the art of flattery.

What is a poem? A poem is nothing. By persistence the poem can be made something; but then it is something, not a poem. Why is it nothing? Because it cannot be looked at, heard, touched or read (what can be read is prose). It is not an effect (common or uncommon) of experience; it is the result of an ability to create a vacuum in experience – it is a vacuum and therefore nothing. It cannot be looked at, heard, touched or read because it is a vacuum. Since it is a vacuum it is nothing for which the poet can flatter himself or receive flattery. Since it is a vacuum it cannot be reproduced in an audience. A vacuum is unalterably and untransferably a vacuum – the only thing that can happen to it is destruction. If it were possible to reproduce it in an audience the result would be the destruction of the audience.

The confusion between the poem as effect and the poem as vacuum is easily explained. It is obvious that all is either effect or it is nothing. What the old romanticism meant by an uncommon effect was a something that was not an effect, an over-and-above of experience. Although it was really not an effect, it was classified as an effect because it was impossible to imagine something that was not an effect. It did not occur to anyone to imagine nothing, the vacuum ; or, if it did, only with abhorrence. The new romanticism remedied this inaccuracy by classifying the poem as the cause of an effect – as both cause and effect. But as both cause and effect the poem counts itself out of experience: proves itself to be nothing masquerading as something. As something it is all that the detractors of poetry say it is; it is false experience. As nothing – well, as nothing it is everything in an existence where everything, being effect of effect and without cause, is nothing.

Whenever this vacuum, the poem, occurs, there is agitation on all sides to destroy it, to convert it into something. The conversion of nothing into something is the task of criticism. Literature is the storehouse of these rescued somethings. In discussing literature one has to use, unfortunately, the same language that one uses in discussing experience. But even so, literature is preferable to experience, since it is for the most part the closest one can get to nothing.

ᔐ

The only productive design is designed waste. Designed creation results in nothing but the destruction of the designer: it is impossible to add to what is; all is and is made. Energy that attempts to make in the sense of making a numerical increase in the sum of made things is spitefully returned to itself unused. It is a would-be-happy-ness ending in unanticipated and disordered unhappiness. Energy that is aware of the impossibility of positive construction devotes itself to an ordered using-up and waste of itself: to an anticipated unhappiness which, because it has design, foreknowledge, is the nearest approach to happiness. Undesigned unhappiness and designed happiness both mean anarchism. *Anarchism is not enough.*

A COMPLICATED PROBLEM

A COMPLICATED problem is only further complicated by being simplified. A state of confusion is never made comprehensible by being given a plot. Appearances do not deceive if there are enough of them. The truth is always laid out in an infinite number of circles tending to become, but never becoming, concentric – except occasionally in poetry.

ALL LITERATURE

ALL literature is written by the old to teach the young how to express themselves so that they in turn may write literature to teach the old how to express themselves. All literature is written by mentally precocious adolescents and by mentally precocious senescents. How not to write literature, how not to be precocious: cultivate inattention, do not learn how to express yourself, make no distinction between thoughts and emotions, since precocity comes of making one vie with the other, mistrust whatever seems superior and be partial to whatever seems inferior – whatever is not literature. And then, if you must write yourself, write *writing-matter*, not *reading-matter*. People will think you brilliant only if you tell them what they know. To avoid being thought brilliant, avoid knowing what they know. Write to discover to yourself what you know. People will think you brilliant if you seem to be enjoying yourself, since they are not enjoying themselves. To avoid being thought brilliant, avoid pretending to be enjoying yourself. Make it clear that you know that they know that nothing is really

enjoyable except pretending to be enjoying yourself.

༄

People may treat themselves as extraneous phenomena or as fundamental phenomena – it does
not matter which. It does not matter, so long as
they behave consistently as one or the other. What
discredits character is not self-importance or self-
unimportance, but the adjustment of personal
importance according to expediency.

MR. DOODLE-DOODLE-DOO

MR. DOODLE-DOODLE-DOO, the great mathematician and lexicographer, then put aside his work and said: '*adultery* and *adulteration* can wait until I return.'

For Mr. Doodle-Doodle-Do was at one thing or the other by turns, and this particular morning he felt his mathematical genius complaining: it was undoubtedly true that it was a long time since he had been out to get Numbers. So, leaving *adultery* and *adulteration* to take care of themselves, he walked out into the Square, and from the Square into the Gardens; and in the Gardens he sat down on a bench near the rockery and began to think with the mathematical half of his brain.

'Let me see. I left off with *honey* last time. Now the problem will be to show that honey as a purely mathematical symbol is equivalent to honey as a philological integer. If I can do this I have once more proved that $2 \times 2 = 4$ is the equivalent of "two times two is four." For it's not enough to show a thing is true: you must also show that true is true. By being a mathematical lexicographer and a lexicographical mathematician, I am therefore able to check the truth with the truth. My last words are never "that's true" but "that's correct," which explains how I can be a philosopher and a gentleman at the same time.'

With this Mr. Doodle-Doodle-Doo crowed three times: once for lexicography (Doodle), once for mathematics (Doodle), and once for himself (Doo), wherein the truth was checked by itself and found correct. The immediate matter in hand, however, was honey. So he left off crowing and proceeded with his calculations, which went so quickly that it is very difficult to record them. But they were something like this: –

$$
\begin{aligned}
\text{H O N E Y} &= \text{HONE} + \text{Y} \\
\text{G O N E} + \text{Y} &= \text{GONEY (sailors' term} \\
&\qquad \text{for albatross)} \\
\text{L O N E} + \text{Y} &= \text{LONE(L)Y} \\
\text{B O N E} + \text{Y} &= \text{BONEY} \\
\text{O N E} + \text{Y} + \text{M} &= \text{MONEY}
\end{aligned}
$$

BONEY	GONEY	HONEY	LONE(L)Y	MONEY
I	2	3	4	5
H	O	N	E	Y
I	2	3	4	5

At this point he stopped following him. But that his researches must have reached some happy conclusion was obvious from the enthusiasm with which he later returned to his lexicography. His calculations then ran something like this: –

$$\begin{array}{c} 1\ 2\ 3\ 4\ 5 \\ H\ O\ N\ E\ Y \\ 1\ 2\ 3\ 4\ 5 \\ A\ D\ U\ L\ T\ [\ E\ R\ Y \\[6pt] 1\ 2\ 3\ 4\ 5 \\ H\ O\ N\ E\ Y \\ 1\ 2\ 3\ 4\ 5 \\ A\ D\ U\ L\ T\ [\ E\ R\ A\ T\ I\ O\ N \end{array}$$

∴ H O N E Y E R Y ∴ H O N E Y E R A T I O N

$$\text{But}\ \begin{array}{c} 1\ 2\ 3\ 4\ 5 \\ H\ O\ N\ E\ Y \\ 5\ 4\ 3\ 2\ 1 \end{array} = \begin{array}{c} 1\ 2\ 3\ 4\ 5 \\ S\ W\ E\ E\ T \\ 5\ 4\ 3\ 2\ 1 \end{array}$$

∴ S W E E T E R Y ∴ S W E E T E R A T I O N

Which went far enough to persuade him that in lexicography he was, if anything, even more skilled than in mathematics.

AN IMPORTANT
DISTINCTION

THE important (but infrequently drawn) distinction between what is gentlemanly and what is dull in poetry. Most people read poetry because it makes them feel upper-class, and most poetry is written by people who feel upper-class; at least by people who take pleasure in describing themselves as upper-class; for instance, by men who make themselves feel upper-class by holding gentlemanly feelings toward woman, and by women who make themselves feel upper-class by acknowledging these feelings. This poetry is idealistic poetry: it dramatizes a non-existent emotional life and seems real because it is not real. It also seems 'interesting' because it is not real.

Practical poetry is written by people who do not feel upper-class: who do not feel anything. It describes themselves, but not as upper-class, not, in fact, as anything. It is real and therefore not dramatic and therefore seems unreal. It therefore seems (and is) dull. The only reason that people ever read dull poetry (such as some of Shakespeare's) is that they mistake it for gentlemanly poetry (such as all of Browning's). For few people are really interested in anyone else's description of himself except as it makes them feel upper-class. They mistake it for gentlemanly poetry because of their inability to distinguish between the interestingness of dull poetry and the dullness of 'interesting' poetry.

THE CORPUS

THE first condition was chaos. The logical consequence of chaos was order. In so far as it derived from chaos it was non-conscious, but in so far as it was order, it had an increasing tendency to become conscious. It therefore may be said to have had a mind of which it was unconscious and of which it remained unconscious in its various evolutionary forms until the mind developed to a point where it in turn separated from order and invented the self. The occasion of the self was a stage in the most anarchic evolutionary form, man, coeval with the general transformation of chaos into a universe. A consciousness of consciousness arose and at the same time divided between order, in which mind was the spirit of cohesion, and the individual, in whom mind was the spirit of separation. In the ensuing opposition between these two, order yielded to the individual by allowing him to call it a universe, but triumphed over him since, by naming it, the individual made the universe his society and therefore his religion. Order was the natural enemy of the individual mind. To conciliate it order appealed to the individual mind for sanction. This sanction, the original social contract, was not between man and man, but between man and the universe as men, or society. Although the sanction was given on the basis of natural instinct, or the non-conscious identity of man and the universe, society has always claimed authority over conscious thought and purpose. In incorporating the man it attempts to incorporate the mind and in turn to give the mind its sanction through the sanction which it first had from the man: it constitutes itself the parent past and the mind present memory of it.

The social corpus is tyrannically founded on the principle of origin. It admits nothing new: all is revision, memory, confirmation. The individual cosmos must submit itself to the generalized cosmos of history, it must become part of its growing encyclopædia of authorities. Such a generalized cosmos, however, must have been formulated more by the desire of people to define themselves as a group than to account for the origin of their personal existence. Origin, indeed, is properly the preoccupation of the individual and not a communal interest. The group is only interested in the formal publishing of individuals for the purpose of establishing their social solidarity. Art, for example, is record not creation. The question of origin is only emphasized in so far as it proves the individual a member of the group, as having a common pedigree with the other members of the group. Thus God, the branding-iron of the group idea, does not appear in societies where as yet there is imperfect differentiation between the individual and the type; where as yet there is no need for branding. Once the distinction between the group mind and the individual mind could be made the group mind really ceased to exist. The distinction, however, could only be made by minds complete in themselves, and as such minds have always been extremely rare, the fiction of a group mind has been maintained to impose the will of the weak-minded upon the strong-minded, the myth of common origin being used as the charter of the majority. The tyranny by which this majority can enforce its will may be either democratic or oligarchic. The only difference is that in the first case, provided that the democracy is a true democracy (which it very rarely is), the group mind is so efficient that it acts despotically as one man; in the second case the group mind is less efficient and, by a process of blind selection, the most characteristic of the weak-minded become the perverse instruments of unity.

Both the individual mind and the group mind are engaged in a pursuit which may be described as

29

mind-making or, simply, truth. The object of group truth is group-confirmation and perpetuation; while individual truth has no object other than discovering itself and involves neither proofs nor priests. In order, however, to win any acceptance it must translate itself into group truth, it must accommodate itself to the fact-curriculum of the group. But not only is such truth forced to submit to group terminology and order, but the group conscience demands that the individual mind serve it by working with the purposes of the group. The group, indeed, tries to preclude all idiosyncratic thought-activity and to use what intelligence it can control against it. This civic intelligence is found simplified in the catechism instructing children 'to order themselves lowly and reverently before their betters and to do their duty in that state of life unto which it has pleased God to call them.'

The confirmation of the candidate as a member of the group establishes the superiority of group opinion over individual opinion and the authority of the group to define this relationship as one governed by civic duties. It is the nature of these duties which determines the categories into which civic intelligence falls. The group can never be anything more than a superstition, but the categories assemble all available material into a textual Corpus. There being no real functional group surviving, this Corpus of group texts is used as the rallying point of the group, the counterpart of the primitive clan totem, the outward and visible sign of a long-extinct grace.

The Corpus, in making categorical demands upon the individual, thus limits the ways in which works may be conceived and presented. These demands become the only 'inspiration' countenanced, and theoretically all creative supply has its source in them. This seems a fairly plausible view of the status of the arts and sciences in human society. The occurrence of a supply independent of Corpus demands, its possibility or presence, is a question that the social limitations of our critical language prevent us from raising with any degree of humane intelligibility.

∽

We live on the circumference of a hollow circle. We draw the circumference, like spiders, out of ourselves: it is all criticism of criticism.

POETRY AND MUSIC

THERE is a weakling music and a weakling poetry which flatter each other by making critical comparisons with each other: there is a literary criticism of music in which words like 'wit' and 'rhetoric' excuse musical flabbiness, and a musical criticism of poetry in which words like 'symphonic' and 'overtone' excuse poetic flabbiness. This mutual tenderness leads to false creative as well as false critical analogies between poetry and music; to the deliberate effort to use the creative method of one art in the other.

I am not distressed by the poeticization of music because I do not much care what happens to music; it is a nervous and ostentatious performance, and little damage remains to be done to it. I am, on the other hand, distressed by the musicification of poetry because poetry is perhaps the only human pursuit left still capable of developing anti-socially. Musicified or pictorialized it is the propagandist tribal expression of a society without any real tribal sense. We get a 'pure' poetry, metaphysically musical, that reveals a desire in the poet for a civilized tribal sense and for poetry as an art intellectually coördinating group sympathies: and we get a sort of jazz poetry, politically musical, that reveals a desire in the poet for a primitive tribal sense and for poetry as an art emotionally coördinating group sympathies.

Art indeed is a term referring to the social source and to the social utility of creative acts. Poetry I consider to be an art only when the poet consciously attempts to capture social prestige: when it is an art of public flattery. In this sense Beaumont and Fletcher were greater artists than Shakespeare – better musicians. Shakespeare alternated between musical surrenders to social prestige and magnificent fits of poetic remorse.

To explain more precisely what I mean by this distinction between what I believe to be poetry and what I believe to be art I shall set down a number of contrasts between poetry and music.

1. All real musicians are physically misshapen as a result of platform cozening of their audience. They need never have stood upon a platform: there is a kind of ingratiating 'come, come, dear puss' in the musical brain that distorts the face and puckers up the limbs. All real poets are physically upright and even beautiful from indifference to community hearings.

33   c

2. The end of a poem is the poem. The poem is the only admissible test of the poem; the reader gets poetry, not flattery. The end of a musical work is an ear, criticism, that is, flattery.

3. A musical work has a composer; it is an invention with professionally available material and properties. A poem is made out of nothing by a nobody – made out of a socially non-existent element in language. If this element were socially existent in language it would be isolated, professionalized, handed over to a trained craft. Rhyme and rhythm are not professional properties; they are fundamentally idiosyncratic, unavailable, unsystematizable; any formalization of them is an attempted imitation of music by poets jealous of the public success of music.

4. Music is an instrument for arousing emotions; it varies only according to the emotions it is intended to arouse and according to the precision with which these emotions are anticipated in the invention of the music. Emotions represent persons; not persons in particular but persons in general. Music is directed toward the greatest number of persons musically conceivable. It is a mass-marshalling of the senses by means of sound. Poetry is not an instrument and is not written with the intention of arousing emotions – unless it is of a hybrid musico-poetical breed. The end of poetry is not to create

34

a physical condition which shall give pleasure to the mind. It appeals to an energy in which no distinction exists between physical and mental conditions. It does not massage, soothe, excite or entertain this energy in any way. It *is* this energy in a form of extraordinary strength and intactness. Poetry is therefore not concentrated on an audience but on itself and only produces satisfaction in the sense that wherever this energy exists in a sufficient degree of strength and intactness it will be encouraged by poetry in further concentration on itself. Poetry appeals only to poetry and begets nothing but poetry. Music appeals to the intellectual disorganization and weakness of people in numbers and begets, by flattering this weakness (which is sentimentality), gratifying after-effects of destructive sociality. The end of poetry is not an after-effect, not a pleasurable memory of itself, but an immediate, constant and even unpleasant insistence on itself; indeed, it has no end. It isolates energies in themselves rather than socially dissolving one in another.

5. Music provides the hearer with an ideal experience, a prepared episode. Poetry is not idealistic; it is not experience in this episode or programme sense. There is an entertaining short-story variety in music; a repellent, austere monotony in poetry. Poetry brings all possible experience to the

same degree: a degree in the consciousness beyond which the consciousness itself cannot go. Poetry is defeat, the end which is not an end but a stopping-short because it is impossible to go further; it makes mad; it is the absolutism of dissatisfaction. Music brings not the consciousness but the *material* of experience to a certain degree, always to different degrees. It makes pleasantly happy or unhappy. It is the vulgarity of satisfaction.

6. Music disintegrates and therefore seems active, fruitful, extensive, enlarging. Poetry isolates all loose independencies and then integrates them into one close independency which, when complete, has nothing to do but confront itself. Poetry therefore seems idle, sterile, narrow, destroying. And it is This is what recommends it.

POETRY AND PAINTING

PAINTERS no longer paint with paint except in
the sense that poets write with ink. Paint is now only
a more expensive, elegant ink. What do painters
paint with, then? They paint with poetry. A picture is a poem in which the sense has been absorbed
by the medium of communication of sense. It is
not an intelligible series of hieroglyphics, but the
poem itself forced into a kind of outrageous, unnatural visibility: as if suddenly the thing mind
were caught in the hand and made to appear painfully and horribly as a creature. The development
of painting is toward this poetic quality; the better
(the more literal, the less realistic) it gets, the more
horrible. So much for the so-called abstractness
of painting: the sense is made identical with the
medium by forcibly marrying it to the medium.
Medium and sense are a legally fictitious One in
which the medium, the masculine factor, forces the
sense, the feminine factor, to bear his name and do
honour to his bed and table. *She* is all meek, hopeless amicability, *he* is all blustering, good-humoured
cynicism.

This poetic progress of painting influences the pictorial progress of poetry. There is a great response in modern poetry to the demand by painters that it should be more poetic. See for yourself how many of the newest poems have not their names lettered in aluminium on their doors, with a knocker designed by the latest French abstract sculptor (master also of golf), humanly visible furniture within (all primary colours), and nobody home.

POETRY AND DREAMS

I DO not believe there is any more relation between poem-making and dream-making than between poem-making and child-making. The making of poems, dreams and children is difficult to explain because they all somehow happen and go on until the poem comes to an end and the sleeper wakes up and the child comes out into the air. As for children, there are so many other ways of looking at the matter that poetry is generally not asked to provide a creative parallel. As for dreams, they are the dregs of the mind, anxious to elevate themselves by flattering comparisons. As for poems, they are frequently (more often than not) concocted in the dregs of the mind and therefore happy in an understanding of mutual support between themselves and dreams.

The only real resemblance between poetry and dreams is that they are both on the other side of waking – on opposite sides. Waking is the mind in its mediocrity. Mediocrity is of such large extent that it pushes off into obscurity the mental degree *beyond* mediocrity, in a direction *away from* sleep. The mental degree *before* mediocrity, *toward* sleep, is the dream. So the stage before the lowest degree of mediocrity and the stage beyond the highest degree of mediocrity are bracketed together by mediocrity because they are both outside of mediocrity – the mind at its canniest intelligence and the mind at its canniest imbecility.

JOCASTA

THE pathetic differences between wrong and right are well illustrated in the persons of Otto Spengler and Wyndham Lewis. Herr Spengler is a pessimist who has succeeded in cheering himself up with a romantic view of Decline. Mr. Lewis is an optimist because he is right, forced into pessimism by the general prevalence of wrong. He sees wrong (rightly) as Time, Romance, Advertisement (forced optimism), Righteousness, Action, Popular Art (Time, Romance, Advertisement, Righteousness, Action, united in an inferiority complex). Since he is right his right quarrels with the various manifestations of wrong he is able to distinguish: the more he is able to distinguish the more corroborations he has of his rightness. Herr Spengler, being wrong, has this advantage therefore over Mr. Lewis: whereas Mr. Lewis's success must be confined to seeing wrong in the most unorganized (that is, various) manner possible, *his* success depends on his being

41

wrong in the most organized manner possible – the more organized he seems, the more right he seems. Unfortunately this situation brings about a competition between Herr Spengler and Mr. Lewis: Mr. Lewis feels obliged to organize his unorganized view of wrong, which cancels the potency of his rightness, which is only valid so long as it is unorganized (that is, commentarial instead of systematic). So he becomes a colleague of Herr Spengler in righteousness, the advocate of a vocabulary. We find him, as he himself admits, trying to give 'compendious' names to what is wrong: which places him immediately in Herr Spengler's class.[1]

To be right is to be incorruptibly individual. To be wrong is to be righteously collective. Herr Spengler is a collectivist: he believes in the absorption of the unreal (right) individual in a collective reality (History or Romance) – by which the individual becomes functionally (as opposed to morphologically) really-real. Mr. Lewis is an individualist

[1] Mr. Lewis takes a fierce, acquisitive joy in being right: as if it were an honour to be right, and his unique honour. But many people, alas, are right, only with more quietness and less joy than Mr. Lewis. To be right (to see wrong) is properly a sad, not a joyous mental condition. To be right in Mr. Lewis's manner is to become a self-appointed destroyer of wrong; and so to make oneself a candidate for destruction, in turn. To be right in his manner – so righteously right – is to be God; and so to chasten every one into wrong.

in so far as he is opposed to organized functional
reality. But he is unable to face the final conclusion
of individualism: that the individual is morphologically as well as functionally unreal, and that herein
alone (in this double withdrawal from both nature
and human society, or history) can he be right. How
does Mr. Lewis come to believe in the morphological reality of the individual? By devoting himself so violently to revealing the sham of historical action in art – the unreality of functional
reality – that he creates by implication a real which,
since it cannot exist in historical romance (society),
which is all sham, must exist in non-historical
romance (nature). Further, both Herr Spengler
and Mr. Lewis think through the same machinery
– the machinery of knowledge. Indeed it appears as
if they thought because they possessed this machinery and had to use it: this is the constant impression made by Herr Spengler, the frequent impression
made by Mr. Lewis. I do not think that Mr. Lewis
really thinks because of and by means of knowledge. I am convinced that he thinks. But I see also
that he is unable to face uncompromisingly the problem of individualism. He is not content with being
right; he is stung by his irritation with what is
wrong into the desire to be real as well as right. He
therefore organizes the same material that Herr
Spengler organizes – to prove that it is sham, as

43

Herr Spengler to prove that it is real. He even uses the same false organizing system as Herr Spengler – analogy. Herr Spengler, by proving the analogical consistency of his views, merely proves that wrong is wrong. Mr. Lewis, by overstudying the analogical consistency of wrong, establishes his right by the same system that Herr Spengler uses in establishing his wrong. He is making of his right a competitive Romance to argue with Herr Spengler's Romance. With both Herr Spengler and Mr. Lewis I feel in the presence of realists. Herr Spengler, I feel, is happy in being a realist, Mr. Lewis, I feel, is not. He is not, I think, because he is fundamentally right, but afraid of facing the unreality of rightness. It is difficult to explain this because it is a difficult situation; and I wish if possible to avoid compendious names. It would perhaps be simplest to say that Mr. Lewis is timid (as he has himself privately admitted).

Mr. Lewis attacks the principle which is to Herr Spengler the right of his wrong. He attacks the reality of the collective-real. But in doing so he opposes to it an individual-real. The collective-real is man in touch with man. The individual-real is man in touch with the natural in him, in touch with nature. Neither Herr Spengler nor Mr. Lewis dares face the individual-unreal: both believe in unity and integration, Herr Spengler in the unity and

integration of history, Mr. Lewis in the unity and
integration of natural as opposed to historical existence. 'I am for the physical world,' Mr. Lewis says.
One of the reasons he is for the physical world is,
apparently, that the historical world, in keeping
up with itself, not only worships the fetich of
Romance, but the fetich of childishness as well. In
pointing this out Mr. Lewis is both wise and cour-
ageous; but he reveals at the same time an important fetich of the individual-real, adultishness. Nor,
maddened by the vulgar success of the historical
world with itself, can he see that the fetich of childishness in only a half-clue to the story of Gertrude
Stein, that Miss Stein has one foot in the collective real and one foot in the individual-unreal –
which is more than can be said of Mr. Lewis,
who has both feet planted in the individual-
real.[1]

[1] The adultishness of the individual-real is an abhorrence
(as Mr. Lewis shows it to be) of intellectualism (organized
fear) in the up-to-date White mass, which to Mr. Lewis is
sentimental Bolshevism, Bohemianism. But such an abhorrence of intellectualism in the up-to-date White mass, if one is
not careful, becomes (as in Mr. Lewis) an adultish championship
of intellectualism (organized bravado) in a privileged White few
(as any *system* of individualism must mean by individualism the
individualism of a few) – a sentimental Toryism, in fact, Acade-
mianism. And in what few ? The few, of course, swept aside
by the time-current; the few, indeed, who might be truly
individual were they not organized into a system of indivi-

45

I must next give an illustration of the individual-real in contemporary literature. This will perhaps not please Wyndham Lewis and will certainly not please its author, Virginia Woolf. I can only say that I do not mean to attack either of them but merely to explain the individual-real. And Mrs. Woolf's most recent book, *To the Lighthouse*, seems to me a perfect example of the individual-real. In the first place, it is individual: not in the sense that it is personal, warm, alive to itself, indifferent to effect or appreciation, vividly unreal, but in the sense that it individual-izes the simple reality of nature, gives it distinc-tion – shade, tone, personal subtlety. In the second place it is real – meticulously, mathematically like life: not historical time-life, which is an easy approximation, but natural flesh-life, which must be laboriously, exquisitely, irritatingly, painfully

dualism. Mr. Lewis's Toryism would be perhaps apt if he were trying to be only politically, not philosophically right as well. But in the circumstances his satire is as irrelevant to his right, which is philosophical, as Swift's would have been, had it been philosophical, to his right, which was political. The only satire relevant to a philosophical right is a satire like Blake's: Blake's faith showed the people who were wrong to be ene-mies, it was not a system organizing himself into an enemy. Mr. Lewis does not like Blake because he said that the roads of genius (right) were crooked : Mr. Lewis believes that the roads of right should be systematic, that the person who is right should be an enemy, a righteous, sentimental Tory rather than a sad though angry spirit.

rendered. To do this language must be strained, supersensitized, loaded with comparisons, suggestive images, emotional analogies: used, that is, in a poetic way to write something that is not poetry – used to argue, prove, prick the cuticle of sense, so to speak, in a way that is extravagant, unpleasant, insincere (since it purports to be pleasant). The method, in fact, has no creative justification: it merely drives home the individual-real, which is physical emphasis of self – individual because it is physically self, real because as physical it shares in the simple reality of nature. All this delicacy of style, it appears, is the expression of an academic but nevertheless vulgar indelicacy of thought, a sort of Royal Academy nudeness, a squeamish, fine-writing lifting of the curtains of privacy. In the third place, it (the individual-real as illustrated in this novel) is adultish – advanced but conservative: it does not belong to childish, democratic mass-art, but neither does it belong to the individual, non-physical, non-collective unreal. It is over-earnest constrained, suppressedly hysterical, unhappy, could give no one pleasure. Pleasure is doing as one pleases. In works like this neither the author, who is obsessed by the necessity of emphasizing the individual-real, nor the reader, who is forced to follow the author painfully (word for word) in this obsession, may do as he pleases. There is only one novel-writer who really did as he pleased, let his characters do as they pleased and his reader to do as he pleased, and that was Defoe. He could do this because he was, as Pope said, 'the unabashed Defoe,' and he was unabashed because he was unreal, vividly unreal – personal, warm, indifferent to effect (consistency). Mrs. Woolf defends herself from any such analysis of her work as I have made here by declaring that there is no such thing as a novel. If *To The Lighthouse* is not to be treated as a novel, then it must, by its language-habits, be treated as a poem. Analyse it then as a poem: what then? It proves itself to be merely a novel; and an insincere novel – the use of the material of the collective-real to insinuate dogmatically the individual-real. Defoe used the material of the collective-real as it could only be used sincerely – to insinuate the individual-unreal: and so Defoe, if you like, did turn the novel into poetry.

I once discussed this point with E. M. Forster and we found that we had each read *Roxana* in entirely opposite senses. Mr. Forster was certain that Defoe followed Roxana in every word he wrote of her, and that Roxana likewise followed Defoe, that there was no do-as-you-please break between her and Defoe or between her and the reader or between Defoe and the reader; that all was one intense, physically compact and consistent exposition of the individual-

real. I pointed out the striking division in, for example, Roxana's long feminist declamation against
marriage to her Dutch lover – a division in which
all the *dramatis personæ*, including author and reader,
are released to accept the declamation with whatever bias they please. In this division I find Defoe's
sincerity. Mr. Forster, on the other hand, under-
stands the declamation as a remarkably unified,
innocent, three-dimensional slice of that individual-
real which is the story. If I thought that Defoe had
written that passage innocently, with realistic consistency, I should catalogue him as a fine writer and
skilful hypocrite. But I am persuaded he was
neither of these. I am sure that the feminist recital
was wilfully unreal, inconsistent, many-dimensional; that it was delicate common sense for the
Dutch lover, frank but sentimental expediency for
Roxana, sound doctrine for Defoe and undisguised
storifying for the reader present in the story; and
that none of these was deceived in his bias, but
could if he wished change it for any other without
damaging the consistency of the piece, since there
was none. *The Tempest* has the same sort of inconsistency as a Defoe novel; it is the most unreal
of the plays and to me preferable to the more
realistic plays. Others are more poetic, as Mrs.
Woolf's *To The Lighthouse* is more poetic than
Roxana. But they do not contain so many poems,

as there is no passage in *To The Lighthouse* with the dimensions (the contradictions) of Roxana's recital to her Dutch lover. In *The Tempest* there is not only a continuous chain of such inconsistencies (poems); the characters themselves have the same many-dimensional inconsistency – the unreal Caliban, the unreal Prospero, interchangeable in their inconsistency.

Before leaving this question and returning to Herr Spengler, whose wrong has not in my opinion been sufficiently disorganized, I must come back to the suffocating, nearly sickening physical quality of what I call the individual-real – not a strong, fresh, casual frankness of flesh, but a self-scented, sensuous, unbearably curious self-smelling of flesh. The collective-real is crude, symbolic, sham; the individual-real is exquisite, more than symbolic – literally, intrinsically metaphorical. I have in mind, in connection with *To The Lighthouse*, a book of E. M. Forster's, *A Room With a View*. Before reading this book I had met Mr. Forster and found him charming; the book was recommended to me by my friends as a charming book. I read it. I could not deny that it was charming. Yet it was to me unpleasantly painful to read. It was too charming. I do not mean to be flippant, or to disgust, or to alter my original conviction of Mr. Forster's personal charm, which I have had an opportunity of confirming since reading this book. But the truth is that it affected me in the same way as would the sight of a tenderly and exquisitely ripe pimple. I longed to squeeze it and have done with it. At the time I could only reproach myself with this rather shameful morbidity and admit that my reaction seemed preposterous. It was a simple, exquisitely written story about simple, unexciting people; and the unpleasant excitement it gave me was unnatural. Since then I have come to be able to identify and understand a little the individual-real, and it is now perfectly clear to me why Mr. Forster's book affected me in that way, although then I could only feel a vague physical reaction to its metaphorical realism. That I recognized it as an essay in metaphorical realism is proved by the persistent image of the pimple with which the book came to be associated in my mind. And indeed, if I had thought a little more closely about metaphorical realism at the time, I might have arrived very soon at the same conclusion that I have here arrived at, *via* Otto Spengler, Wyndham Lewis, and so forth.

In the ordinary time-world or art-world of the collective-real, symbolism, however romantically it may be used, never denies that it is symbolism. Its very effectiveness depends on its being recognized as such. Further, since symbolism is here collective rather than individual, since the symbol, that is, is *chosen* to collectivize individual emotions which would otherwise have separate and presumably weaker communication with the thing for which the symbol stands, it is clear that the symbolic method of the collective-real is selective: it implies a graded choice of the things which it seems necessary and important to symbolize. This method, whose psychology Herr Spengler attempts to discover, is all that Mr. Lewis says it is (it is really the symbolic method of the time-world that he attacks). In the literature and art of the collective-real it is easy to recognize because they are frankly symbolical: it is part of their technique to insist on the symbolic quality of the symbol. This means that symbolic art is generally bad art, full of double meanings, vulgar obviousness, facile concessions to sentimentality, flattery of the mass-emotions which confirm the relation of the symbol with the thing it represents.

Yet there is a proficiency, a vulgar good in this bad art that gives great and pure pleasure – great because it has the strength of what is purposively, defiantly bad, pure because it makes no attempt to conceal its badness. And there is one further virtue in the symbolism of the collective-real, that, being a selective symbolism, it does not symbolize everything – if it symbolized everything it would destroy the time-world, the organ of communication and author of symbols. Instead, it lets pass much which it realizes would be proof against symbolism and thus threaten its prestige: it admits that there is much that is unreal and, in so far as is consistent with its authority, leaves it alone. Poetry, therefore, in the world of the collective-real, is given a little chance.

Symbolism, in the nature-world of the individual-real, denies itself to be symbolism. It uses all the tricks of the symbolism of the collective-real, but to insist that it is individually, not collectively real, that it is, therefore, not symbolic but literal, not 'artistic' but natural. It is not selective, since if it were it would admit itself to be symbolical, but makes everything it touches equally significant, physical, real. Its technique is to insist on the authentic quality of the symbol. This means that it is only a more ambitious, expert, clever symbolism than the symbolism of the collective-real. It is literally instead of suggestively symbolic. It is morbidly physical instead of merely morbidly sentimental. It is difficult (not by nature but by art), adult, aristocratic, *better*. The difference between the collective-real and the individual-real as revealed by their respective methods of symbolism proves itself to be no more than a snobbish difference of degree: the art of the individual-real is self-appointed good art. And as such it is strained, unhappy-hypocritical, slave to an ideal of superiority that I can only properly describe as the ideal of slickness. There is no opposition here of right to wrong, only a more academic, individual wrong (or real) than even the best democratic, collective wrong. The right (the unreal) remains (as it should) categorically non-existent.[1]

[1] The symbolism of the individual-real in its scientific aspects is best explained in C. K. Ogden's and I. A. Richards' *The Meaning of Meaning*. In this confused mixture of philosophy, psychology, ethnology and literature it is just possible to distinguish between what is meant by 'bad' and 'good' symbolism. To begin with, the assumption must be made for both varieties of symbolism that words mean nothing by themselves. Bad symbolism is apparently the use of words for collective propagandist purposes which distort the 'referents' (original objects or events) of which the words are signs; good symbolism makes language not an instrument of purposes but of the 'real' objects or events for which it provides a sort of mathematic of signs. Words in this reformed grammar are thus not vulgar stage-players of images; they are certified scientific representatives of the natural objects, or constructions of objects called events, which man's mind, like a dust-cloud, is assumed to obscure from himself. To Mr. Ogden and Mr. Richards language is ideally a neutral region of literalness between reality and its human perception. Signs (of which language is this precise mathematical grammar), being the closest the perceiving mind can come to reality, must for convenience be regarded as reality itself; the more faithfully they are defined as signs, the more literally they represent reality. There is no evidence anywhere in this book that perception is properly anything other than a slave of

I recall with pleasure an outrageous example of the vulgarity, sentimentality, proficient badness of collective-real literature; a novel by Rebecca West. It is a long time since I read it, and what I can reproduce of it is from memory. I remember in particular one passage, in which it was told how delightful it was to hold an egg in the little hollow in the front of the neck, and in which baked pota-

reality. Disobedient perception – language by itself – is an 'Enchanted Wood of Words.' There is no hint that individual perception, instead of making a separate approximation of the general sign conveying the object, does in fact where originality is maintained experience a revulsion from the object or event concerned. No hint that the very genesis or *utterance* of a sign is an assertion of the independence of the mind against what the authors call the sign-situation. Or that the mind is a dust-cloud only when perceptively organized to define reality. Or that language is only an Enchanted Wood of Words when the dragon Reality is searched for in it. Or that words are literal man, not 'main topics of discussion,' not literal perception or the science of reality.

The conclusion of this study, if one has patience to extract a conclusion from this science-proud collation of verbal niceties, is that man has no right to meaning: meaning is the property of reality, which is to be known scientifically only through symbols, which in turn are to be regulated as to interpretation by limitations on the use of symbols, called definitions. 'But in most matters the possible treachery of words can only be controlled through definitions, and the greater the number of such alternative locutions available the less is the risk of discrepancy, provided that we do not suppose symbols to have "meaning" on their own account, and so people the world with fictitious entities.'

55

toes were charmingly mixed up with cirrus clouds.
It was all so frankly false, so enchantingly bad, so
vulgarly poetical without the least claim to being
poetic, that it was impossible not to enjoy it and not
to find it good: one was being sold nothing that

But what, then, in this stabilizing of the scientific or symbolic
use of words, is to happen to poetry, which is assumed as the
deliberately unscientific use of words? Poetry, it appears,
deals with evocative as opposed to symbolic speech. 'In
evocative speech the essential considerations is the character
of the attitude aroused.' The corollary to this proposition,
which the authors imperfectly and insincerely develop, is that
there is no true antithesis between evocative (partisan)
speech and symbolic (logical) speech. We deduce that
evocative speech is in fact not an independent speech of its
own but a persuasive quality that may be added to symbolic
speech: the 'attitude aroused,' that is, is an attitude toward
something – evocative (poetic) speech is false *by itself* (in opposition to symbolic speech), it is scientifically admissible only
where it shows close dependence on symbols meaningless
in themselves but showing close, scientific dependence on
reality.

This deduction we find confirmed in a little book by Mr.
I. A. Richards, *Science and Poetry*. 'The essential peculiarity of
poetry as of all the arts is that the full appropriate situation is
not present.' The fact that poetry is evocative rather then
symbolic gives it a freedom from the hard-and-fast laws of
reality that often enables it to convey a more faithful impression of the 'real thing,' by a sort of loyal lying, than would
painfully truthful symbolic speech. Thus, by making symbolism the purpose of science rather than of art (as it is in the
vulgar collective-real) Mr. Richards is able to allow poetry
(always by scientific leave, of course) certain aristocratic

was not obvious. After Rebecca West put Katherine
Mansfield, a cross between the collective-real and
the individual-real, a perplexed effort, a vapour.
Then put the development of the individual-
real, culminating in the art of Virginia Woolf, in

latitudes of expression – a certain rhetorical *finesse* – that it
lacks when it is erroneously used as symbolic (pseudo-scien-
tific) speech. Poetry as symbolic speech is only figurative
speech; it invents a fairy-story of reality. Poetry as evocative
speech takes its clue from external (scientific) symbols of
reality rather than from internal (imaginative) symbols of
reality – it means, in Mr. Richards' words, 'The transference
from the magical view of the world to the scientific.'

In the magical view the 'pseudo-statements' of poetry were
connected with belief. In the scientific view they are disconnected from belief; we are returned to the assumption scattered
through the pages of *The Meaning of Meaning*, that man has no
right to meaning. The poet armed with the scientific view
accepts the 'contemporary background' as tentative meaning:
so that 'the essential consideration is the character of the attitude aroused.' This attitude has literary licence according to
the degree of scientific acceptance: the more complete the
acceptance, the greater the 'independence' (meaninglessness)
of the poetry.

Poetry is according to such criticism, therefore, a socially
beneficial affirmation of reality by means of a denial, or phan-
tasization, of individual mind. In symbolic (magic) poetic
speech reality itself is the principal of the fairy story; in evocative (scientific) poetic speech the principal of the fairy-
story is the individual mind. In both cases the one belief from
which the poetic mind must not disconnect itself is the belief
in reality; which proves itself in either case to be only the most
advanced 'contemporary background' appreciable.

which nothing is thrown out since it admits no unreal, in which poetry has no chance because the individual-real itself is so poetic, in which one is sold poetry without being aware of it; this super-symbolical, unsufferably slick alchemy that takes poetry out of the unreal and turns it into the dainty extra-pink blood by which reality is suffused with reality:

'She looked up over her knitting and met the third stroke and it seemed to her like her own eyes meeting her own eyes, searching as she alone could search into her mind and her heart, purifying out of existence that lie, any lie. She praised herself in praising the light, without vanity, for she was stern, she was searching, she was beautiful like that light. It was odd, she thought, how if one was alone, one leant to things, inanimate things; trees, streams, flowers; felt they expressed one; felt they became one; felt they knew one, in a sense were one; felt an irrational tenderness thus (she looked at that long steady light) as for oneself. There rose, and she looked and looked with her needles suspended, there curled up off the floor of the mind, rose from the lake of one's being, a mist, a bride to meet her lover.'

I submit that this is *more wrong* than Rebecca West's writing because it is better, slicker. It bends the bow of taste (to use the manner of Mrs. Woolf) back into a contorted, disdainful, monotonous, sensuously bulging circle. The collective-real, when a revolution takes place in it (when it is threatened by the unreal and makes a violent gesture of self-assertion), acknowledges the shadow that has passed over it, accepts the consequences of pledging itself to be with time: shortens its skirts, chops an inch off its hair, puts a cheerful face on its modernity – its progressive retreat from the unreal. The individual-real, on the other hand, secure in Nature's fortress, insists that no shadow of the unreal can fall upon it. It is everything – real because it is individualistic, unreal because it is symbolical: it cannot come to harm. If it is threatened, it lengthens its skirts, swishes grandly along the ground, grows its finger-nails, scratches exquisitely the plaster wall that surrounds it, sharpens its pencil till it has nerves and writes just a little more finely than is possible. And whatever it touches turns to spun-silk under it. It is the delamarish memory-fairy.

Yet certainly there is much that cannot, except in the fairy-tale of memory (the individual-real) be turned into spun-silk. To make everything real, no matter how unreal, how personal it may have been in its occurrence, is to symbolize it for the democratic mass. Thus psycho-analysis is not unacceptable to the individual-real, thus in individual-real literature we find grating public exhibitions

59

of individuality. Any personal incident may be stroked, coaxed, maddened by fine torture into symbolic existence. For example: when I was fourteen I used to read the *New York Times* every afternoon for an hour (for a pittance) to an old man whose eyesight was poor, a veteran of the Civil War. He had a most eccentric mispronunciation, which I had to adopt in reading to him. It was very difficult, as on the other side, at school, I was being trained in pronunciation. I concentrated on mispronunciation, and one day, when I had just about become expert in it, I knocked at his door to find that he had died. There I was, with all that mispronunciation on my hands; and to a certain extent it is still on my hands. Now, if I were a psycho-analytic individual-realist, I should symbolically refine this. I should have a mispronunciation complex, I should say that life was like that and associate it with other incidents in which life was like that, I should have a mental ejaculation every time I mispronounced, and so on. As it is, it is merely an incident – what I may call a statistical incident. It happened, I occasionally mispronounce, it is all very personal, unreal, illogical, unsymbolical and poetic to me. I have never told it, poetically, as a good story to illustrate this or that or to mean this or that.[1] And in treating it in this way I am

[1] Except here!

sure I am closer to the incident as it happened and as it affected me, though I am not closer to what is called the reality of the incident. This is perhaps trivial and even irrelevant to the argument. Yet it is to me an exposition in life of the always threatening danger of the individual-real in literature and art.

§ 2

I have already said that I considered Herr Spengler wrong and Mr. Lewis right. To say that Herr Spengler is wrong is to say that he is wrong. To say that Mr. Lewis is right is to imply, because I place his right side by side with Herr Spengler's wrong, that I regret the argumentative rightness of his right: I not only object to Herr Spengler's systematic wrongness because it is wrong, but also because it is systematic. Herr Spengler perceives a conspiracy and is delighted, Mr. Lewis perceives a conspiracy and is infuriated. Therefore, though I admire Mr. Lewis because he is right, I restrict my admiration in so far as he is systematic: the obsession with conspiracy is no more wrong in Herr Spengler than in Mr. Lewis. I regret to see Mr. Lewis decorating his right with the trappings of argument: I regret to see him dramatizing his right realistically to impress the same audience as Herr Spengler does – emphasizing the individual-real as Spengler does the collective-real. I should like to

61

see Mr. Lewis being right, being unreal, being himself, rather than sending out his right to instruct the democratic mass on the same stage on to which Herr Spengler sends out his wrong. It is none of my business, of course, what Mr. Lewis does with his right; but in admiring Mr. Lewis and not admiring Herr Spengler it is only fair to point out that the former as well as the latter is guilty of realistic projections.

By projections I mean saying more, thinking more, knowing more, observing more, organizing more than is self. I mean creating the real. In Herr Spengler's writing I find nothing unreal; I find no self. In Mr. Lewis's writing I find a considerable unreal projecting itself realistically, organizing itself against, for example, James Joyce. I do not speak merely of attacking James Joyce or Sherwood Anderson or D. H. Lawrence. I speak of attacking by advocating a system to take the place of the system which certain aspects of James Joyce's work, say, represent to Mr. Lewis. I think this system should indeed be attacked in so far as it is a system and in so far as is necessary for a preservation of integrity. I do not think it should be replaced. I want the time-world removed and in its place to see – nothing. I do not want to see the unreal – Mr. Lewis's, mine, anyone's – become more than itself, become either intellectual (Spengler) or physical

(Lewis). I want it to remain inhuman and obscure. Both Herr Spengler and Mr. Lewis make it, the one in his wrongness, the other in his rightness, human and glaring. To me the secularistic subjective softness of the first is no more aggressively realistic than the secularistic 'objective hardness' of the second. For all Mr. Lewis's unreal, the question remains to him 'whether we should set out to transcend our human condition or whether we should translate into human terms the whole of our datum.' I agree with Mr. Lewis in discarding the first alternative, but I submit that the second contains in it two other alternatives and that in choosing the *wrong one* of these (as he does by creating the original pair of alternatives) Mr. Lewis leans towards rather than away from transcendentalism. For what he calls the datum is nothing but the unreal; to call it the datum and, further, to suggest the necessity of its translation from the unreal into the real, the personal (inhuman) into the human (physically collective) is only to oppose one kind of transcendentalism to another – the individual-real to the collective-real. In this he is identifying himself with critics who, like I. A. R. Richards, wish to find a place for literature and art 'in the system of human endeavours,' to prove the unreal to be but 'a finer organization of ordinary experiences'; that is, in order to combat the gross romanticism and rhodomontade of democratic realism, he turns merely to a more classical, aristocratic realism.[1] He thus reduces the difference between himself and Herr Spengler to a difference in taste rather than in principle; the distinction between right and wrong, unreal and real, which Mr. Lewis might be one of the few people able to maintain, becomes, as has already been pointed out, merely the distinction between good and bad, between two types of the real or between degrees in the real.

Man, as he becomes more man, becomes less nature. He becomes unreal. He loses homogeneity as a species. He lives unto himself not as a species but as an individual. He is lost as far as nature is concerned, but as he is separated from nature, this does not matter. He is in himself, he is unreal, he is secure. This sense of unreality, however, varies in individuals: it is weakest in the weakest individuals. These weakest individuals, missing the physical homogeneity which reality in nature would give man, construct by analogy an ideal homogeneity, a history, a reality of time. 'The means whereby to identify living forms,' Spengler says, 'is Analogy.' As systematic analogy with nature be-

---

[1] As instead of opposing a fine sexual indifference to the sexual impotence or sentimental feminism that he finds in modern life he flaunts a sentimental Spartan masculinity.

comes more and more difficult, the basis of analogy,
parallelism with nature, is removed; but the system
of analogy remains. A transference is made from
what Herr Spengler calls morphological equivalence
to functional equivalence. Instead of being nature-
like (like the species *man* in nature) he becomes man-
like (like the species man in man). The individual
is like himself collectively, really, not like himself
individually, unreally. It is now possible perhaps to
discuss more clearly the significance of the terms I
have been using: pessimism, optimism; collective-
real, individual-real; unreal. Herr Spengler, I
should say, is pessimistic at the sight of the disintegration of man as a natural species; he consoles
himself with a vision of man as a consistent analogous rather than homologous social mass. He has,
we might say, a melancholy, mystical vision of an
eternal structure of decay, whose processes may
be collectively appreciated and participated in.
His vision is the collective-real, by which he
manages to transcend the unreal. Mr. Lewis, I
should say, is fundamentally optimistic at the sight
of the disintegration of man as a natural species.
He is not distressed, I believe, by the fact that there
is a problem of individualism. He would face it
cheerfully if he were not so annoyed by Herr Spengler's gloomy evasion of it – by the whole time-
philosophy for which Spengler is but one of many

spokesmen. But he is distracted from his pursuit of the problem of individualism into the unreal, where is to be found its only satisfactory conclusion, by his annoyance with evasions of it like Herr Spengler's or Dr. Whitehead's. And in his annoyance he remains permanently distracted; he succeeds in doing no more than substituting for it another kind of evasion. I do not say that Mr. Lewis is an official spokesman of the individual-real in the way in which Herr Spengler is an official spokesman for the collective-real. But in opposing him without fully acknowledging the unreal he seems to me to be identifying himself with a brand of realism that is in its way as obnoxious as collective realism.

Let me elaborate what I consider to be the viewpoint of the individual-realists. They perceive the disintegration of man as a species and resent the philosophical substitute which the collective realists, with the help of history, make for the natural species – this analogical instead of homological species. They recognize that however removed man may now be from nature, analogies of the individual with natural history are less false than analogies of the individual with human history. Analogies of the individual with nature will become less and less exact as man becomes more and more removed from nature. But it is at any rate true that these analogies will hold as long as it will be possible to make them. Analogies of the individual with history will, on the other hand, become more and more exact, since they are invented rather than discovered analogies, analogies maintained by a system of representational cohesion. Historical analogy thus stands for the tyranny of democracy, while physical analogy stands for a Toryish anarchy – the direct communication of a few individuals with the physical world without the intervention of the symbolic species.[1] I think that anarchism is very nice;

[1] Deity to the collective-realist is reality as symbolic oneness; to the individual-realist, reality as rationalistic oneness. To the former therefore personality is an instrument for conceiving emotionally the mass character of this oneness; to the latter, an instrument for corroborating intellectually the individualistic character of this oneness. (Intellectual democracy as opposed to intellectual anarchy.) Mr. Lewis says: 'We have a god-like experience in that only' (personality). The collective-realist would say: 'We have a god-like experience in that only' (personality). The only difference between these two expressions is political. 'Evidences of a oneness seem everywhere apparent,' Mr. Lewis says. 'But we *need*, for practical purposes, the illusion of a plurality.' The 'practical purposes' are, presumably, the necessity of protecting this democratic oneness from the democratic mass: 'plurality' here means the plurality of the few. It is comprehensible, then, that Catholic thought should, by its scholasticism, appeal to Mr. Lewis – the political wisdom of an institution that keeps a small body of well-paid intelligentsia to administer Godhood to the not so individualistic, the not so well-paid worshipping mass. And Mr. Lewis is here at one with his rather more scholastic colleague in individualism, Mr. Eliot, who with his

but I do not think that anarchism is enough. I agree that morphological analogy is more literal than functional analogy; but as morphological analogy is bound to become less and less exact as the individual's memory of himself as a member of a species becomes more and more shady, it seems to me idle to maintain it at all (except humorously); especially idle to maintain it, this individual-real, categorically against the collective-real, and in doing so to lose sight of the only quality in which the individual is secure, in a certain personal unreality not affected by analogy of any kind. I am not much concerned about the philosophical invalidity of the individual-real; I am ready to admit that it is philosophically a more tenable position than the collective-real. Philosophical positions have all to do with versions of the real, and have varying degrees of tenability:

French co-littérateurs phrases the conflict between symbolic oneness and rationalistic oneness, or symbolic personality and rationalistic personality, more elegantly as the conflict between intuition and intelligence (between the feeling whole and the thinking whole, in Mr. Lewis's language). Individuality to the individualist is thus an intellectual fiction, as to the collective-realist it is the oneness which is the fiction ('Human individuality is best regarded as a kind of artificial Godhood' – Mr. Lewis. And again: 'We at least must *pretend* not to notice each other's presence, God and ourselves to be alone.') – the difference here being merely the difference between a sentimentalized Tory absolute and a sentimentalized Communist absolute.

but if a philosophical position have the maximum degree of intelligibility it does not alter the fact that any philosophical position is irrelevant to the individual and relevant only to a symbolic mass of individuals. The only position relevant to the individual is the unreal, and it is relevant because it is not a position but the individual himself. The individual-real is more indulgent of the individual-unreal than any other philosophical position; but this is a disadvantage rather than advantage to the unreal, since it actually means an encroachment upon, a parody of the unreal by the individual-real. It is about this encroachment and parody as it takes place in literature that I am really concerned. To put it simply, the unreal is to me poetry. The individual-real is a sensuous enactment of the unreal, opposing a sort of personally cultivated physical collectivity to the metaphysical mass-cultivated collectivity of the collective-real. So the individual-real is a plagiarizing of the unreal which makes the opposition between itself and the collective-real seem that of poetic to realistic instead of (as it really is) that of superior to inferior realistic; the real, personally guaranteed real-stuff to a philosophical, mass-magicked real-stuff. The result in literature is a realistic poeticizing of prose (Virginia Woolf or any 'good' writer) that competes with poetry, forcing it to make itself more poetic if it would count at all. Thus both the 'best' prose and the 'best' poetry are the most 'poetic'; and make the unreal, mere poetry, look obscure and shabby. And what have we, of all this effort? Sitwellian connoisseurship in beauty and fashion, adult Eliotry proving how individually realistic the childish, mass-magicked real-stuff can be if sufficiently documented, ambitious personal absolutes proving how real their unreal is, Steinian and Einsteinian intercourse between history and science, Joycian release of man of time in man of nature (collective-real in individual-real), cultured primitivism, cultured individualism, vulgar (revolutionary) collectivism, fastidious (anarchic) collectivism – it is all one: nostalgic, lascivious, masculine, Oedipean embrace of the real mother-body by the unreal son-mind.[1]

---

[1] Spenglerism is male religiosity and symbolism of the vulgar romantic as opposed to the refined classical kind. 'The Faustian soul looks for an immortality to follow the bodily end, a sort of marriage with endless space . . . till at last nothing remains visible but the indwelling depth-and-height energy of this self-extension.' The historical mind (the 'Faustian soul') overcomes its perpetual temporariness by a perpetual give-and-take between itself and the Great Mother reality, whom it honours with its philosophical erections (what Herr Spengler calls third-dimensional extension) and from whom it receives sensations of infinity – the Great Mother's gratitude for this masculine 'conquest' of herself. To the Spenglerist (the modernist) this infinity is vague, collective,

§ 3

In showing how the distinction between the collective-real and the individual-real meant really no more than a difference of degree – between degrees of good, for example – I might have carried the argument further. I might have shown that in thus revealing themselves as merely differences of degree, they reduced all oppositions that might be made between them to differences of degree. Take the opposition of *intellectual*, of the time-world (collective-real), to *physical*, of the selves-world (individual-real): *intellectual* proves itself to

metaphorical: 'somehow we are in nature'; somehow 'the "I" overwhelms the "Thou." ' The scientific world, the Great Mother, is dead; it is the fairy-tale brought to life in each fresh embrace of it by the historical world. To the individual-realist (the classicist) the masculine extension is actual and personal rather than metaphorical and collective: the fairy-tale individual mind acquires an immediate ahistorical liveliness from its intercourse with the Great Scientific Mother. Herr Spengler despises the classical ahistorical attitude to reality. But overstudiously; for it is rather more than less than modern; it is based on the minute of the moment, not on the age of the moment. Both the collective-realist and the individual-realist function by sexual phantasia; the only difference between them being that the latter claims to be able to have closer contact with the Great Mother than the former – one merely historically, through the experience of the time-group to which he belongs, the other scientifically, through *his* experience *now*.

mean based on an emotionally maintained unity; *physical* proves itself to mean based on a unity maintained by reason. The opposition then of *intellectual* to *physical* (of Herr Spengler, say, to Mr. Lewis) or of intuition to intelligence (of John Middleton Murry, say, to T. S. Eliot) is a restatement of the more hackneyed opposition of *emotional* to *intellectual*; which in turn proves itself to be not an opposition at all but an expression of degrees of historical advancement.

Thus to Herr Spengler 'Soul,' the felt self, is an eternal, romantic youthfulness in man; which expresses itself by comparing itself (analogy) continually with the world, the not-self, the unfelt self; which is the permanently aged, self-apprehending, being self of nature. Herr Spengler does not see that once having made this opposition he has placed himself in the position of choosing between them, that one or the other must represent the illusion of one or the other. Failing to do this, by maintaining a communicative opposition between them, he shows that both are illusions (mutually, one of the other). To compare mathematics and logic is to show wherein both are false, by reason of their resemblance to each other. If the likeness were true, it would be a complete likeness, it would be identity, and one or the other must disappear; and it follows that the one in whose terms the likeness is stated is the most false, the most illusory. The likeness is maintained by the self's fear of self, the fear of personal loneliness. The mathematical unity of the world sets an example for the historical unity of the Soul, the time-child of the world; a community self, a Culture, is invented to keep the self company. All the values by which this self is organized are derivative values. 'Logic is a kind of mathematic.' Language is an expression of functional relationships, it is not just language, the tongue of a self; it must co-ordinate, *express* the members of the community self rather than *say* each self; it must be comprehensible, that is, it must show likeness – if it does not show likeness it is attacked as obscure. A painter or a composer or a sculptor is one who demonstrates, through his medium, this communicative opposition between the world of reality and the world of self. The poet is one who, by personal duplicity, takes it upon himself to prove that the opposition is so and not so; his poetry is a demonstration of the righteousness of duplicity. 'Nature is to be handled scientifically, History poetically.' Self is poetic self. Nature, mathematical life, is the become, the eternally grown-up; History, logical life, is the becoming, the eternally childish.

The time-advocate, whom I shall call the philosopher, does not see, or is afraid to see, that the become and the becoming are both mutually illusory Worlds of reality: that they are self-created refutations of individuality to which the individual succumbs from imperfection. He forgets, that is, that the individual is an *unbecoming* and that the categories 'becoming' and 'become' are really a derivation from him, a historical reconstruction. Unbecoming is the movement away from reality, the becoming unreal. What is called the become is therefore really the starting point of the unbecoming. What is called the becoming is therefore really a hypothetical opposition to the unbecoming. The become and the becoming are both oppositions to the unbecoming; the become from which the becoming is derived is a static order organized against the unbecoming, the become is the material of disintegration. The becoming is an attempt to check the disintegration of the become from real to unreal by reversing its direction, turning it from real to more real, making Nature suggest History. This is done by reading into Nature a necessity and inventing for the species man, a digression from Nature, an analogical Darwinistic Nature. The necessity of Nature is then called Causality, the necessity of History, Destiny.

The philosopher, then, is the formal opponent of

the unreal. To him the individual is a piece, Nature is a whole, and the individual cannot match the wholeness, the real of Nature, except by sharing in a community self, the collective-real. To one who recognizes the reality of the unreal, each individual is a positive unit produced by the disintegration of the reality of Nature. Nature is a process; and the pieces of this process are the wholes, not Nature. To the philosopher thought is a reintegration of the scattered pieces into a symbolic whole, which may then be related to the literal whole of Nature; it also brings about a close interrelation of these pieces among themselves, a functional conformity. To a believer in the unreal, thought confirms disintegration. It is not a collective system. It is each self.

This opposition of the philosopher to the individual-unreal remains merely a philosophical opposition. For it is the nature of the believer in the unreal to be without a system – a system implies collective association (it is even impossible to give him a label, like 'philosopher'); and the philosopher could only be opposed by a system. Indeed so thoroughly 'unselfish' is the character of the unreal self that its just conclusion is a sort of social disappearance. This is practically impossible because to the unreal self is attached a physical memory of the process by which the self was made, a birthmark of piecemealness opposing to the complete unreal self a reconstructed, ideal whole of origin. The unreal self is forced to indulge this. Sex, for instance, is an indulgence by the unreal self of romantic physical nostalgia. To the unreal self this indulgence is incidental, to the philosopher it is fundamental. Herr Spengler's whole inspiration is nostalgic. (So is T. S. Eliot's. So is Mr. C. B. Cochran's – every 'Cochran's Revue' is a variation on the theme of the integration of historical pageantry, an epistemological medley of primitivism, Shakespeareanism, Charlestonianism, etc.)

The philosopher has, however, his formal opponent. His formal opponent is one who resents the gross personification of man as the ideal individual of the species; to whom Spenglerish dualism is only 'bad philosophy' (Mr. Lewis); to whom good philosophy is a severe monism, a literal, aware dwelling in the mathematical (being) self of Nature. Instead of History we have Criticism: the formal opponent of the philosopher is the Critic. And, once more, the difference between them shows itself to be only a difference of degree; criticism defines itself as 'better,' more intellectual philosophy than 'intellectual,' 'bad' philosophy. The critic (this new, anti-philosophical type that I am speaking of) dismisses the childish, historical self as a travesty of the adult self of physical

76

reality; as that sick, inner-eyeish, Strindbergian 'subjective' self, which has poisoned instead of nourished itself on reality, that the psychologist, physician of reality, attempts to redeem from the subconscious (run-down, pathological reality). For the philosophical system of logic the critic substitutes the mathematical system of reason. The world of Self is not to be deduced from the world of Nature; there is but one world, and the self is in this, a like fact with other facts, not a subjective fact in a shadowy world of analogy. What Mr. Lewis calls the 'success of reason' would permanently establish self as objective fact, as the individual-real. The language of the individual-real neither expresses the members of a community-self nor isolates each self. It expresses the extrinsic value of the self for a system in which there are only extrinsic values; as the language of the collective-real expresses its intrinsic value for a system in which there are only intrinsic values, which are made valid, however, by means of oppositional relation to a system of extrinsic values. So that for the individual-realist, the self is also poetic self; rational instead of intuitive, 'physical' instead of 'intellectual'; a poetic detail of real reality rather than a real detail of poetic reality.

The critic, then, like the philosopher, is an opponent of the unreal. The unreal self is intrinsic self, intrinsic without respect to a system of extrinsic values; it is without value. It is more than anarchistic; it does not treat individualistically with values; it supersedes them. The unreal self is not poetic self, it is self. It is not a detail of co-ordinated reality.[1] It is an absolute, disconnected, hopeless whole. To the philosopher thought is memory of Mother-Nature. To the critic thought is thoughts

[1] These positions might perhaps be more clearly illustrated in their respective attitudes to place. The collective-realist is poetically attached to the idea of the *there*; reality is romantic, far-away, collective – superior to the personal *here*; it is the eternally old fountain of eternal youthfulness. From this feeling comes the morbid fondness of Western man for other races, so severely condemned by Mr. Lewis. The individual-realist is poetically attached to the idea of the *here*; reality is classical, local, individual – superior to the collective *there*; it is the eternally old fountain of eternal adultishness. The first attitude ends in doctrinaire universalism, the second in doctrinaire provincialism: both the collective-realist and the individual-realist believe in the social significance of locality, differing only in their location of locality. Both, in fact, suffer from this obsession with social significance. Take, for example, niggerish jazz: its real strength and attraction is that it is movement free from significance; pure, ritualistic, barbaric social pleasure that can only be properly understood and enjoyed by those who understand and enjoy the civilized individuality of significance. To the romantic universalist niggerish jazz is a religious devotion of the sensations to eternal youthfulness. To the classical provincialist it is a depraved, democratic infantilism. Both emotionalize it, the one as elevation, the other as degradation: to one the jazz

– diverse, objective, related facts of reality. There is
no antithesis between the position of the philosopher
and that of the critic: the philosopher invents instruments for observing and measuring reality from afar
and has dream-embraces of reality: the critic says:
'Sentimental stuff and nonsense! I am *in* reality.'
The critic, that is, is a little more sentimental,
ambitious, intellectual, poetic, snobbish than the
philosopher. To both of them thought means connection with reality. To both of them poetry means
eloquent consciousness of life. To the unreal self,
to whom they are both brother-opponents, thought
is separation from reality, and poetry is the consciousness (the perhaps ineloquent consciousness)
of what is not life, of what is self. A tree (even this
is doubtful, for it is a late, nearly human form) is
not born; it lives. What is born ceases with birth
to live; it is self, unreal self. For this reason it
is impossible to call the unreal self poetic self:
'poetic' and 'poetry' are words drunk with reality,
they have indeed become by popular use rhetorical
substitutes for 'real' and 'reality.' By reality I mean
organized, 'universal ' reality. It would be possible
to speak of the unreal self as the real self, the self of

nigger is the angel-symbol, to the other the devil-symbol.
While the only one able to intellectualize it properly is the
jazz nigger himself – generally an individual, unreal, paleface
Jew with a dusky make-up of social clownishness.

separate reality, were it not for the community sense that belongs to philosophical or critical reality. I might have said, instead of unreal self, dissociated self. The problem of the right word is more difficult in the case of 'poetic' and 'poetry.' I can point out that the real self is poetic, and, in opposition to both real and poetic, put the unreal self. It is painful, however, to be forced to leave 'poetry' to the real self and to call the poetry of the unreal self unreality. Poetry is a stolen word, and in using it one must remain conscious of its perverted sense in the service of realism, or one suddenly finds oneself discussing not poetry but realism; and this is equally painful. But if poetry is a stolen word, so is reality: reality is stolen from the self, which is thus in its integrity forced to call itself unreal.

Poetry may perhaps for the moment be saved for the poet and for the unreal self if the collective-real, the individual-real, philosophy, criticism, are denominated 'literature.' Literature then clearly represents the symbolical, the rational, the romantic, the classical, the collective, the individualistic reality of man. Further, if we make it clear to ourselves that all literature is poetic, then we are separating poetry from literature and drawing a sharp line between what is poetic and what is poetry. Further still, we are discovering that literature is everything but the unreal self, it is the society of reality; it is History, it is Nature, it is Philosophy, it is Reason, it is Criticism, it is Art. Most of all perhaps literature is Art, the seizure and confirmation of reality by the senses, the literalizing of the world of reality. The more 'abstract' Art is (the less symbolical) the more real it is. Poetry is thus seen to be neither literature nor Art. Literature is the ladder of reality: the historian yields to the scientist, the scientist to the philosopher, the philosopher to the critic, the high-priest of Reason, of which 'great works of art' are the visible signs: for Reason is Reality.[1]

§ 4

This has been, so far, the elaboration of a point of view. From here on will be found various applications of this point of view. Generally in exposi-

[1] Or again, these positions might be illustrated in their respective attitudes to size. The collective-realist thinks of society as a big, symbolical unit, the individual-realist as a small, concrete unit. The unreal self does not think of size, or of society, as significant concepts at all. The collective-realist makes the individual emotionally as large as the many. The individual-realist makes the individual intellectually as large as himself – that is, of a standard realistic size. The unreal self gets rid of even the fractional reality of the self of the individual-realist: it is not the quantitative nothing derided by Mr. Lewis, but a sizeless invisibility from reality. Mr. Lewis disapproves of nothing; and he disapproves of Bradley's Absolute because 'he did not succeed in relieving it of a

tive writing there is no distinction made between what is organically elaborative and what is incidentally applicative: all is elaborative and therefore over-elaborative. The argument continues to elaborate itself even though it has come to an end; it incorporates the application of the point of view in the development of the point of view; it does not distinguish between argument and comment. I wish to distinguish carefully here between argument and comment. A certain very small amount of illustration and instancing is necessary to focus an argument properly: the smaller the better, since most specific reference and substantiation is a concession to the audience, which generally cannot think purely, that is, without the machinery of learning. Once the argument is focused, it should not develop further. It should repeat itself, like an acid test, in each fresh application. All philosophical or critical systems are the absorption of an original point of view by the facts to which it applies itself: the force of the point of view is lost, it becomes a

certain impressive scale and impending weight.' What he seems to imply is an Absolute temperately placed between all and nothing – a sort of safely quantitative qualitative absolute; a short, certain, academic eternity as opposed to a vulgar, tentatively eternal eternity; a small, well-bred, provincial church in which to worship a congregationalist Absolute as opposed to a popular arena erected to a universalist (demogogic as opposed to pedagogic) Absolute.

convenience by which facts organize themselves and eventually dominate the point of view. All philosophical or critical systems are no more than learning, a synthesis of instances, and therefore develop generalizations that mean nothing without instances. I have no philosophical or critical system to advance; I am interested in generalizations that mean something without instances, that are unreal, since they mean something by themselves. Generalizations of this sort, when applied to instances, should not be absorbed by them. The argument should dismiss instances with comment on instances, remain meaning in itself. If it does this then it is capable of maintaining an opposition between right and wrong. If it does not, it only becomes a better wrong than the wrong it attacks. It becomes real.

By this I do not mean that I am a subjective critic. A subjective critic is one who converts his point of view into a system, makes it real: his point of view must be continually fed by works of art, otherwise it ceases. I propose here a point of view that is completely unto itself, that is unreal, that is independent of instances. When it meets instances it comments on them by repeating itself. Nor is it subjective, since subjectivity implies an objective world of experience from which it must perpetually derive itself. I speak of a point of view which is self and only self, of an unreality which is every one's to the extent to which he is able to extricate himself from quantitative reality and be, instead of a purse-proud something, a proud and purseless nothing. What is this I am describing? – the poetic (a stolen word) self.

I

Mr. Herbert Read (*Reason and Romanticism*).

'That the critical spirit, expressed in reason, will ever evolve a synthesis capable of fulfilling the functions of religion is evidently impossible. Reason and emotion only unite in very rare and special perceptions; such perceptions are not capable of generalization. . . . Emotions are too diffuse, too widely distributed, ever to be unified in reason, which is an evolved possession, never perfect at all, and only approaching perfection in the rarest individuals.' The impossible, Mr. Read admits, is attainable in the rare 'universal mind.' Universal in the strict critical sense proves itself to mean 'broad' in the eighteenth-century sense – aristocratic. So Goethe (both for Herr Spengler and Mr. Read) is the ideal universal type; so is Leibnitz, so is Diderot. Mr. Read confirms my description of the philosophico-critical system in his definition of universality as 'a capacity *to receive* all knowledge

84

and events with equanimity and unprejudiced per-
cipience; and to build up a positive attitude on this
clear and perceptual basis.'[1] From here we are
gently conducted to the proposition that 'poetry is,
in short, delectation.' Poetry is, in short, a game-like,
sporting, snobbish exercise of reason, the most
ambitious display of knowledge possible: 'and the
greater our knowledge, the more surcharged it is
with the perception of values, the deeper will be the
delight aroused in us.' What is reason? Reason is

[1] We observe the same aristocratic bias in Mr. Lewis. The
universal mind (the artist's or seeing mind) is not lodged in a
collective all but in a selected few for all: individual-real
(cultured anarchism) opposed to collective-real (cultured
democracy) and to individual-unreal (anarchism is not
enough). The anarchistic, artistic, critical mind is not interested in individuality as individuality but as superior individuality, as reason: it is an expert in reality, it sees what is
'here.' It is a poetic common-sense seeing (through its
monocle) a vision 'classical,' 'geometric,' 'severe' (' "Classical"
is for me anything which is nobly defined and exact, as
opposed to that which is fluid' – Mr. Lewis). It does not
believe in lower-class doing but in upper-class thinking:
laissez-faire anarchism. It is against violent sympathies and
antipathies; it is provincial but informed. Reason is aloof,
courteous prejudice ('we should grow more and more polite' –
Mr. Lewis); intelligent conventionality, haughty submission
to reality. For example, Mr. Lewis's objections to Bolshevism
only apply to it where it is in action, not anarchistic; not to
Bolshevism as a polite 'vision' – that is, in so far as it is the
gospel of an uncultured many rather than the dogma of a
cultured few.

socialized reality, 'the sum total of awareness, ordained and ordered to some specific end or object of attention.'

Mr. Read on metaphysical poetry: metaphysical poetry is 'emotional apprehension of thought.' This means, we discover, individual mind systematically apprehending reality: '. . . we find in Donne a mind poised at the exact turn of the course of philosophy drawing his inspiration right back from scholastic sources, and yet at the same time eagerly surveying the new future promised by the science of Copernicus and Galileo. Chapman, on the other hand, is in a remarkable degree the forerunner of humanist philosophy – of Hume and Spinoza in particular. He is aware, above all things, of 'the constant and sacred harmony of life.' In this way criticism classifies poetry according to the poet's intelligence of reality – that is, according to his conventionality, his politeness; whereas that Donne wrote poetry at all was because he was able to separate himself rudely from the reality of which he was in a class sense a privileged agent.[1]

[1] Again we perceive the same emphasis on superior as opposed to plain, ordinary individuality. The man of reason is an aristocrat of race-individuality; the race, of course, being a superior race – if it were not superior it would be unendowed with reason. But (and this is a point for which we must be grateful to Mr. Lewis) race-superiority (individuality) is administered for the whole race by only one class in the

86

On Dante and Guido Cavalcanti: 'Or, more exactly, all experience, whether intellectual or sensual or instinctive, was regarded as equally and

race; so that while 'char-lady' is lady by race, she is not lady by class (lady of reason). Char-ladies who confuse race with class and forget their place do so 'to their undoing.' Their undoing is apparently a muddy-watery, unladylike laughter that is not, of course, reason. What is reason? Mr. Lewis tells us: 'Let us rather meet with the slightest smile all those things that so far we have received with delirious rapture.' The change is not so much from laughing rapture to haughty smiling as from one we to another kind of we – a democratic we to an aristocratic we. Thus, the true we of the Machine Age is not, according to Mr. Lewis, the mob but the capital-istic, anarchistic individualists – the Mr. Ford's. Mr. Ford admits, Mr. Lewis points out, that he could not live the life of one of his workmen. While in a ruthlessly democratic scheme (Bolshevism or Spenglerism) there is only a mob-life disguised as Culture. Spengler would be the ideal romantic mob-historian; Tacitus, possibly, the ideal classical, urbane, polite, smiling, anarchistic, *laissez-faire*, perspectiveless, ahistorical, geometric individualist-historian. To the collec-tive-realist the mob moves, to the individual-realist it is static ('The Russian workman and peasant under the Bolshevik is the same as he was under the Tsar, though less free and minus the consolations of a religion ' – Mr. Lewis). Mob-philosophy (mob-individualism, liberty, organized *laissez-faire*) is 'against human reason, motiveless and hence mad' (again Mr. Lewis). What is human reason? Mr. Lewis's 'young catholic student' tells us: 'not that some bank-clerk on a holiday has dis-covered that trees have something to say for themselves.' But when some bank-president, superman or Saint 'traverses a wood with complete safety' – that is with proud, rational, individualistic submission, with sedate, conventional, geo-

87

contemporaneously the subject-matter of their poetry. The result was a desirable continuity or coherence; imagination, contemplation, and sensibility becoming fused within the perfect limits of a human mind.' Mr. Read then quotes from William Walrond Jackson, D.D., 'Introduction' to his translation of the *Convivio* (Oxford, 1909), p. 18: 'The poet was inspired by an overmastering desire to link the present with the past and with the future, to blend all knowledge into one coherent system, and to bring the experiences of life into one harmonious whole. . . .' Plainly, this donnish, publicly fostered service of the poet to reason would be absorbed, if he were a poet at all, in his essential, enduring unreality by the time his work reached

metric curiosity. Human reason is Authority, authority received and authority administered; and it is interesting that both Mr. Lewis and his young catholic student emphasize this sexual duality of reason. To Mr. Lewis reason is the quiet, conventional, slightly smiling she availing herself of her feminine privilege to remain seated, and also the conventional, brainy, impressive, standing-up he, viewing the general situation with brilliant restraint. The young catholic student outlines Baron von Hugel's definition of authority: 'By it, the force and light of the few are applied to the dull majority, the highest in a man to his own average.' Baron von Hugel's own words on this Church of Individualism (for the few), quoted by him, are: 'The Church is thus, both ever and everywhere, progressive and conservative; both reverently free-lance and official; both, as it were, male and female, creative and reproductive. . . .'

the criticism of four hundred years later. Instead criticism keeps artificially alive the derived reality of the work, submerging in it what intrinsic unreality it may have had. 'The true metaphysical poet is conscious of no such dualism: his thought is in its very process poetical.' Poetry is reason. 'Leibnitz has defined an intelligent author as one who includes the most of reality in the least possible compass.' And further . . . 'the poet is in a very real sense the product of his age – witness especially Dante' ('age' meaning 'the most of reality in the least possible compass'). These two statements comment sufficiently on themselves. What recommendation has Mr. Read for the modern poet? He looks 'to the modern physicists, whose work would seem to provide a whole system of thought and imagery ready for fertilization in the mind of the poet.' This again, is its own best comment on itself.

2

Mr. Lewis is merely a pamphleteer of anarchism, T. S. Eliot is a serious moralist, bent on professing rather than on attacking. We therefore look to Mr. Lewis for explanatory rhetoric and to Mr. Eliot for explanatory ritual: in many respects his modest behaviour is more illuminating than all Mr. Lewis's language. After years of hard and brilliant service as a poetical yogi Mr. Eliot suddenly discovered that he had all the time been acting on behalf of the universe of man, of human nature, instead of in behalf of the universe of reason, of natural nature. So he replaced religiousness by priggishness; he went from a popular, mystical cult to an exclusive Thomist club; from large, symbolical (ironic) outer circle abstractions to small specific (concrete) inner circle abstractions.

Instead of attacking the time-mob, like Mr. Lewis, he withdrew himself from it and left it to carry on the orthodox, unanimous flux so obnoxious to Mr. Lewis, yet so necessary to both Mr. Lewis' and Mr. Eliot's anarchism: the basis of anarchistic individuality is not authentically individualistic, but snobbish. Mr. Lewis's incentives to anarchism are political – 'for the sake of the ride'; Mr. Eliot's are moral, that is, self-protective – the ride was for the sake of running away. He ran away from the collective-real to the individual-real (the *Criterion* furnishes us with a progressive record of Mr. Eliot's movements). Like Mr. Lewis he opposed aristocratic orthodoxy (anarchism) to democratic orthodoxy (co-operation); he deserted the collective dogma of periods for the collective dogma of individuals. 'For those of us who are higher than the mob, and lower than the man of inspiration, there is always *doubt*; and in doubt we are living parasitically (which is better than not living at all) on the minds of the men of genius of the past who have believed something' (from the *Enemy*, January, 1927). Mr. Lewis advocates grandiloquently but vaguely aristocratic orthodoxy in general; Mr. Eliot is dryly and specifically in pursuit of *the* or at least *an* aristocratic orthodoxy. The difference is that between irritated rightness and alarmed priggishness. Mr. Lewis is merely led astray by his extravagant though praiseworthy fury with democratic orthodoxy; his worshipful enthusiasm for the classical man of quiet is not dogma but pique against the modern romantic man of action (time-flux, space-motion). Mr. Eliot upholds the man of quiet from dogma. He is a minority-representative, as the man of the time-flux is a majority-representative. Mr. Eliot's position demonstrates clearly the relation of the individual-real to the collective-real: it is a priggish, self-protective minority-attitude to the same material which is the substance of the dogma of the collective-real. But he objects to 'mentalism' not only, I should say, because it generally means mob-mentalism, but equally because it may mean unreal, unorthodox individuality; his anarchism is timidity fallen between two stools. Mr. Lewis, however, objects to mentalism, I feel, chiefly because it generally means demogogic mob-mentalism. 'By this proposed transfer from the beautiful *objective*, *material*, world of common sense, over to the "organic" world of chronological mentalism, you lose not only the clearness of outline, the static beauty, of the things you commonly apprehend; you lose also the clearness of outline of your own individuality which apprehends them.' I do not think Mr. Eliot would have been capable of saying 'your own individuality'; I do not indeed believe that Mr. Lewis is naturally an individual-realist, but that he has been unfortunately stung into a pose.[1]

[1] Mr. Lewis's predominant emotion is disgust and he is therefore snobbishly old-fashioned; Mr. Eliot's is moral anxiety, and he is therefore snobbishly 'advanced' – what seems old-fashioned or mediæval or Thomist in Mr. Eliot is really his greater (than the silly emotional orthodox mob's) strictness in keeping up-to-date, in time with the universe of reason. He is at pains to discover the right side and to fight on it. Mr. Lewis is so disgusted with everything that he has abandoned all positive questions of right, and like a Swiss, retained nothing but his fighting conscience, a haughtiness of bearing in which alone he finds himself in sympathy with Mr. Eliot. In matters of faith they must certainly disagree. Mr. Eliot's Toryism is modern, intellectual, in sober perspective. Mr. Lewis's is petulantly old-fashioned, sentimental, 'geometric': the good, Swiss stern old days when everything happened anyhow, without historical significance or morality, are his fighting, anarchistic slogan against the presumptuous mob-consciousness of modern life. What Mr. Lewis fails to see is that if he devoted his energy to individualism (cultivating his own individuality) instead of anarchism (knocking the mob on the head with his individuality) the mob might develop a social regularity, an automatic geometricity that even he might

Aristocratic (as opposed to democratic) orthodoxy is not, as I have already indicated, a pose with Mr. Eliot. I said he had *an* orthodoxy. It would be helpful to an understanding of the problem to discover what the nature of an aristocratic orthodoxy may be. In Mr. Eliot's case, this is all too obviously: a humble, up-to-date respect for the best, internationally sifted great names. A practical-minded Toryism, which says, in gently criticizing Mr. Anthony M. Ludovici's more journalistic Toryism (The *Monthly Criterion*, July, 1927): 'Mr. Ludovici is engaged in forming what might be called a myth or idea for the Tory Party. Such a myth or idea has much to commend it; and I sympathize with so many of his views that I may declare at once what seems to me the great weakness of his construction: he isolates politics from economics, and he isolates it from religion.' What Mr. Eliot's attitude to economics is it is difficult to determine; I should say from various evidences that economics to him did not mean a human problem but an academic tradition worthy of study. Mr. Eliot has, from time to time, spoken more specifically on religion. In the review from which I have just quoted, Mr. Eliot further says: 'Toryism is essenti-

share in without disturbance to his individuality; that it is the anarchism of a few that gives false historical significance to the days of man, not the co-operative unanimity of the many.

93

ally Anglican; Roman Catholicism, which in our time draws its greatest support from America, is more in harmony with Republicanism. The problem of Toryism should be rather to make the Church of Laud survive in an age of universal suffrage. . . .' Further, he ardently seconds Mr. Ludovici in his recommendation that the Conservative Party should encourage *thought*, 'the activity of men of thought who are not and who do not desire to be parliamentarians.' In such quiet language does Mr. Eliot phrase his gospel of timid, aristocratic mentalism – a kind of politico-literary extract of Anglo-Catholicism, if we may judge by signs. His demands are familiar to every properly brought-up British schoolboy: that the Church must have more power, that the Kingship must be strengthened, and that Aristotle must be studied, supplemented by an Anglican reading of St. Thomas if the lad is to enter literature. Yes, literature. I had nearly forgotten that Mr. Eliot began his Progress as a Poet. But Mr. Eliot, finding himself higher than the mob and lower than the man of inspiration, is modest; he does not ask to be considered, or consider himself, as a poet. Unless we are deceived by his modesty, he would be content to be Bishop or to be Professor Saintsbury.

3

Mr. Roger Fry in *Transformations* concerns himself with the distinction between pure and impure art – 'a distinction which Mr. Richards has the good fortune to be able to ignore.' Mr. Richards, we learn from his *Principles of Literary Criticism* (published in 1925, the first text-book of psychologico-literary criticism) is interested in value rather than in purity. Criticism is to him a minute and comprehensive gradation of what T. E. Hulme called the world of religious and ethical values; purity, a social rather than æsthetic attribute; a moral term, by which a work is described as a public act of its author. To Mr. Fry a work is not conduct, it is a thing; its purity as a thing depends on its dissociation from authorship. It is impossible not to prefer Mr. Fry's criterion to Mr. Richards'; the former is plainly trying to discover the laws of goodness in works, the latter, the laws of goodness in humanity. The works we have with us; humanity, the idea of species, must be philosophically evoked.

But what is the nature of the work as thing? According to Mr. Fry its nature would seem to be reality. It is created by a sharp separation of the author's personality from the material with which he works, so that his work, when complete, is to be classified with nature, the world of mathematical reality, rather than with man, to whom reality is a sentimental objectification of his subjectivity. I should say that Mr. Fry's criticism made possible a clearer sense of a work's *self* than Mr. Richards', but that it created a misunderstanding of the nature of this self by identifying purity with reality. In Mr. Fry's criticism the homologue of a work would be a thing. But what is a thing and how is it pure? Pure means being whole, single in element, nothing but self, thoroughly new and fresh. Impure means being more and less than whole, complex in element, not possessing thoroughly new and fresh selfhood. The 'things' of what is called reality are mere interpretative morsels, tainted with pedigree. To me the thingishness in a work depends on no real homologue; the work is a thing of its own kind, without homologue. The material with which an author works is not reality but what he is able to disentangle from reality: in other words I think the identity is rather of purity and unreality. An author must first of all have a sure apprehension of what is self in him, what is new, fresh, not history, synthesis, reality. In every person there is the possibility of a small, pure, new, unreal portion which is, without reference to personality in the popular, social sense, self. I use 'self' in no romantic connotation, but only because it is the most vivid word I can find for this particular purefaction. When this self has been *isolated* from all that is impression and impurity of contact in an individual, then a 'thing,' a work, occurs, it is discharged from the individual, it is self; not *his* self, but self. If it is not discharged, it is immediately reabsorbed in that composite accident of reality by which he is known to others as a person. Thus many people without creative ability – the ability to discharge self – must feel for one passing moment that isolated purity in themselves which might, if they were able to sustain it a little longer, turn into 'things.' In those who can from time to time discharge self, the power is not constant: if it were, 'creation' would cease – creation is intermittent recurrence and repossession of this power – and there would be death, bright death.

The power, then, is not synthetic, is not to compose things, but to isolate them; it is an analytic power. Mr. Fry describes the reaction to works of art as a reaction to a relation. This could only refer to works which were compositions, attempts to create, by a synthetic, material (non-personal) action of the senses, real things; for relation can only result from synthesis. A work-thing of this kind is a pattern of reality, an arrangement of elements; and pattern is accident. The author of a synthetic work can choose the elements of which it is to be composed, but they work themselves out: the so-called neces-

97   G

sity of reality is really *accident*. The reaction therefore to the kind of work Mr. Fry speaks of, a 'real'
work, is a reaction to accident: the critic, himself
presumably a pattern of reality, experiences a shock
from meeting another pattern which is command-
ingly different and hypnotizes him into a rearrangement of the elements of which he is composed –
'the esthetic emotion' is here a sensual recombination of personality. For this reason I consider such
esthetic emotion false and escapist. The experience,
on the other hand, of a critic confronted with an
'unreal' work, would, I believe, be this: if it were a
thing of pure, isolated self, he could not perceive
it except with what was pure, isolated self in him.
He would be forced for the moment to discard what
was real in him; he might, by means of the thing,
succeed in discharging self: the operation of the
thing on him would have an analytic effect separating in him the pure from the impure, protecting
him for the moment from the 'esthetic emotion'
with which in fact he generally reacts to everything.
When Mr. Fry says 'In literature there is no immediate sensual pleasure,' he is really commenting on the
analytic, unreal quality of the word as opposed to
the synthetic (sense-combining), real quality of the
instrumentalities of the material arts. Word-works
in which there is an immediate sensual pleasure are
ones which have been artified, realized. Words in

their pure use, which I assume to be their poetic use, are denials rather than affirmations of reality. The word *hat*, say, does not create a real hat: it isolates some element in the real hat which is not hat, which is unreal, the hat's self.

But my description of this unreality would at first seem to correspond with the unreal world of poetry described by A. C. Bradley. Mr. Fry quotes Dr. Bradley: 'For its (poetry's) nature is not to be a part, nor yet a copy, of the real world (as we commonly understand that phrase), but to be a world by itself, independent, complete, autonomous.' The key-word in this definition is *world*: Dr. Bradley is not writing about unreal self but about romantic humanity. Poetry represents to him the world of fancy; and by fancy he means ethical, realistic fancy – the real world of man as opposed to the real world of mathematical nature. Nor is this a true opposition: it is impossible to overlook the significance of the term *world* – we have here all over again the ambitious, analogical Soul-World of Herr Spengler.

Mr. Fry is at pains to point out the alien, psychological, literary element in various plastic works, in determining what is 'pure' art. The very term 'art' forces him to confine his definition to the purely real. So that he can do no more than make a sharp distinction between the art of the real world and the art of the unreal (psychological, literary) world. We are to conclude that in its way the art of the unreal world (literature) is pure: what is impure is a mixing of these two worlds. Mr. Fry is only annoyed by literary art, not by artistic literature.

But the unreal, literary, psychologically organized self-world is the collective-real: its existence depends on a belief in reality, though in reality as a myth. Nor is the self of Mr. Fry's real world any less 'psychological': but merely a more anarchistic, individualistic associate of reality, reality hence as reason rather than myth, or, as Mr. Lewis might put it, as God Himself rather than religion. And so the issue between realism and idealism is no more than a quarrel over methods of affirming reality: rationalistic instinct as against emotionalistic intellect, short-way-round as against long-way-round, anarchistic as against communistic psychology. Realism is the method of artistic art, idealism, of literary art. Art is the use of self to make syntheses – things *like* 'real' things: all controversy about art-methods narrows itself down to a disagreement over what real things are *like*.[1]

The controversy, that is, is not over principles but over style; and style is, ultimately, not so much

---

[1] See, for example, in Mr. Lewis's *Time and Western Man*, the chapter *The Object as King of the Physical World*.

the manner of a work as the manner in which it is talked about. The end of most criticism is not to determine what a work must be but to fix the language of criticism; and it follows that most works are therefore without the quality of self: they are made merely to fit the language of criticism popular at the time or that happens to have made an impression on the author.

Criticism has to do with what is already done, with what has already happened: it is a cataloguing of reality, and reality is the past. A work that invites criticism is an exercise in history, whether its author has the man-history point of view or the nature-history point of view; it is the creation of old stuff. Most works are old stuff, differing only in style; in how they innovate old stuff; in their critical language: they agree in principle, that only old stuff is possible – reality, synthesis, pattern, recombination.

Mr. Read blames Mr. George Moore for using the word 'objective' to describe what he means by 'pure poetry' – 'objective,' Mr. Read complains, is a psychological term. It is not one of the what Mr. Read calls 'universal terms.' A universal term should convey 'an inner conviction of necessity.' What Mr. Read is really complaining of is the unsystematic use of a psychological term. Criticism should use the same language about art as it does about reality; it should unite philosophy and art in Reason. Reason is personal, direct, conscious traffic in reality. It is enlightened magic ('an inner conviction of necessity'). Primitive man, being more instinctively aware of reality, did not need to have his magic (his art) enlightened. The primitive artist was a seer, the civilized artist is a visionary: to Mr. Read reason is the ability to have correct visions of reality. It is interesting to find that Mr. Lewis uses the same language of criticism. The artist is to him a wide-awake dreamer; 'Don Quixote, or the Widow Wadman, is as *real*, to put it no higher than that, as most people ostensibly alive and walking the earth to-day'; 'For me art is the civilized *substitute* for magic.' To both Mr. Read and Mr. Lewis purity means that magical intelligence, that inspired (rather than primitive, stupid 'objective') literalness which may be philosophically defined as the individual-real. Both, moreover, object to art that is magical in the primitive sense as to an anachronism; it is fabricated sensationism, it is the collective-real, it is ideological rather than natural symbolism.[1] They are interested in getting man into proper focus in

[1] To Mr. Lewis, Science, popularized magic, rather than Reason, the artist's personal magic. (Compare, similarly, New Testament pseudo-primitive communism, with properly modernized Old Testament individualism.)

reality, and in his usefulness as an instrument of measurement: they are interested, that is, in psychology, in the language of criticism, the mathematics of synthesis.

Mr. Richards, too, is primarily interested in the language of criticism. He condemns Beauty-and-Truth terminology – the criticism that treats civilized art as unintelligent magic, in fact. He not only recognizes Reason as man's participation in the patterns of reality; he insists on Reason as social duty; criticism is to him morality. The mathematics of synthesis by which reality may be accurately apprehended are to be developed by turning the human world into a world of values: making conduct (communication, relation) achieve significant pattern. Conduct is then the training of the community as a whole in traffic in reality, with the artist as band-master – 'the arts are the supreme form of communicative activity.' Value (the graded necessity of reality) is to be discovered by a 'systematization of impulses.' We have here that intelligent, superior, adult instinct which Mr. Lewis believes should supply the civilized substitute for magic – the instinct equally of the collective-real, with only a difference of degree in sophistication, manners. Instinct in the collective-real is always either unconsciously or consciously flamboyant, grossly poetic; in the individual-real always consciously reserved, meticulously poetic (art, Mr. Richards says, deals with 'minute particulars'). But it is always the same instinct, the nostalgic desire to reconstitute an illusory whole that has no integrity but the integrity of accident.

Respect for this accidental quality of reality (necessity) may be expressed either by the enthusiasm of what Mr. Lewis calls the Revolutionary Simpleton, who is always religiously anticipating accident, or by what I should like to call Mr. Richards' Moral Simpleton, who observes a reverent plasticity in the development (accidental rearrangement) of custom. And I should like to add Mr. Lewis's own hero, the Individualistic Simpleton, who is to be forced 'to remain absolutely alone for several hours every day.' Why? To become unreal? No, to become more real, to be made into 'much better people.' But if they were much better people already (if a kind of criticism of reality prevailed which satisfied Mr. Lewis), then Mr. Lewis, however free he might permit himself to be, would certainly not worry them with individualism.[1] He wants them free now only as a protest, an act of spiteful superiority against the collective-real. The individual-real is not concerned with self but with exposing the stupidity, the hypocrisy of the fanatic

[1] 'I, of course, admit that the principle I advocate is not for everybody.' – Mr. Lewis.

mob. Instead of freeing the self to self, it frees it
to Reason, to prove merely that intelligent civilized
individuals can be in closer touch with reality than
a stupid civilized mob: that they can know more,
conform more perfectly to customs of more perfect
taste, control what is unreal self in them more
systematically, respond more respectfully, regularly
(classical-poetically) to the stimuli of accidental
reality. That they can behave, that is, by finding a
civilized substitute for magic, like a perfect primitive mob of philosophy-fed art students.

4

Mr. Richards quotes Dr. Bradley's definition of
poetry as an illustration of the sort of criticism to
which he is opposed. In principle, however, I do
not think they are opposed. Dr. Bradley's 'world
by itself' is fundamentally allied with Mr. Richards'
world of values: the difference is that Dr. Bradley's
world – not 'a copy of the real world,' not bound
up with human affairs – gets its revelations of reality
through the imagination, that is, dreaming, while
Mr. Richards' world gets its revelations of reality
through waking. Both worlds are trying to prove
how real they are, the one lying down, the other standing up. They are the same world in different attitudes, the æsthetic attitude and the moral attitude.
The protagonist of the first says, 'I cannot do two

things at once – apprehend reality and make money or eat my supper at the same time, I must set aside a part of the day sacred to reality, in which I do nothing else, sleep over it, as it were.' The protagonist of the second says: 'Pshaw, affected sensitiveness. I can sharpen knives, shave, cook, travel, marry, go to church and apprehend reality at the same time: in fact, whatever I do is all the better done for this, and I apprehend reality all the better for what I do.' Whether a person apprehends reality from the moral or from the æsthetic point of view is all a matter of energy: what seems easy to one person may seem difficult to another, and *vice versa*. Thus, to Mr. Richards, the moral theory of art 'has the most great minds behind it,' 'the most prominent of these great minds being Plato, Aristotle, Horace, Dante, Spenser, Milton, the Eighteenth Century, Coleridge, Shelley, Matthew Arnold and Pater.' Which leads us to believe that as a 'moral' critic Mr. Richards is something of an æsthetician.

5

Modern criticism has supplemented itself with psychology, or rather with its literary version, psychoanalysis. If criticism is primarily interested in the language in which reality is discussed, then it must have a partner to deal with the rough physical side

of reality – a field worker in reality. Criticism con-
fines itself to taste; psycho-analysis to substantiating
taste with practical data.

'We are our bodies,' Mr. Richards says: that is,
we should try to be our bodies, to exist psycho-
analytically, to provide criticism with data. The
view that we are our bodies, Mr. Richards says,
should not be described as Materialism – 'it might
equally well be called *Idealism*.' All criticism, he
means to say, is an appreciation of reality; criticisms differ in method, never in principle. With the
help of psycho-analysis we pay reality the compliment of saying 'we are our bodies'; and reality, with
the help of criticism, returns the compliment, per-
mitting us to say 'our bodies are us.'

As bodies we are acted upon by reality; this is
the psycho-analytic half of the trick. The action of
reality on us produces effects which reveal the
nature of this reality which acts on us; a description
of this nature is the critical half of the trick. It is
not suggested that as bodies we may act on reality,
for this would reveal the fact that bodies were not
like reality a solid lump, but separate and inde-
pendently acting; it would indicate a break-up of
reality, open up the problem of the unreal, and
O! What a mess we should be in then. Let us have
order while we can.

'To know anything,' Mr. Richards says, 'is to be

influenced by it.' This makes things still more simple and comfortable: we do not have to worry about anything which is not *here*, which does not affect us, which is not reality. We are what we know, and what we know is also what we know. The echo of matter in mind proves that there is matter, and also that mind is matter. The mind need have no fear of becoming lost in itself so long as it continues to know, to be affected. It need not be afraid to produce art so long as art remains a knowing of reality; knowing of reality is reality: as echo of sound is also sound. Mr. Read quotes sympathetically Professor Sonnenschein's learned expression of this echo-theory as applied to poetry: 'Rhythm is that property of a sequence of events in time which produces on the mind of the observer the impression of proportion between the duration of several events or groups of events of which the sequence is composed.' 'A good artist,' Mr. Read says, 'is firstly a good critic.' He predisposes his mind materially to apprehend reality, to receive echoes: 'The work of art emerges within a radiation of critical perceptions.'

If every one began systematically treating himself as mind, we should all quickly become separate individuals and know ourselves, and the symbols we used would not be echoes of reality but themselves, and then indeed we should be in deep water. To prevent this possibility psycho-analysis is called on to supplement 'the narrowness of criticism' (Mr. Read's phrase. Criticism is presumably narrow because it deals with forms, while psycho-analysis can roll up its sleeves, poke around in the stuff from which the symbol is derived, and 'help us test its social validity' (Mr. Read) – 'social' meaning pro-matter, anti-mind: mind can only be pro-matter when it is collective mind.

Psycho-analysis divides people into two types – introverted and extraverted. Introversion represents error in man, a straying away from reality into self, a going of the mind into mind. Both psycho-analysis and criticism agree that this process cannot, or rather *should not* produce art. Both processes, *or their possibility*, exist in each individual (psycho-analysis is forced to admit that introversion always exists; extraversion exists if the individual is 'successful'). They may, it is held, be combined in *phantasy*; and phantasy produces 'living reality,' art. But what is this phantasy but the whole introversive world of man behaving extraversively – the collective-real? Unless it is introversion actually transformed in the individual into extraversion, individual mind into matter of 'more than individual use' (as Mr. Read defines creative phantasies) – the individual real? The opposition between collective-real and individual-real disappears in the general agreement between all parties that, by no matter what method, introversion must be extraverted. Likewise the opposition between romanticism and classicism: romanticism is acceptable if it has an extraverted, classical touch; classicism is not necessarily damaged by an introverted, romantic touch, so long as it does not lose complete hold of extraversion.

Extraversion, it is clear, is intelligent body-being. What introversion is it seems difficult to say, since it is always defined by defamatory comparison with extraversion. 'Jung,' Mr. Read says, 'further differentiates *active* and *passive* phantasy – the latter a morbid state which we do not need to stop to consider here.' Complete introversion is presumably not intelligent mind-being, but a pathological condition. Individual mind-being is not intelligent, pathological, because it does not make for unanimity. And both psycho-analysis and criticism want some unanimous, collective mind in contemporary man like the collective mind in primitive man, with the distinction – made in consideration of the grown-up, individualized character of modern man – that this must be an intelligent collective mind, inspired with Reason, a refined version of brutish objectivity. 'We need some unanimity,' Mr. Read says, 'to focus the vague desires that exist in the collective mind.'

But what is the collective mind? A herd of deer clinging together may be said to have unanimity, but it can scarcely be said to have a mind: it has unanimity because to the extent to which it clings together it *is* brutish, natural reality. And the same is true of primitive man up to the point where individual works of art occur; at this point the hold on reality has been lost, unanimity can only be maintained by force, and by the force of a few masterful but pathological, introversive, mind-being individuals. Collective mind is a contradiction in terms: what is meant is intelligent (self-enslaving) collective matter.

And here psycho-analysis is more consistent than criticism because it is frankly interested in extraversion rather than in extraversive works: it would not seriously worry psycho-analysis if works and their authors were discontinued: it would still have Case B, in which Mr. X and Miss Y. . . . Criticism, on the other hand, cannot get along without famous works by famous authors, which are, moreover, a continual source of discord since they are all introversive in origin and cannot be allowed to take their place in literature until they have been rigorously extraversified.

6

Psycho-analytic criticism makes the emotion with which a work is experienced merely a more complicated, appreciative kind of sensation. In sensation the cause of sensation, a real object (experience), attacks the individual; he is helpless *not* to respond, he can only classify his response according to whether he does or does not enjoy it. Every sensory experience is a destruction of his originality. The work of art presented to him on this response-basis is a deliberately aggressive real object intended to usurp his originality in a more constructive way than ordinary sensation. Even the freedom of classifying sensation according to its enjoyableness is denied him: a forced classification is contained in the object-work, representing not a principle of personal preference, but of social preference, expressing the criticism, or Reason, of the time. The ordinary object has generally only an immediate, disorganized sensory effect; the object-work reaches back into the whole past of the individual, re-adapting it to itself by means of memory. All image-making involved in so-called appreciative, reactive experience is a perversion of originality, of the independent power of acting upon initiative, to the derived power of acting upon incentive: the critical bias, first interpreting works as object-works, then inspiring works to be object-works means 'imitation'.

So little does pure, original action seem possible or desirable that we have no word for an impulse contrary in its nature to the nature of reaction, for dissociative rather than associative conduct – dis-action. To the psycho-analyst all activity is inter-pretable only as reaction to sensation; to the pro-fessional critic (Mr. Richards, for example) all critical conduct is imaginary re-activity: we have the individual's originality not momentarily eclipsed, but actually engaged in destroying itself, enriching sensation with the complicated depth of personality.

Art so conceived thus becomes a skilful thwarting of originality. The immediate shock to the con-sciousness which a work brings, which might be expected to encourage an independence in the consciousness, a dissociation from reality (influ-ences) and a development of its differences from reality, is utilized to possess the consciousness for reality, to force it to organize itself according to its resemblances (responses) to the particular ob-ject-work by which it is attacked. Art is an ex-aggeration of the hostile operation of reality on the individual consciousness, an exaggeration pro-portioned to overcome the originality which offers a casual, disorganized resistance to ordinary objects.

Between object and object there is a complete hypnotic interaction by which reality is maintained and which exists only partially between man and object because man is possessed of originality. The object-work is therefore an object especially designed to correct this originality in man by ensnaring him in a more than ordinarily intense field of hypnotic action.

A poem, then, in the critical scheme, is only a work in the sense that it achieves a value equal to an exceptionally 'good' experience; it is an especially high-class object, one that makes use of all man's powers for reconstructing reality: a model object, as the poet is supposed to be a model man. But man's powers for reconstructing reality are really a misuse of his powers for constructing himself out of the wreckage which is reality. The only true entity possible to man is an analytic entity: the synthetic entities of art are all parodies of self. An original poem is only seemingly synthetic; the words of which it is made are both the instrument of the analysis and the substance of the pure self of the poem which emerges from the analysis. Every poem of this kind is an instance of fulfilled originality, a model, to the reader, of constructive dissociation: an incentive not to response but to initiative. Poetry is properly an art of individualization as opposed to the other arts,

which are arts of communication. To compare a
poem with a picture or with a piece of music
or sculpture, is to treat analytic entities and synthetic entities as if they were objects of similar
reality. Synthetic entities are imitative, communicative, provocative of association: their keynote
is organized social sanity. Analytic entities are
original, dissociative, and provocative of dissociation: their keynote is organized personal insanity.
This is why, in hurried scientific fear, the shamen
of psycho-analysis and criticism explain as pure
introversion only obviously morbid conditions,
making out art to be, wherever possible, redeemed
introversion. If criticism of this sort persists there
is no doubt that art will in time produce only
synthetic entities: that is, poetry will disappear.
Indeed it may be the prevalence of such criticism
that is responsible for the present situation of
poetry; why, in Mr. Read's words, there is 'no
adequate literary equivalent in England for the
impressive organization and intellectual content of
the modern movement in painting.' For poems as
synthetic entities must obviously always run a very
poor second to pictures.

7

As to the problem of rhythm and the point
of view I have been applying. Rhythm in the

decorative poetic sense in which it is generally used is, I believe, a strictly prose property. Prose is an inclusive medium, its merit depends on its fullness. The more rich in illustration, detail, rhythmic intricacies it is, the better prose it is, the more effective as an instrument of synthesis. It is poetry, on the other hand, which is properly harsh, bare, matter-of-fact. Punctuation, the notation of rhythm, is essentially a prose development, a means of managing the intricate language-flow. Prose is the social, civilized instrument of communication. The restraints put on it are like the complicated conventions that govern an apparently free-and-easy but actually rigidly prescribed drawing-room atmosphere.

The purpose of poetry is to destroy all that prose formally represents. It is an exclusive medium, and its merit depends on the economy with which it can remove the social rhythmic clutter of communicative language. The savage *tom-tom* is poetry of a brutally specialized kind used to eliminate everything in the listeners but the purpose with which it has been argumentatively overloaded. Non-purposive poetry has all the eliminating force of the *tom-tom* without the grotesque effects of special pleading. A suppression of all associative obligations that might hinder analysis takes place in the poet: by this narrowness he is free as by the synthetic broadness of prose the prose-writer is bound. And it is this narrowness that is the only rhythm proper to poetry. Metre is an attempt to soften the economy and narrowness requisite in poetry; and it is likely to cause, and in the main has caused, only a more fancy, mannered prose than prose; to misrepresent the nature of restraint and limitation in poetry. The end of poetry is to leave everything as pure and bare as possible after its operation. It is therefore important that its tools of destruction should be as frugal, economical as possible. When the destruction or analysis is accomplished they shall have to account for their necessity; they are the survivors, the result as well as the means of the elimination. They are the pure residue, and the meaning if there is any; and they vary in each poem only according to the amount of destruction they have done and the clutter with which they began. The greater the clutter attacked and the smaller, the purer, the residue to which it is reduced (the more destructive the tools), the better the poem.

Rhythm in poetry is therefore a deadly hammer, hammer away in which each word demonstrates its necessity and in which each word is accented. In prose there is accenting, then a long period of relaxation, the harshness of the important words is absorbed in the unimportant words: it is rhythmic.

Prose is skilful manipulation of the whole standing vocabulary, and a great deal of poetry merely competes with prose in vocabularistic manipulation. Poetry is a selection of a few words from this inert mass, which justify, quicken themselves, in its destruction. The abruptness of poetry, commonly softened into prosaic musicalness, is due to the implied omission at every point of rhythmic prose language. Poetry is narrow (like the poem on the page), broken, quick; prose is broad, rhythmic, slow. Poetry is personal, prosaic. Prose is social, dressed out in verbal amenities, poetic.

8

As to the application of the kind of point of view that I have outlined to an individual's relations with his fellows and, beyond that, to the relations of a poem with reality. As to fellows: the unsocial, ascetic concentration of self on self, the analytic intensification of personality to a state of unreality, makes personality a pure, not diffuse, a restrained and completely private activity. Where personality was of this nature, all synthetic, public, real life would be impersonal and formal – it would have manners for the sake of communicative ease, not for the sake of concealing or discovering, or suppressing or standardizing personality. Real life, I mean, as an abstract, general life would be happier so than as a concrete synthesis of personalities. It would not be a source of physical nourishment for personality. The unreal person would not feed on or be absorbed in the pattern; he would sharpen and try his asceticism in it. A view of this kind, making society an artificial pattern based on accident instead of a 'real' pattern based on necessity, is the only possible clue to the reconciliation of freedom and formality. To attempt to discover and form personality in the social pattern is to make social life dull, vulgar and aggressive, and life with self, dull, morbid and trivial. To treat social life as an impersonal pattern is to give it the theatrical vitality of humour and to make life with self strong and serious. The social problem is for each individual how to reach the proper degree of humorous formality in his communicative language, his clothes, his home; not how to acquire a vicarious personal life which has no content but a gross synthetic personality-desire. Social life (life with others) as opposed to personal life (life with self) should be as dancing opposed to walking – formal meaningless gesture as opposed to eccentric significant character. Certain strictly social arts such as music would become immediately tolerable and desirable if treated as arts of gesture rather than of character.

Now as to poems and reality. A poem is an advanced degree of self, as reality is an advanced degree of social life. The poem dances the dance of reality, but with such perfect artificiality that the dance, from very perfection, cancels itself and leaves, as far as reality is concerned, Nothing. But as far as the poem is concerned, Nothing is a dancer walking the ruins; character, by the ascetic nature of its energy, surviving gesture. This asceticism is the creative formality of the poem. Its critical formality is its original deadly participation in the dance. Where we find no critical formality the poem represents diffusion of self in the literary, synthetic self of reality; wantonness of gesture; sentimental corruption of character; tedious extension of reality beyond decent limits of sociality; instead of the dance, an orgy of improprieties. Where we find only critical formality, there is the same moral laxity, but concealed under a squeamish disciplinary veneer; the difference between 'romantic' and 'classical,' merely.

9

Mr. Lewis's ambitious offensive against wrongness makes a nice point of conclusion, as it made a nice starting-point, for this exercise. Most of Mr. Lewis's confusions are due to his attempt to correlate his political system with his taste. His political system is consistent with itself; we agree with it unreservedly or we agree with it not at all. His taste is inconsistent with itself wherever it has been made to conform with his political system: it becomes a nagging, expedient right, lacking the proper indifference of taste and the proper consistency of a political attitude. It is therefore obviously futile to treat with Mr. Lewis on matters of taste; while, on the other hand, it may be helpful to consider certain clear features of his political system.

(*a*) To the popularist progress is socially continuous; culture is the large-scale, accumulative participation of everyman in progress; conduct is behaviourism, perfect social automatism. To the individualist progress is political rather than social – aristocratically hereditary through that bluest blood, Reason; culture is eclectic, conduct is anarchistic, the perfection of the individualism of the few who are in this system responsible for the social conformity of the rest. They differ in their opinion of the size of a potent political group: the former believes that the entire social group may form the political group, the latter that the political group is an independent minority representative of the social group. But both support the idea of a progressive tradition; to the one it is mystical and collective, to the other rationally and personally maintained. And to both the idea of a non-social self outside the tradition and without reference to a cultural line of succession (a self, rather, 'beginning again and again and again') would be equally foreign and repulsive. Mr. Lewis's concrete, 'stable' person is only an upper-class version of the hysterical, hypnotic, mass social self – more realistic, steady, decorous, common-sensible. The suppression of individual will by mass-will of which Mr. Lewis complains refers only to checks on political opportunism: what he is really interested in is power not individuality. He appreciates the fact that sociality means loss of personal consciousness. His solution is that the few strong individuals who object to loss of consciousness should benefit by an anarchistic dispensation that leaves them their consciousness intact in order that they may politically administer sociality to the unconscious.

(b) Mr. Lewis's individualistic compromises come from his unwillingness to face the dualistic character of the individual – his real, social effect, his unreal, more-than-anarchistic self-subtraction from the social group for purposes of identity. For various reasons Mr. Lewis has not been able to shake himself free of the academic, philosophical force of the language that he uses; the problem is in any case too fine for his rough argumentative methods. He would have first to overcome his prejudice against dualistic concepts arising from their shady association with romantic ventures in philosophy, a task of patience not in harmony with his temperament. In any case, his political sense is too strong, too orthodox, to permit of his admitting that the identity of the individual may be established outside the social group. We may find the clue to his dogmatism in this respect in the accent of philosophical awe with which he pronounces 'reality.' Reality's the thing; the individual is only (in a few individuals specializing in individualism) an honourable second. Even unreality may not be a thing by itself: it is (and this seems to be Mr. Lewis's general conclusion) the queer slant at which reality is seen. To say that reality is unreal, from Mr. Lewis's viewpoint, is like saying that sugar is sweet: the queer slant is in reality, not in the individual, as the sweetness is in the sugar, not in the tongue. 'Unreal' is in this usage merely a more philosophic-sounding word than 'pretty,' 'spiritual,' 'mysterious' or 'queer.' 'The reality,' Mr. Lewis complains, 'has definitely installed itself inside the contemporary mind' – it has become what I have called the fairy-tale of the collective-real. Mr. Lewis, that is, is more interested in the prestige of reality than in the general integrity of the individual mind. His implication being that if the contemporary mind had definitely installed itself in 'the reality' all would be well. We should have a social group psycho-physically imbedded in reality, the individual consciousness

being in this case the fairy-tale – with a few independent individual consciousnesses wagging themselves wisely and anarchistically in political appreciation of the situation. Farther than this Mr.
Lewis is unable to go. He contents himself with
establishing the concreteness, the social security of
the wiseacres. His brand of individualism depends
on the social setting for authentication; he does not
dare to separate the fact of individuality from the
fact of sociality and reveal how they maintain themselves in one person through a contradiction, not
through 'reason.' The contradiction is difficult to
grasp, as is the dualism from which it proceeds, and
difficult to persevere in clearly and equitably once
it is grasped; demanding infinite precision and much
active distress and conferring few brilliant occasions
on those who do grasp it. And Mr. Lewis's brand of
individualism is more immediately ambitious, more
impatient, more realistic. He does not trust himself to wait upon successes or brilliant occasions.
He skilfully glozes over the fine distinctions, makes
politic compromises with the reality sufficient to
assure the more astute members of the social group
of a few ready individualistic privileges, and sneers
down with aristocratic scorn the political idealism
of the mob. He is willing to go all the way back to
wipe out the effects of historical romancing; he is
unwilling to come all the way forward again and

risk doing the job thoroughly (the job, that is, of thinking through to the fine distinctions), as it might be now done. And so he remains, for all his intellectual swagger, a mere reactionary and anarchist. Another hero who, having fought just hard enough to permit him to celebrate a triumph, but not hard enough to force a conclusive battle, has claimed his laurels in Rome and retired to live upon them; the fine distinctions still untaken. 'For the former generals, as soon as they believed their exploits had entitled them to the honour of triumphal distinctions, always abandoned the enemy. Insomuch that there were already in Rome three statues adorned with laurel; but still Tacfarinas was ravaging Africa. . . .'

(c) Mr. Lewis's world of reality is what we see plus what we know: what we know is the queer slant in what we see, not the queer slant in us. Our knowledge is the poetic touch in reality. The world of reality for the collective-real is what we see, alone; the fact itself of reality is poetic. But the differences are fundamentally slight. Knowing is the individualistic comprehension of seeing; conscious, literal perception versus crude, mystical mass-sensation; private ownership of reality versus the vulgar, public, figurative participation in reality of the impoverished working-class mob – that is, anarchistic, personal seizure of reality made possible by the philosophical vagueness of the mob. (For example, Mr. Lewis could not argue his position either with success or impunity in Russia.) I repeat, then, that the differences between the collective-real and the individual-real are fundamentally slight. Both defer to the snobbism of reality: it is reality and not the individual that matters. And both are poetic, a sentimental fusion of two contradictory categories, a wilful blurring by the intelligence of the dualism upon which it is based. Both, for example, have difficulty in defining 'the object,' due to their unwillingness to admit this duality; so that the same fusion and blurring that takes place in the individual takes place in the object as well. The romantic inwardness of the one inflates its faults and delusions to a degree of obviousness that invites and facilitates attack. The common-sense outwardness of the other is more aggressive, but more discreet, hiding under its well-bred anarchism and upper-class self-deprecation an enormous greed of possession. The one is childishly content with a fairy-tale of possession; the other insists haughtily upon a true story. But for both the problem, whether as seeing or seeing and knowing, is essentially the same: to have or not to have. As for being, it is not a proper poetic, not a proper philosophical and therefore not a proper political question, and therefore out of order.

(d) The evasion of both of these two systems of

the dualism that I have attempted to suggest without romantic prejudice is reflected in their respective treatment of time and space. Recognizing the antinomy of time and space, they dismiss the possibility of enforcing it practically as too frightening: if what is is made to be what is, then we have nothing but what is; we cannot fool ourselves; therefore evasion and philosophy. The antinomian pie is cut. Mr. Lewis's side takes space; the other side takes time; and both sides now devote their energies to proving that each has the better piece. And certainly both have very good pieces. In space occurs a disintegration that may prove space, through its particulars; in time, an assemblage of particulars that need not however develop particularity, but merely prove time, through the standardizing of its particulars. Good pieces. But only pieces. Space suffering from excessive definiteness; time from excessive indefiniteness. Each trying to pretend it is the whole pie, but each remaining just a self-infatuated piece. Space-synthesis, time-synthesis – philosophical impostures with different political methods, one conservative, old-fashioned, the other revolutionary, modernist. Time a sort of negative space, space a sort of positive time. Space-ist philosophy belied by its individualism, time-ist philosophy by its generalism. To the time-men the wholeness, the reality, is administered by a democratic Self; a Self not sufficiently self-ish, nothing-ish, unreal, small, instantly conceived, to be real in a time-scheme; therefore mystical, poetic. To the space-men, the wholeness, the reality, is administrated by an anarchistic, aristocratic God; a God too personal, too concretely particular, too specially knowable, too real, in fact, to be real in a space-scheme; therefore rationalistic, poetic. The time-men re-inforce the democratic Self with Everybody. The space-men reinforce God with Art, which is a few superior minds capable of animating the material world 'with some degree of mental existence.' For by itself – and this is Mr. Lewis's astounding conclusion – the material world is unreal. And we, too, are unreal – we should regard ourselves, he thinks, as surface creatures. But his conclusion is less astounding if we understand it as the debater's final shock that clinches the argument: the material world is unreal and we too are unreal *if* we do not believe in reality. If we believe in reality 'God becomes the supreme symbol of our separation and of our limited transcendence.' God is the queer slant which through faith (the proper geometric point of view) may be conceived as ultimately (that is, in the absolute sense) straight. And faith is reason. In the time-scheme the democratic Self is the queer slant; it is a sceptical, an ultimate queer slant. And scepticism is romanticism: vague, insincere, sweeping transcendence of the material world. Mr. Lewis, then, is not, as it at first seemed, against transcendence, but only against temporal transcendence. He does not object to evasion and philosophy, but rather wishes them to be more zealous, individualistic, spatial; more evasive and philosophical; to be Art. The temporal what-may-be comes too carelessly close to the what-is. Art, backed up by God, begs the question more efficiently; anarchistic but timid instead of socialistic but bold. It now only remains to be decided whether Mr. Lewis's stand-by is Art or God; and since God was a late-comer in his scheme we can decide in favour of Art – and Mr. Lewis.

(e) But Art. Art is artists. And what is artists? Artists is a few superior minds. Artist is short for artists. Mr. Lewis is not short for artists but long for himself. As between artists and himself, Mr. Lewis decides in favour of himself; it is therefore still easier for us to decide in favour of Mr. Lewis. Against artists. What is artists? For example, Mr. E. M. Forster is artists, as is to be seen in his book *Aspects of the Novel*. The novel is a 'spongy tract.' It is 'bounded by two chains of mountains . . . Poetry and History. . . .' The novel tells a story. The characters are either flat or round. The 'element of surprise' . . . is of great importance in a plot. Then Fantasy. (Here compare Mr. Lewis's treatment of *Ulysses* with Mr. Forster's and you will understand perhaps why Mr. Lewis is not artists.) Then prophecy: 'In Dostoevsky the characters and situations always stand for more than themselves; infinity attends them; though they remain individuals they expand to embrace it and summon it to embrace them; one can apply to them the saying of St. Catherine of Sienna, that God is in the soul and the soul is in God as the sea is in the fish and the fish is in the sea.' D. H. Lawrence is 'the only prophetic novelist writing to-day . . . the only living novelist in whom the song predominates, who has the rapt bardic quality, and whom it is idle to criticize.' (Compare Mr. Lewis's criticism of Lawrence with Mr. Forster's, and you will understand further why Mr. Lewis is not artists.) Then Pattern and Rhythm. *Thais* is the shape of an hourglass. *Roman Pictures*, by Percy Lubbock, is shaped like a grand chain. Also Henry James. But a pattern must not be too rigid. If it is, 'beauty has arrived, but in too tyrannous a guise.' For 'the novel is not capable of as much artistic development as the drama: its humanity or the grossness of its material hinder it. . . . Still, this is not the end of our quest. We will not give up the hope of beauty yet. Cannot it be introduced into fiction by some other method than pattern? Let us edge rather nervously towards the idea of "rhythm." ' We then learn that 'rhythm is sometimes quite easy.' And so to bed and pleasant dreams about the development of the novel mixed up with the development of humanity ('the interminable tape-worm,' as Mr. Forster had called it earlier in the day when it was 'wriggling on the forceps'). No, Mr. Lewis is not artists. He is not an aristocrat, but a distracted and disaffected rough-neck. He has no more real connection with aspects of the novel than Nietzsche with any of the numerous 'æsthetic revivals' of his time. Like Nietzsche his politics and philosophy are æsthetic only in the sense that they are personal. His few 'superior minds' are himself. If he had made this clear in the very beginning he would have saved himself and those who have been good enough to follow him a great deal of unnecessary distraction. Politeness, God, reality – these are all Mr. Lewis in kid gloves embracing himself. His rightness consists in his embracing himself, his wrongness in his wearing kid gloves. For anarchism is not enough. It is obviously not enough for Mr. Lewis. The kid gloves which enabled him to rush into society confused the dualism on which selfhood certainly depends. When he takes them off (as it is probable he will in time, for he does not seem happy in them) and shakes himself by the bare hand, his enthusiasm over his own unreal individuality will have a bare-handed social concomitant more like Bolshevism than anarchism. Or rather, Mr. Lewis will find that not even Bolshevism is enough. What is enough? Nothing is enough. And until Mr. Lewis finds this out he will go on celebrating more and more ferociously his ferocious pangs of hunger, seconded by dozens of famished æsthetic revivalists.

HOW CAME IT ABOUT?

How came it about that Mrs. Paradise the dressmaker is here to dress me, and Mr. Babcock the bootmaker to boot me and a whole science of service to serve me, and that I am precisely here to be served? Do not speak to me of economics: that is merely a question of how we arrange matters between us. And do not speak to me of genesis: I am discussing the question of Mrs. Paradise and Mr. Babcock and myself and the others as immediate causes of one another, I am not discussing creation. Personally, I do not believe in creation. Creation is stealing one thing to turn it into another. What I *am* discussing is existence, uncorrupted by art – how came it about, and so forth. Do not speak to me of love: Mrs. Paradise and Mr. Babcock and myself and all the others do not like each other, in fact, we dislike each other because each of us is most certainly the cause of the other. I am the reason for Mrs. Paradise's making frocks and Mrs. Paradise is the reason for my wearing frocks. If it were not for each other we should be occupied only with ourselves; we should not exist. How then came we to exist? I ask this question. Mrs. Paradise asks this question. I am Mrs. Paradise's answer. Mrs. Paradise is my answer. As for Mr. Babcock, he has hair on his nose and I never look at him. As for all the others, I must put up a notice asking them to ring the bell gently.

&

There is a woman in this city who loathes me. There are people everywhere who loathe me. I could name them; if they were in a book I could turn to the exact page. People who loathe me do so for one of two reasons: because I have frightened them because I have loathed them (that is, made my death-face at them, which I shall not describe as it might in this way lose some of its virtue) or because they are interested in me and there seems no practical way of (or excuse for) satisfying their interest. As to love, that is another matter – it has nothing to do with either interest or fear. Love is simply a matter of history, beginning like cancer from small incidents. There is nothing further to be said about it.

But as to loathing: I feel an intense intimacy with those who have this loathing interest in me. Further than this, I know what they mean, I sympathize with them, I understand them. There should be a name (as poetic as love) for this relationship be-

134

tween loather and loathed; it is of the closest and more full of passion than incest.

To continue about this woman. What is to her irritation is to me myself. She has therefore a very direct sense of me, as I have a very direct sense of her, from being a kind of focus of her nervous system. There is no sentiment, no irony between us, nothing but feeling: it is an utterly serious relationship.

For if one eat my meat, though it be known
The meat was mine, the excrement is his own.

I forget in what context these words were used by Donne – but they express very accurately how organic I feel this relationship to be. The tie between us is as positive as the tie between twins is negative. I think of her often. She is a painter – not a very good painter. I understand this too: it is difficult to explain, but quite clear to myself that one of the reasons I am attached to her is that she is not a good painter. Also her clothes, which do not fit her well: this again makes me even more attached to her. If she knew this she would be exasperated against me all the more, and I should like it; not because I want to annoy her but because this would make our relationship still more intense. It would be terrible to me if we ever became friends; like a divorce.

HUNGRY TO HEAR

HUNGRY to hear (like Jew-faces, kind but anti-cipating pain) they sit, their ears raw. The conversation remains genteel, of motor cars: her brother bought a car, he was having a six months' vacation from an Indian post, he should have known better than to buy an American car, the value depreciates so, and *she* (his sister) should not have lent it to *her* (her friend) even though it wasn't her fault that the car only did fifteen miles to the gallon after she returned it. A clear situation like this, in which life is easy to understand, is cruel to them. It leaves no scratches in the mind around which opinions, sympathies, silly repetitions can fester and breed dreams and other remote infections – too remote always to give serious pain. They long to be fumbled, to have confusion and uncertainty make a confused and uncertain end of them. There they sit, having pins-and-needles of obscurity which they mistake for sensation. They open their newspapers: 'I suppose it is foolish to spend all this time reading newspapers? They are lying and dishonest and de-

136

voted to keeping a certain portion of the population in ignorance and intellectual slavery? Or is it foolish to take it so seriously? I shall go on reading them out of sophistication? . . .' Oh, go to hell.

IN A CAFÉ

THIS is the second time I have seen that girl here. What makes me suspicious is that her manner has not changed. From her ears I should say she is Polish. If this is so, is it not dangerous to drink coffee here? Does anyone else think of this, I wonder? Yet why should I be suspicious? And why should her manner not remain unchanged? She has probably been cold, unhappy, unsuccessful or simply not alive ever since I saw her last. Quite honestly I wish her success. The man who is making sketches from pictures in the Art Magazine may find her little Polish ears not repulsive. For good luck I turn away and do not look at her again. I, who am neither sluttish nor genteel, like this place because it has brown curtains of a shade I do not like. Everything, even my position, which is not against the wall, is unsatisfactory and pleasing: the men coming too hurriedly, the women too comfortably from the lavatories, which are in an unnecessarily prominent position – all this is disgusting; it puts me in a sordid good-humour. This attitude I find to be the only way in which I can defy my own intelligence. Otherwise I should become barbaric and be a modern artist and intelligently mind everything, or I should become civilized and be a Christian Scientist and intelligently mind nothing. Plainly the only problem is to avoid that love of lost identity which drives so many clever people to hold difficult points of view – by *difficult* I mean big, hungry, religious points of view which absorb their personality. I for one am resolved to mind or not mind only to the degree where my point of view is no larger than myself. I can thus have a great number of points of view, like fingers, and which I can treat as I treat the fingers of my hand, to hold my cup, to tap the table for me and fold themselves away when I do not wish to think. If I fold them away now, then I am sitting here all this time (without ordering a second cup) because other people go on sitting here, not because I am thinking. It is all indeed, I admit, rather horrible. But if I remain a person instead of becoming a point of view, I have no contact with horror. If I become a point of view, I become a force and am brought into direct contact with horror, another force. As well set one plague of cats loose upon another and expect peace of it. As a force I have power, as a person virtue. All forces eventually commit suicide with their power, while virtue in a person merely gives him a small though constant pain from being continuously touched, looked at, mentally handled; a pain by which he learns to recognize himself. Poems, being more like persons, probably only squirm every time they are read and wrap themselves round more tightly. Pictures and pieces of music, being more like forces, are soon worn out by the power that holds them together. To me pictures and music are always like stories told backwards: or like this I read in the newspaper: 'Up to the last she retained all her faculties and was able to sign cheques.'

It is surely time for me to go and yet I do not in the least feel like going. I have been through certain intimacies and small talk with everything here; when I go out I shall have to begin all over again in the street, in addition to wondering how many people are being run over behind me; when I get home I shall turn on the light and say to myself how glad I am it is winter, with no moths to kill. And I shall look behind the curtain where my clothes hang and think that I have done this ever since the homicidal red-haired boy confided his fear to me and I was sorry for him and went to his room and did it for him. And my first look round will be a Wuthering-Heights look; after that I shall settle down to work and forget about myself.

I am well aware that we form, all together, one

monster. But I refuse to giggle and I refuse to be frightened and I refuse to be fierce. Nor will I feed or be fed on. I will simply think of other things. I will go now. Let them stare. I am well though eccentrically dressed.

FRAGMENT OF AN UN-FINISHED NOVEL

WHAT could I do but treat my secret as if it did not exist, that is, as my mother did hers until she confided it to me? which was not confiding, but a necessary explanation of the curious gift or curse (you will decide which for yourself before many pages) that I had from her (the flesh only knows how) when she put me into this world fifty-four years ago in a carved bed made of an old sea-chest that she had of her father (together with many other things) who was a Dutch Jew of a family that had fled from Spain and made its fortune as merchants and traders and in African mines and which disinherited him when he ran away to sea from school and saw things in China which neither white man nor Jew might see without death, but which long afterwards recalled him when he was in America and too proud to accept the portion denied him in his youth, which my mother never forgave him but continually during her lifetime besought me to apply for in my own person, which was pleasing and persuasive.

My mother, I say, broke her secret to no one, excepting me, and this was not breaking it, since I had the same secret, and I broke my secret to no one, which was either wise or foolish (I can't say which) but not wicked, for had I wished it was a thing that could go against no one but myself (as you shall see). How my mother had it, she did not know, although she was of the opinion that she caught it from a travelling bookseller who secretly sold romances to the pupils of the French convent in New Orleans where her father kept her – over the garden wall. It could not be the books, she said, for they were as innocent as the Bible, with no more rapes and indeed fewer mysteries. The contamination, if it was such, must have been from his eyes, if at all, which were long-lasting ones, she remembering them many days after each visit and for a long time seeing through them, as it were. She knew nothing about him but that he was Mexican, of a poor breed but of such charm (he dressed in the Mexican manner) that she would have run away with him had not her strange possession come over her at about this time and changed the whole course of her life.

'Perhaps,' I suggested, when she told me this, 'he used a charm against you. It is known there are certain herbs to be found in Mexico which may be used to cunning ends.'

'That may indeed be so,' my mother said, 'for I remember he once gave me a fine gold chain to wear on which was suspended an image of a pale blue stone, and I could never make out what it represented, as it was all twisted and seemed a different thing each time I looked at it, now like a snake, now like a clenched hand or like a troll's face.'

'Surely,' I cried, 'it was this charm that brought the thing upon us.' For I thought, if it was a charm that brought this thing on my mother, it might be a charm that would take this thing from me; and for this reason I have ever been one easily affected by superstitions of all kinds and ready to put my faith in what is but circus farce to others, a weakness that has been as great a source of misfortune to me as my possession.

'It might indeed have been so,' replied my mother, 'but I cannot be sure. At about the same time Sister Mathilde began praying for me, as if God had sent her against this journeyman for my sake. She prayed in my room and soon she slept in my bed the better to protect me, and I began strongly to dislike it for she sweated powerfully and loved me more tenderly than is good for girlish sleep. Wherever I was between these two I shall never know. If one was of God and the other of the Devil, then there is a third power which exists to

144

save the human soul from both, I hesitate to say with what intentions or effects. For as I was one morning sitting on my pot and enjoying innocent conversation with myself, suddenly I looked up, feeling myself not alone. Think how my modesty fainted to behold the room full of people all looking intently (and kindly) at me. I covered my face with my hands. I dared not rise.

' "Never mind, child," said a shrill voice at my ear that sounded like an aunt's, "it will soon be happily over."

' "Happily over!" I tried to shriek but could not, trying to rise and button myself.

' "Leave your dress alone, chicken, you could not look better," said another voice at my nose, a third cousin's by its sound. Nor could I have – I caught a glimpse of myself in a mirror just then, and I was a bride! This is how I found myself married to Mr. Pink, whose calling was jobs for which no name could be found, and could ask no questions for shame, since the last I knew of myself was on a chamber-pot, but only pretend to be possessed, as seemed reasonable in the principal party of the event, of full knowledge of what was going on about me.'

This martyr's discretion in my mother has ever been a noble example to me in my own endurance of that cruel idiosyncrasy which she, to her everlasting grief, passed on to me. 'Never lose self-possession,' she continually besought me, 'or contradict circumstances, which cannot lie and which know you better than yourself.' Dearest Mother! Shall I blame her for that inheritance she gave me against her heart and will and by which I had the blessing of her eternal (so long as she lived) solicitude? Not to mention (petty recompense and enjoyment) the liberty she gave me beyond all reasonable expectation I could have had of remorseful indulgence from her, which included the privacy of her papers which I could not read since she wrote always in bed and upon brown paper, from sombreness of spirit, and the treasures her father gave her out of spite to her mother, for bearing him a black child by perfidy of blood or whoring, it exasperated him not to know which, and of which, though all were mine from childhood, I loved and attached to me but one shabby trifle, a totem six inches long that did me for a doll while I remained a child and for a child when I became a woman and dared not breed, confide, form honourable attachments or soften my heart save to that which, being wooden, could not soften its heart to me.

My mother, as I said, having once grasped her unspeakable peril, resolved to protect herself with the means at hand, that is, to remain Mrs. Pink, if she could, until she found herself something else.

146

And to further her security in this she formed a second painful resolve, never while she could help it to leave her bed, thinking that she might thus restrain her visitations or at least govern the place in which they seized her. Alas! restrain them she could not, and alas! a bed (as she learned too late) was more ungovernable than a chamber-pot, for in this bed she got me, in a cruel lapse when Mr. Pink her husband was in the Argentine collecting the names of common tropical plants for the Secretary of State known in private life as a gifted maker of South American tales, and when she must undoubtedly have been visited by hundreds of Mr. Pink's friends and relatives, Mr. Pink, who understood my mother's infirmity and never blamed it except as such, insisting that it was his uncle the Chicago photographer who had nearly an artist's appreciation of the human form, of which my mother being half Jew and perhaps a dash negro, was an exotic and irresistible example.

This unavoidable slip, of which I was a living and growing reminder, never prejudiced Mr. Pink my mother's husband against me, but on the contrary seemed to stimulate his curiosity in me. He was a thin man, but I think of a passionate imagination, and I wanted nothing. Nor was he quite certain that it was his uncle the Chicago photographer, but in the wistful hope that it might have been Prince

Moredje, the famous Balkan adventurer whom he used to decorate official banquets of which he was responsible for the seating plan, he provided me with a riding master though we lived in an unimproved flat in the rear and bought me when I was quite young a green plumed hat from an auctioneer friend of his who specialized in theatrical costumes. Himself he dressed shabbily, as his profession required. I never knew him otherwise than in his black and white checked suit and red tie, and it was one of the sorrows of his life that he could not wear black, for he was a quiet man, since his greatest attraction to his clients was that he was not genteel, by which he seemed more efficient, mysterious, quaint and criminal. My mother required very little beyond bed shawls, of which she kept two, one for company and one for private, the company one being pure white, that she might be thought of by visitors as a pale object martyred to her bed and so not excite experiences; I have this very shawl to thank for myself, which she was wearing when her sense was suddenly transported in time and she found herself with me in her womb and could make no denial or protest, and her white shawl on her shoulders though in private, that is, alone with her husband Mr. Pink who had just let himself in at the door from the Argentine, whence he had come in all haste to embrace her, having been made anxious by certain reports which his friends and relatives maliciously wrote him of my mother. Her private shawl, a red cashmere, she consoled herself in; she only wore it when she felt safe. In this shawl too she consented to rise for her needs and melancholies. How often have I come upon her standing in her shirt at the window, only half of her decently covered, the rest of her naked and unhappy – a pair of pretty buttocks that she could scarcely trust as far as the door and ready to betray her at the least winking of her eye and plant her where she must acknowledge her position by that she sat in it with them. It was to our further mortification that our sad affliction only came over my mother and me when we were sitting, an attitude that by its ease soothes suspicion, and that we have never come to ourselves except in this attitude, which may try dignity painfully, as I have reason to know. 'To find one's feet' – how well, alas, do *I* know the tragic significance of that phrase. . . .

W I L L I A M   A N D   D A I S Y :
F R A G M E N T   O F   A   F I N -
I S H E D   N O V E L

WILLIAM and Daisy lived in Cemetery Street.
They had no connection with each other except that
they were not attracted by life or death; so they
lived in Cemetery Street. William was pessimistic
because he disliked life a little more than death,
Daisy was optimistic because she disliked death a
little more than life. William had two memories:
one, that he had been familiar with harlots; two,
that he had been familiar with famous writers.
These two memories mixed and he could make nothing of them. Daisy had two memories: one, that
she had once been a harlot; two, that she had in her
time known several famous writers. These two
memories mixed and she could make nothing of
them. They could make nothing of their memories
except that they both felt dignified and did not wish
to end their days in a workhouse. So they lived in
Cemetery Street.

Every night Daisy went for a walk down Cemetery
Street and said 'What a lovely night,' and passed

William on her walk and said 'What a coincidence';
and every night William, too, said 'What a lovely
night' and 'What a coincidence.' They began to
know each other's thoughts and were more bored
with each other than ever.

They had their shoes mended by the same shoemaker. Each knew the shoemaker had taken a girl
to live with him behind the shop and then thrown
her into the street when his wife had learned about
it. Yet each continued to think him a nice man because they could not be bothered to think him a
mean man. They became more and more absolute
in their thoughts and habits until . . .

I do not know what happened to them, nor do
they.

AN ANONYMOUS BOOK

§ 1

AN anonymous book for children only was published by an anonymous publisher and anonymously
praised in an anonymous journal. Moreover, it imitated variously the style of each of the known writers
of the time, and this made the responsibility for its
authorship all the more impossible to place. For
none of the known writers could in the circumstances look guilty. But every one else did, so this
made the responsibility for its authorship all the
more difficult to place. The police had instructions
to arrest all suspicious-looking persons. But as
every one except the known writers was under suspicion the department of censorship gave orders
that the known authors should be put in prison to
separate them from the rest of the population and
that every one else should be regarded as legally
committed to freedom. 'Did you write it?' every one
was questioned at every street corner. And as the
answer was always 'No', the questioned person was
always remanded as a suspect.

The reasons why this book aroused the department of censorship were these. One – it imitated (or seemed to imitate) the style of all the known authors of the time and was therefore understood by the authorities to be a political (or moral) satire. Two – it had no title and was therefore feared by the authorities to be dealing under the cover of obscurity with dangerous subjects. Three – its publisher could not be traced and it was therefore believed by the authorities to have been printed uncommercially. Four – it had no author and was therefore suspected by the authorities of having been written by a dangerous person. Five (and last) – it advertised itself as a book for children, and was therefore concluded by the authorities to have been written with the concealed design of corrupting adults. As the mystery grew, the vigilance of the police grew, and the circulation of the book grew: for the only way that its authorship could be discovered was by increasing the number of people suspected, and this could only be done by increasing the number of readers. The authorities secretly hoped to arrive at the author by separating those who had read the book from those who had not read it, and singling out from among the latter him or her who pretended to know least about it.

All the stories in the book were about people who did not like the world and who would have been glad to be somewhere else. Some were irreligious, some were ungrateful, some were scornful, some were openly rebellious, some were secretly rebellious, some were merely ironical, some were merely bored. Many were too good, many were too bad. All were disobedient, and all wanted to go away. Wanting to go away to somewhere else did not mean wanting to go away to somewhere else with the rest of the entire population of the world. It meant in all the stories wanting to go away alone. All the stories in the book were about people who wanted to go away to somewhere where they would be, no matter how many other people they found there, the only one. All the people in the book thought the world fit only for light, heat, moisture, electricity, plants, the lower animals, and perhaps for occasional parties, excursions, commemoration days, Sunday afternoons, exhibitions, spectacles, concerts, sight-seeing and conversation. But none of them thought it fit for higher creatures to live in permanently, because all who were in it, they said, were the only one, and were thus objects of hate, ridicule or mock-adoration for one another, being each by his mind freakish and uncommon but by his brain natural and common.

Such was the philosophical import of this book. But its philosophical import was got only if the reader had a taste for, a passion for, a suspicion of,

an obsession with, or instructions to look for philosophical imports. Or if he shrank from stories. What
was plain and comprehensible before all philosophical imports was just stories. The four upon
which most suspicion was fixed were *The Flying
Attic, The Man Who Told Lies to His Mother, The
Woman Who Loved an Engine,* and *The Woman Who
Was Bewitched By a Parallel.*

It was impossible to say particularly which story
was written in the style of which author. The effect
of imitation that the book gave was rather a mixed
one; that is, it was generally and throughout a
witty, energetic, beautiful, simple, earnest, intricate,
entertaining, ironic, stern, fantastic, eloquent, modest, outspoken, matter-of-fact and so-forth book,
so that generally speaking it could not be read but
as a conglomerate imitation of the noted literary
manners of the time, of the well-known author who
wrote so wittily, of the well-known author who
wrote so energetically, of the well-known author
who wrote so beautifully, of the well-known author
who wrote so simply, of the well-known author who
wrote so earnestly, of the well-known author who
wrote so intricately, of the well-known author who
wrote so entertainingly, of the well-known author
who wrote so ironically, of the well-known author
who wrote so sternly, of the well-known author who
wrote so fantastically, of the well-known author who

wrote so eloquently, of the well-known author who wrote so modestly, of the well-known author who wrote so outspokenly, of the well-known author who wrote so matter-of-factly, and of the well-known author who wrote and-so-forthly.

It is not the object of this account, whose purpose is chiefly historical, to transcribe in detail all or even many of the stories of which the book was composed, or to analyse, criticize, praise or condemn the few that shall be reproduced (in whatever way seems most economical) here. It is rather intended to give an honest, accurate, elementary notion of the book from which the reader may form a scholarly opinion of its character that shall be in restrained harmony with his own. Several of the stories (those cited above, for example) will be elaborately summarized, according to the degree of eccentricity they possess in comparison with other stories which fall more naturally into a group-significance or classification. Some will appear only in a table of constructional correspondences; others as interesting or corroborative or contradictory points of reference: still others as problems of too fine difficulty for the moment, here put aside and marked out for the future specialist.

§ 2

The Flying Attic is the first of the miscellaneously significant or dangerous stories. The central char-

acter is a cook who had never in her life been guest
to anyone and who had never in her life ascended
above the kitchen floor of any house. No description of the character's appearance, age or parentage
is given, so that the atmosphere of the story, inten-
tionally or unintentionally, is one of allegory, or
morality, or symbolism – as you like. This creature,
the story tells us, conceived the fantastic ambition
of living permanently in a guest attic, descending
only at the new moon, and then to find herself each
time in a different house, each time guest to a
different host or hostess.

The realization of this ambition is made techni-
cally possible by the dismissal of the cook for serving
a custard made from a manufactured pink powder,
instead of from original ingredients. No complaint
seems to have been made against the excellence of
taste or quality of the custard. Its very excellence
in fact is what arouses suspicion. And so after coffee
the cook is dismissed. The family chats, finally goes
to bed. Then the cook steals out of the kitchen and
up to the attic, at the moment unoccupied but in a
state of preparation for a guest who is expected to
arrive the following day. The cook draws the curtains, lights a candle, gets into bed. The beams are
made of old ship's timber; the sharp-ribbed roof
suggests an inverted ship's bottom. The candlelight, the drawn curtains, the architectural irregu-

larities of the attic, the distorted, ship-like sense of motion faintly conveyed by the crazy contour of the attic in candlelight to the mind of the cook now floating in the unreality of the fulfilment of an impossible ambition – all these factors contribute to what must count – in the story at any rate – for a genuine disturbance of forces: the attic moves, the cook's mind swoons with pleasure, day and night the curtains remain drawn (otherwise the problem of *locale* would seriously interfere with the narrative device), she passes her time in a passive delirium of satisfaction, and at the morning of new moon punctually descends. The first and last descents will be given in detail, the intervening ones only listed.

First descent: as the breakfast bogy, in the costume of a German peasant – green jacket, flat, ribboned hat; into the house of a country lady, mother of three young children, recently widowed. Cook unlatches the attic door and walks slowly downstairs – a heavy male step. Cultured and terrified children's voices are heard as the steps pass the night nursery: 'Oh mother, the breakfast bogy – we are afraid to get up.' 'Nonsense, children,' the mother calls back, 'come down immediately.' The steps continue, Cook enters the dining-room, sits down at the table in the chief chair as master of the house. The mother enters from the kitchen with large porridge basin, sees Cook, screams. Children come running down. 'The breakfast bogy, the breakfast bogy!' they cry. 'We told you so, Mother.' Cook says: 'I am master here now. We will all have breakfast together and you will pay me every respect. After breakfast I shall go away and not return till luncheon. The same for tea and dinner. You must guess what I like to eat and after each meal thank me for the food. And you must kiss me good night. That is all.' It is to be noted that whenever the central character of any of these tales gives an order, it is always obeyed without question, however wicked, unreasonable or fantastic it may be. Thus in *The Dishonest Scales* the grocer-woman not only cheats her customers in the weight of what they buy (though the scales whenever tested seem to record quite honestly), but after taking their money she says firmly 'Now that is all,' and sends them away unprotesting without their purchases.

After breakfast Cook retires to the attic and appears again at luncheon. All this happens in the most orderly manner imaginable. The widow even smiles prettily to Cook after luncheon and 'hopes the gentleman finds all satisfactory.' Cook here nods stiffly. There is no clue given as to what either Cook or the family do during the intervals between meals. Only one rather shocking mischance occurs: the oldest of the children, a boy, spies upon the cook between tea and dinner and is snatched angrily into the attic. At dinner only two children appear, and Cook announces quietly: 'Your oldest child attempted to spy upon me, so I turned him into an eiderdown to keep me warm.' To which the widow replies 'It serves him right,' and goes on eating. After dinner Cook is kissed good night affectionately by the widow and her two remaining children, goes up to the attic, fastens the door, gets into bed and tucks herself round with her new eiderdown.

Second descent: Cook comes down into a prison tower as a captive queen, murders her warder, takes upstairs with her her warder's poodle, the pillow she stabbed him on, and his wife's lace cap, saying: 'All this will contribute to the comfort of my old age.'

Third descent: Cook comes down into a full-rigged ship about to sink in a storm off the Gold Coast, rescues the captain, a villainous but hearty old man, and carries him off to her attic with great satisfaction.

Fourth descent: Cook comes down into a great kitchen as a cook and carries the whole kitchen up with her in one armful.

Fifth descent: Cook comes down into a library as a respectable young working man inquiring from the lady librarian for a book on how to mend leaking roofs. The lady librarian strongly resembling Cook in her youth, the young working man is smitten with a great fancy for her, marries her, takes her up to the attic, where she becomes cook to Cook.

Sixth descent: Cook opens her attic door to walk out as herself for a breath of fresh air, steps upon nothing and begins to fall. While falling she looks up, sees her attic far above her, flying off at great speed toward the east, where it is growing dark. 'However will I get back to it?' she thinks mournfully to herself. At this point there is a long passage describing intimately all of her anxieties in her fall, such as what will happen to her poodle, who will smooth out her eiderdown, what will her captain have for dinner all by himself, down to the last, which is, what shall she give them for a pudding to-night? She decides, since it is so late already (it is now quite dark in the east and her attic has completely disappeared) to give them a custard made from a manufactured pink powder, which will take only a moment to stir up and only fifteen minutes on the window-sill to cool. It would be impossible without exact quotation from the original (which is outside the modest scope of the present volume) to reproduce the delicate transition that takes place just here from one level of the episode to the next (from the higher to the lower, or the fantastic to the factual, I might say). Suffice it for our purposes that there occurs at this point a shock, the contact on the one hand of Cook's feet with the ground, on the other of Cook's right ear with church clock just striking seven. 'And there will be a guest to-night,' she exclaims to herself, tasting and stirring, chopping and sprinkling. At last dinner is served, eaten, over. 'Dear kind Cook,' Mistress says to her before retiring, 'aren't you going upstairs to-night?' 'My goodness, is it so late?' replies Cook. 'I was just cooling myself a bit' – for Cook was standing on the kitchen doorstep gazing east. So she goes upstairs to her attic and fastens the door behind her. Upon which unsatisfactory note this story concludes, leaving the reader uneasy and somewhat cheated of that general resolution of himself in the story which it is his right to expect from every upright invention – an effect all the more disquieting in that it seemed everywhere in this work arrived at rather by art than by accident or inferiority of execution.

§ 3

It would be well at this point to uncover a little of the philosophical skeleton of this book for the benefit of the reader likely to become too absorbed in the narrative surface, so to speak. It would also be well to emphasize, on the other hand, the fact that the anonymous author was if anything over-precious in the technical brilliance of his stories: he seemed to wish, by ringing from them a pure, glassy artificiality, that their perfection as stories should make them as trivial and false-true as stories, so that they held the moral more obediently. There is therefore little or no hint of moral in any of the stories, the sincerity of the narration in every particular being the best guarantee (according to the principles of his writing) of the presence of the skeletal sense beneath it. We might, for the purpose of analysis, call this obsession with fictitious fact an obsession statistical. And we might likewise call (for the same purpose) the style of the book the style of curiosity. The effect of this style on the reader is indeed an effect of curiosity – curiosity in the general usage of the word. That is, it makes the reader first inquisitive of the course and conclusion of the narrative, then suspicious of the philosophical import of the narrative, and finally resolved to track down angerly (as our Elizabethan might have said) the chief mystery of each narrative, namely the anonymity of the author: as indeed the police of his time were angered into doing (without success). The style of curiosity, itself, however, was of a different order of curiosity from this. If you will look out this word in any full contemporary dictionary you will find that while the current meaning is this precise *effect* of curiosity, the two first (and previous) meanings have a more particular application:

(1) Scientific attentiveness; technical nicety; moral exactness; religious fastidiousness. Obsolete.

(2) Honest or artistic workmanship; generous elaboration; charitable detail. Obsolete or archaic.

And such, in fact, was the style of curiosity: so that the effect of curiosity on the reader had in it a touch of quaintness; which is the reason why, in fact, the anonymous author seemed to his critics, censors and readers to be imitating the style of all the well-known writers of the time and yet to be clearly not among them.

Perhaps I can best illustrate this obsession statistical and this style of curiosity (both in origination and effect) by a direct transcription. It is to be found (by those fortunate enough to lay hands upon the book itself) in the story (untitled) about the man who could not help stealing his friends' matches though his father was a prosperous match-manufacturer, though he had a generous allowance from him and though he had no interest in the match business:

'He paid his fare exactly, having the scale of fares off by heart (more thoroughly than the conductor) and having always in his pocket such a variety of small coins as should make it unnecessary for him to be given change in his fares, purchases and contributions to charity. He sat on top, on the left, in the fourth row from the front, by the rail, a habit so strong and methodical in him that he never thought (and was never obliged) to sit elsewhere. He made a minute comment to himself upon the flower stalls or stands along the route, concluding with the generalization that the predominating colour among the flowers sold by the lame or the ugly was mauve. He then went to sleep, timing himself to awake a minute before the arrival of the bus at the railway station. He rehearsed his itinerary, which was to miss his train at the first change and so at the second change and so to have to wait an hour there and two hours there and to examine more particularly during this time the generalization regarding lame or ugly flower-vendors. While asleep he followed his usual practice of descending from the state of personality to the state of thingality, and in this dreamy condition of passive matter he enjoyed the same security that an apple has up to the moment of its fall. And so upon waking he fell from the top of the bus – as if blown down by a strong wind – and broke his nose, one leg, two fingers, cut his left cheek beneath the eye and sustained an injury to his back that left him upon his recovery with a permanent thoughtful posture.'

From this short extract it will perhaps be clear how he teased his reader with sincerity and how his statistical straightforwardness carved out patiently a mysterious block of significance which was not brought upon the platform of the story but which the reader found obstructing his exit, as it were, when the curtain had come down and he attempted to leave the theatre. It was this seemingly innocent obstructionism of course that aroused the authorities to such a violent pitch of antagonism to the book; and which remains to this day a challenge almost impudent (so it sometimes seems) to the endurance of all scholars, philosophers and simple lovers of knowledge. For often, at our greatest moments of ingenuity and science, indeed, we find ourselves suddenly uncertain of our premises and forced to begin once more at the beginning, yielding our own philosophical curiosity to the statistical curiosity of the author. It might therefore be wise, before we entangle ourselves further in scholarly ramifications of our own, to return to the document itself. In this sober intention I mean to present, in as unmeddlesome and economical a fashion as I am capable of, the conspicuous features of one of the most baffling (though to outward appearance one of the most unaffected) stories in the collection, *The Man Who Told Lies To His Mother*.

§ 4

He was an author. He wrote books one after the

other. It was impossible, we are told, to understand, say, the tenth book without reading all the preceding nine. And it was impossible to understand the tenth without the book that followed it. And whatever number the book was, there was always one following it, so that the author was continuously being understood by his readers. The chief character in each of the books was always the same. Half of him was the author himself, the other half of him was the only son of the author's mother. He called the first half I, the second half He. I thought, wrote books, knew all about everything, did nothing. He knew nothing about anything but could do everything. I was wise, He was happy. I was careful to keep himself to himself so as not to have his wisdom spoiled by He or He's fun spoiled by his wisdom. I kept himself in his study, He in the world. I did not permit He to share his study with him because this would have been like denying that there was a world outside of his study and, since he knew there was such a world, making a ghost of himself. I did not want to be a ghost and yet he wanted to remain in his study, so he supported He in the world on the books he wrote in his study. This kept up the world, it kept up He, it made I complete without his having to be complete, that is, to be both I and He. Moreover, though I supported He in the world, he made no attempt to track him, curb him or even share occasionally in his activities. I was continually disciplining himself against such temptations: in order not to corrupt his wisdom by making it a criticism of He and in order not to corrupt the fullness of He's pleasure by making it have anything to do with sense. The important thing for I, inasmuch as He existed and the world existed, was to keep them employed in each other, so that he could be truly, wisely, actually, employed in himself. I said: I am I, therefore I am true, I am not He, therefore he is false; but He is He, therefore He is false-true so long as I encourage him in falsehood. He could not, however, be false by himself – this would have eventually made him true. To be false he needed something to be false with, he needed the world, he needed other He's. For a long time He and the world conducted each other toward themselves with the closest and strictest falsehood; so close and strict in fact that the world, this conglomeration of other He's, became a single close, strict, false She. He and She went on loyally enjoying themselves in each other as He and the world had done, until this falsificatory attachment became so utter that it reproduced I in his study. It reproduced I, it reproduced He and She. It did all this without giving to her only son's mother a grandchild.

And so, the story goes on, the books went on. And

so we the readers of the story (story-readers of the books described in the story) witness how I told lies to his mother without committing a single falsehood. For he sent his books to his mother in her province in place of letters, saying: This is a true account of the doings of your only son. And she read them lovingly as a true account of the doings of her only son, whom she always thought of as He, taking I to be merely the I authorial, which it was. And so I told lies to his mother and they were not lies but a true account of the doings of He.

Now when the author of the story has trained his reader to understand the author in the story who was one-half of the chief character of his own stories, he begins without further explanation a long chronicle of the experiences of the other half of the chief character of his stories under the title of *Lies To His Mother*. We do not know whether these stories are supposed to have appeared in the author-in-the-story's books as they appear here in the story: probably not, since there is in them no mention of I, and I, we must remember, was one-half of the chief character of these books. Or perhaps so, since it is not unlikely that everything relating to I in his books was meant to be supposed to have been described separately, as for example in the form of authorial interludes between the passages relating to He. At any rate, for our convenience it may be best to retitle the stories (a few of which are here summarized) which the author introduces to us under the title of *Lies To His Mother*, as *What His Mother Believed Of He*. It might also be helpful for me to announce here that since further analysis seems hopeless I shall add nothing to these summarizations; except to say, perhaps, that they all confirm us in what we have already observed of the temper of the anonymous author of the book that we are studying: his statisticality, his curiosity and, we might now add, his falsificality.

(*a*) That He one day drank water in such a way as to be drunk of it, and in this condition found himself the hero of an Arabian Nights Entertainment, bathing, with the privilege of a jokester, in the women's pool. And they would not let him come out for a whole day. They kept him in the water a whole day, a whole long day, during which they did many things to him, all of which are faithfully recorded in the original, of which two may with propriety be given here: that they would at intervals very slowly drain all the water from the pool and then as slowly let it fill up again; and that they fed him on nothing but fish, and would not give him drink, forcing him to water himself from the pool. He was allowed to leave the pool at sunset, on the promise that he would amuse them with tales for three days, which he promised. For three days then He amused them with tales, two of which may with propriety be outlined here: the first, of a man bewitched in such a manner that he would do on every occasion the opposite of what it was his will to do; the second, of a far-off city in which the people were silent and their clothes spoke, and of how a quarrel arose between two identical black lace frocks, as to which was which, and of how in anger they tore themselves off their wearers, and became confused in the broil that followed, so that their owners were also confused and uncertain, when the frocks were put on once more, whether their speech matched their silence.

(*b*) That He another day woke to find himself speaking a strange language, in which everything was known and clear – as if all difficulties of the intelligence were difficulties of language alone: in this language He had but to speak to discover, as, for instance, the word for *horse* here not only stood for horse but also made plain the quality of horseliness, what it was. He woke to find himself speaking this language, he was a boy, he was in a classroom, he had blue eyes (they were actually grey), his teacher was a remarkable woman in a pompadour and a large hat who was fond of him, fixing her gaze on his blue eyes when she entered the room and keeping it there until she left; who knew everything and recited it without pause, without sympathy, without antagonism, so that whatever she said meant all and nothing – history, the uses of waste paper, the traditions of pawnbrokers, anything, everything. Then He woke up again to find himself no longer speaking the strange language but as dumb, in his ordinary language, with dumb memory of it. So when He spoke his ordinary language he found it all twisted of sense, which made him abandon it: he uttered only expressive sounds, which others disregarded as nonsensical, composed as they were of soft and shrill shrieks, whistlings, bellowings and blowings. So He went mad and in his madness began speaking his ordinary language again, all nonsensical, but conceived sane by others because it was the ordinary language. And so He was discharged from the madhouse raving and only by slow stages came to regard himself, since others did so, as sane. The theme of a language of complete intelligence, it is to be remarked, occurs in two other stories in the book – in one there is even an attempt, impossible to reproduce here, to give specimens of the language. To all appearances indeed it is the ordinary language in which he (the anonymous author) wrote, with perhaps an outlandish twist due merely to an increase of his usual severity – the authorities explained it by reading it as an imitation of the style of the most wilfully ingenuous author of the time. But it might very well have meant something to the author it could not mean to the reader, which is not at all improbable, since to myself, after long study and, I may say, an application it would be difficult to surpass, it meant only what it said – and this only with the greatest imaginative stretch possible to me in my liveliest moments of inquiry. The story, for the benefit of those few who may have access to the book, is, of course, *The Whisper*.

(*c*) That He one day woke to find himself Professor in Time at the University of Colour: he was addressing a class of old, old men on the principle of greenishness. 'For example,' he said, 'there are many modern artists who will not use green at all in their pictures: it is a foreign colour, an outside colour, an extra colour – the colour of conclusion. Therefore the colour of haughty youth, which is final, and of weird old age, which is beyond finality. The modern painter who banishes green does so from ambition: he means to show that he can give his pictures an effect of conclusion without making use of the wittiness of green. Primitive people make use of green with religious brutality to clinch any argument in colour. Flowers, on the other hand, never use green, nor the sky; unless unwholesome – an eccentric avoidance of a banal they-know-not-what. Earth-green is the symbol of time overcoming time. Green is a colour of sophisticated crudeness and of crude sophistication. A brute thing is in its heart of hearts green, and a casuistical mind is in its heart of hearts green. The grave mathematical most is green, and the silly poetical least is green. The new-born baby is green and the newly-dead person is green. And the extreme of tragedy is green, and the extreme of comedy is green.'

At this moment the oldest of the old, old men got up and shrieked, smilingly through his three teeth, saying: 'I spent my whole fortune in one night in music and food on a girl whose mother was a singer and whose father was a chef. "Trrup," she said, snapping her fingers, "you are an old man, and I love a boy who blacks my boots." ' 'Trrup,' he shrieked, smiling through his three teeth, 'I am green, I am green, and this is my life's story.' And 'Trrup,' shrieked all the old men, 'we are green, we are green.' Until He could not bear the noise and stopped his ears with his fingers, and closed his eyes.

When He removed his fingers from his ears and opened his eyes, he was sitting by his own fireside, and his cat was on the hearth-rug and She was near him, knitting him a green jacket. 'Trrup,' said the cat's eyes, 'what a fool you are to dream such sense,' and 'Trrup,' said She, 'what a dear silly you shall be napping in my green jacket.'

'I,' said He to himself, 'must tell this story to my mother, it will amuse her.'

And it was told, and it did, and she believed it of He, and everything else that was told of him, and put another lump of sugar in her tea, near the bottom of the cup, saying to herself: 'Is it not so? Sometimes I like Mrs. History, and sometimes I do not. Sometimes I pity her, and sometimes I wish her worse trouble. And what does it matter, since she is all this, and I am all that, and each of us always, no matter what happens, a bit of herself? When I am angriest I am nearest to kindness, and when I am clearest in my head I am nearest to confusion. Is it not so? I am sure I never know what I am going to do next. For instance, there are those wicked loves who follow a certain red flag: I am sure I should forget myself and join them if it were a green one.' For she, taking after her own son, was also a liar.

§ 5

The most curiously integrated of the groups of stories which may be classified as a single dramatic (or philosophical) unit of the book is the queen-group. Indeed it is possible to discuss this group as if it were but one story, the episodic variations seeming no more than caprices of style – the same story told in different degrees of earnestness and so in different personalities, as it were. The one fixed personality of the group is the Queen herself; the others are all stylistic personalities. The Queen began as a photograph used by a newspaper at discreet intervals to represent the female bandit of the moment or the murder-victim or the fire-heroine or the missionary's bride. By experience and variety she became a personality, and a fixed personality. It is quite remarkable in fact how under our very eyes this anonymous author should be able to transform a fiction into a fact: for the Queen is as true for always as the photograph is each time false. Indeed, the whole transformation is merely a matter of style. To illustrate: 'As Maxine, the world's sleeplessness champion, the photograph had great momentary importance but did not know it because it was part of a newspaper dynamic in which everything happened with equal fatalistic effect, everything was accident, in the moment succeeding accident it was always clear that nothing had happened. As photograph therefore the photograph saw all this; it was permanently unimportant but it knew this. And as it had a knowledge of its unimportance, it also had a knowledge of the importance of accident; and as the first knowledge made it insignificant so the second knowledge made it Queen. The Queen, the photograph without identity, this anonymous particularity, did in fact dwell in a world in which she was the only one and in which the world of many was only what she called "the

chaotic conversation of events." So she resolved
to put her queendom in order, not by interrupting
the conversation, which would only have increased
the chaos, but by having minutely recorded whatever "happened," whatever "was." Nothing then in
her queendom contradicted anything else, neither
the argument nor its answer, neither the burglar-
proof lock nor the burglar against whom it was
not proof: everything was so, everything was statistical, everything was falsification, everything was
conversation, and she was an anonymous particularity conversing with herself about her own
nothingness, so she was outside the chaotic conversation of events, she was Queen.'

Her three chief statisticians (we learn) were
publishers. They were all pleasant fellows, each
with a touch of the universal in him, and came and
went without suspicion everywhere in the queendom because of their peoplishness: they too, like
all the rest, were statistical, so statistical indeed that
they were statisticians. They went about preaching
the gospel of the communal ownership of events.
They said: 'Primitive man believed in things as
events. As civilized man it is your duty to believe
in events as things.' And the people did. And they
permitted the statisticians (or publishers) to know
what happened to them and what they did with
what happened to them as faithfully as they reported

their possessions each year in the great Common Book. In this queendom there was no loss and no mystery and no suffering, because everything was reported as conversation and nothing therefore thought about. All was automatic spontaneity, even their love for their Queen. As for the Queen, she would walk (we are told) through the dark rooms of her palace at night, having each room lit only upon her leaving it, until she reached her own small chamber, which remained unlit all night while the others shone; until morning, when in her own small chamber the curtains were drawn, the lamps lit, while in all the other rooms of the palace there was daylight. The meaning of this is plain: that in the anonymousness of the Queen lay her non-statistical, her non-falsificatory individuality. She is the author, the Queendom is her book. She is darkness and mystery, the plain, banal though chaotic daylight is her unravelling. By making the unravelling more methodic and so more plainly banal she separates in people the statistical from the non-statistical part, the known from the anonymous. She shows herself to be a dualist of the most dangerous kind.

For a long time the authorities from the internal evidence of the queen-stories suspected the anonymous author of being a woman. They said that it was not improbable that the book was the Bible of an underground sect devoted to educating female children to be statistical queens. But this view had to be abandoned as unscholarly, even ungentlemanly, because in nothing that the Queen said or did was there any accent of disorder or ambition: she merely, with miraculous patience and tact, saw to it that records were kept of everything. The authorities eventually concluded that she was a Character of Fiction, and so stainless, and could not help them. For some time their suspicion was fixed on a character in one of the stories with whom the Queen fell in love. But as he was Minister of Pastimes to the Queen it was thought that it might prove generally disrespectful to State officials to pursue the matter further (as when, in the story *Understanding*, suspicion was fixed on the character who bribed the magistrates to convict him, the inquiry was stopped by the authorities – the detectives even put on the wrong scent – as too metaphysical and cynical).

It must now be clear that the strain of my task is beginning to tell on me. I have become very nervous. In the beginning my emotions were all scholarly, my task was a pleasure, I had the manner of calmness with an antiquity. Toward the end fear has crept upon me. I must speak, and after that go on till I can go on no longer: till I am prevented. I say *prevented*. For I am haunted by the obsession that the authorities are still watching. They do not suspect the Queen. She was or is a fixed personality, so anonymous as to be irreproachably a Character of Fiction. The others vary in earnestness; in anonymity; they are, as I have suggested, personalities of style; they point to the probability that the author was not or is not a Character of Fiction. I dare go no further. I have become very nervous. I shall nevertheless attempt to continue my task until – I am prevented.

One of the three publishers was a Jew. He was tall, his ears outstanding, his grin long, his voice loose in his mouth. He had been financial adviser to a charitable organization and had had much general statistical though humane experience. He was gross but kind and therefore in charge of all sentimental records: his grossness assured accuracy, his kindness, delicacy. He had the historical genius, and several specimens of his work are given – though with a touch of dryness in the author himself which makes it impossible to enjoy them as we might have were the book without an author. Indeed, they were not meant to be read at all, but merely written to satisfy the political instincts of the Queen, who never read them herself. I find it difficult to pass over them myself, for aside from their part in the book they are very interesting. There are several small extracts that might be used here with complete propriety and even in a scholarly way. And after all, the author wrote them down himself, did he not? But he was writing and not reading. But am I not writing and not reading? My position becomes more and more uncertain. I shall hurry on.

I shall give one of the Queen's monologues, to tide us over this difficult period. The monologue does not appear in the book itself: it would have been a piece of naturalism contrary to the theory on which the book was built. Therefore I give it here, as reading. No questions must be asked of me, for as a scholar I should feel obliged to answer them; and the passage would then become writing; and I should have produced a piece of naturalism. Here then is, shall I say, a variety: which is not the anonymous author's writing but we might almost say his reading, and after that my writing but of his reading, which remains reading for all my writing. My conscience is in your hands: the burden of curiosity and falsification falls upon you. With you rest also the rights of anonymity, the reputation of style, the fortunes of publication, the future of philosophy and scholarship and the little children, for whom these contrive sense. Sense, I say, not satire.

And now for the Queen's monologue, which the anonymous author did not write and which for this very reason requires, as the reader's part, sense, I say, not satire, even more immediately than what he did write. Furthermore, you will have to discover for yourself where it begins and where it ends: were I to mark it off it would become writing and so a piece of naturalism and so bely sense and give encouragement to satire. I mean: restraint, statistics, falsification, is more accurate than courage, reality, truth, and so truer. For the Queen's monologue, since the anonymous author did not write it down, is true; had he not statistically, falsificatorily, restrained himself from writing it down it would have become a piece of naturalism and so a subject of satire. To tide us over a difficult period I set myself the difficult task of writing down the Queen's monologue without turning it into writing, and so defying satire (if I succeed, which depends on you). The important thing is to defy satire. Satire is lying: falsity as opposed to truth and falsity as opposed to falsification. It is betwixt and between; against sense, which, whatever it is, is one thing or the other – generally the other, it being for practical purposes impossible for it to be perpetually one thing. By practical purposes I mean of course the question of boredom, as truth finding truth monotonous. Therefore things happen. Sense, I say, not satire. Imagine a woman has her heart broken and imagine a man breaking it, then her heart heals and he ceases to be a villain, and then they meet again and her heart is whole and he is not a villain. Does she weep because her heart was once broken and does he blush because he once broke it? This would be satire. No, they both smile, and she gives him her heart to break again, and he breaks it. This is sense. Or they both smile and turn away from each other, and this, too, is sense, but sense too academic to survive the strain of academically enforcing itself. The One Thing must be saved from itself, it must not be allowed to overwork itself or go stale. That is why sense is one thing or the other and generally the other: falsification to relieve truth, broken hearts to protect whole hearts, weakness to spare strength. Fact is fancy and fancy is desire and desire is puff! puff! everything that satisfies it and which must be carefully recorded in spite of contradictions and lengthiness. Desire is the other things, in great number. And what is satisfaction? Not the other things, that satisfy, but the one thing, that cannot satisfy or be satisfied, and so, though but one thing, equal to desire, and so to all the other things. Fact is *it* not *me*; fact is fancy and fancy is desire and desire is the other things. Satisfaction is *me*, which *it* calls Queen. *It* is a lot of him's, *it* is a queendom, *it* is desire speaking the language of satisfaction, *it* is a great looseness and restlessness of fact and confusion of eyesight and

183

costume, into which the Queen brings sense through order. And what is order? Order is observation. Her first publisher (or statistician) is a gross, kind Jew. Her second is a subtle, cruel Turk, who brutally forced events: he has the political genius. But the people do not mind, since the events happen anyhow: they shrug their shoulders good-naturedly and say 'Old Hassan Bey smiling with Turkish teeth,' and call on the first publisher to take notice how smilingly they wince back. Her third is a Christian, and he does nothing: he has the philosophical genius. His idleness and talkativeness exasperate the other two into efficiency. His favourite harangue is: 'Let the people create their own order.'

'But how, their own order?'

'Let them think.'

'But if they think, they will all think differently, and not only differently – some will think more powerfully than others.'

'Exactly: those who think more powerfully than others will create order.'

'But this would not be real order, rather the disorder of a false order created by the most powerfully thinking individual or individuals of the moment. This would be anarchism, and anarchism is not enough.'

'I have heard that said before, but how is the order created by the Queen not anarchism?'

'The Queen does not create order, she observes methodically, she creates *her* order. That is why *it* is *her* queendom.'

'But is this not merely a refined form of anarchism?'

'No, it is more than anarchism. The Queen is not the chief individual of her queendom; she is the *me* of the *it*; she is the one thing, her queendom is the other things; she is satisfaction, her queendom is desire, a lot of *him's*. The more *me* she is, the more *it* it is, and the more anonymous she is, and the more she and her queendom are diplomatically indistinguishable. The domestic situation is of course another affair. But to carry the distinction beyond the boundaries of the book is to fall betwixt and between, into satire.'

§ 6

Therefore the time has come to close. I am discovered, or rather I have discovered myself, for the authorities lost interest in me when they saw that I would discover myself before I could be officially discovered, that I would in fact break through the pages and destroy the strongest evidence that might be held against me, that is, that 'An anonymous book ——' etc. I understand now that what they desired to prevent was just what has happened. You must forgive me and believe that I was not trying to deceive, but that I became confused. I over-distinguished and so fell into satire and so discovered myself and so could not go on, to maintain a satiric distinction between authorship and scholarship.

And what of the woman who loved an engine? I cannot say. And the woman who was bewitched by a parallel? I cannot say. They come after the place where I left off.

THE DAMNED THING

§ 1

'SEX' is crude sex, resembling other crude appetites which similarly lose significance as soon as satisfied; and it is translated sex – sex surviving the satisfaction of the appetite. As the first it applies to the mechanics, as the second to the sentiment of sex.

The child begins with crude sex alone. It innocently indulges itself in sensual pleasures. It loves kissing and to be kissed, stroking and to be stroked, fondly contemplating its excretions. The civilized society into which it is born magnifies the importance of these insignificant local sensations, gives them intellectual depth. It creates a handsome receptacle, love, to contain the humours of this unnaturally enlarged instinct.

So much at any rate for the male child: parental care nurtures masturbation into love and marriage. Sex may stop short of love at lust. It may be anything it pleases, so long as it satisfies the standard measurements for social impressiveness.

The female child has a different history. She

shares a short period of sexual casualness with the male child, at the end of which she immediately becomes a candidate for the recipience of masculine love; while the sexual training of the male child is intensified at this point. This difference accounts for the so-called early maturity of the female child. For at the time when her male contemporary is only a first-year man she is already a graduate without benefit of education; and her proper mate is therefore a graduate.

Although intelligent people are generally aware of the equivocal background of love and marriage, they nevertheless go on marrying for the relaxation and social ease that comes of doing what every one else is doing. Any other course would be socially unintelligible; and explanations are indecent. Imagine a man and a woman both undeformed by sex tradition and that an intimacy exists between them. The intelligent major part of their intimacy incorporates sex without sentimental enlargement: it is an effect rather than a cause. And it is eventually absorbed, it undergoes a diffusion, it is the use of an amenable physical consciousness for the benefit of mental consciousness.

But traditionally sex would be the cause not the effect of such an intimacy. The conventional language of love could scarcely express it otherwise; the only diffusion recognized would be the verbal substitution of commendable emotions for gross passions. When the lover said 'I love you' it would be socially impossible for him to mean: 'Our personalities have an intense and irresistible sympathy. I am so conscious of you and myself together that sometimes my sexual glands are stimulated by the very thought of you.' It would be impossible for him not to mean: 'My sexual glands, by the ingrowing enlargement of my sex instinct since childhood and its insidious, civilized traffic with every part of my mental and physical being, are unfortunately in a state of continual excitement. I have very good control of myself, but my awareness of your sexual physique and its radiations was so acute that I could not resist the temptation to desire to lie with you. Please do not think this ignoble of me, for I shall perform this act, if you permit it, with the greatest respect and tenderness and attempt to make up for the indignity it of course fundamentally will be to you (however pleasurable) by serving you in every possible way and by sexually flattering manifestations of your personality which are not strictly sexual.'

The diffusion which modern society calls love is the colouring of sex with sentiments which have no connection with sex, sentiments which are not served by sex but serve sex, by making attractive to the finical civilized mind an instinct naturally repulsive to it. They are literary. Sex, in the imagery of Stendhal, is the naked branch which, when introduced into the sált mine, comes out covered with crystal formations: love is the imaginative crystallization of naked instinct. The naked instinct is the monstrous male instinct. The crystallization is an aphrodisiac for the female, in whom sex is comparatively casual: the sparkling branch creates in her an appetite for love equal to the male's tremendous sexual offering, which she would otherwise shrink from accepting. By this stratagem the male himself does not seem to the female to be touching her; in love virginity remains spiritually undamaged. It is like the doll in a recent Oxford smoker. Whenever the doll was touched, the young person of the piece, who had a psychic connection with the doll, was affected, though untouched herself, so the nun conceals carnality from herself by washing herself in dollish instalments. Love is Masoch's stately and marble-like Demon of Virginity ('the deeply rooted fear of existence every creature feels'), a lewd and prudish Shepherdess.

The only courses possible in sex then are love and marriage, misconduct and perversion. Misconduct is masculine brutality, the male's refusal to dress up the overgrown branch; and feminine indelicacy, the female's willingness to accept the overgrown branch in spite of its unromantic nakedness. Per-

version varies in character. It may be mere animal-
like sexual levity. Or the biological cynicism of the
species. Or it may occur in the male when love and
marriage or ordinary misconduct seem insufficient
to his exaggerated sex instinct, which can only be
satisfied by an instinct as exaggerated as his own.
Or it may occur in the female as a feministic improvement on man-made sex, nevertheless imitating
it in its mechanism from an irrepressible sexual
nostalgia. Or it may occur, as also in the male,
through deprivation of normal sex life – though
more rarely than in the male, since her sex instinct
is less demanding. Active Lesbianism is a form of
sexual derangement resulting from the female's mistaken effort to become sexually equivalent to the
male: passive Lesbianism is a romantic substitution
of the feminine branch for the masculine branch
in the forced absence of the latter, the crystallization remaining the same.

There is an intellectual side to masculine homosexuality that is never very strong in Lesbian alli-
ances. Homosexuality in men indeed is more often
intellectually induced than in women: it is ascetic,
whereas women are not sexually fanatic enough for
sexual asceticism. The disgust of homosexual men
with civilized heterosexual love becomes a disgust
with the crystalline aggressiveness of the female
body. If a woman is attractive to a homosexually

minded man it is because she seems what he calls 'pure and virginal' – aloof, that is, from her sexual uses. The disgust is really with the aggressive male sexuality which is responsible for the crystallization. Wherever there is great cynicism about sex, in Islam, say, or in France, homosexuality is connived at as an intellectual supplement to heterosexual life. The classical type of homosexuality was far less exclusive and severe than the modern type: it was sophistication rather than specialization.

Whether or not homosexuality is found a satisfactory intellectual supplement, it is at any rate so that it is easier for male than for female mentality to escape from socialized sex. Woman has been too much under the necessity of self-preservation to lay down the weapons of feminine personality and risk the disarmed independence of sexual impersonality. She is the object, or prey, of male sexuality, and her strength lies in the pride and in the obstacles with which she conditions her capture. Much modern feminism is only a sentimental enlargement of this pride, only a shrewder insistence on her value as a prize. For the most part the feminist still has the mentality of the recipient in sex demanding compensation for the indignity of her position; feminism is an unnatural preoccupation in woman with her sexual self.

Woman's case is nearly hopeless, then. Man is just a little better off: his position affords him the relief, if he is intellectually capable of taking it, of sexual suicide.

§ 2

Often we spend hours disposing of some small thing not worth five minutes' thought. We have had it a long time, it is occasionally useful, some one has given it to us, it would be a pity to throw it away, it has become quite a part of us, and so on. And yet it is in the way. Yielding to the tyranny of the trivial hanging-on thing is adaptation. Outwardly we seem to make the thing adapt itself to us. Actually we are adapting ourselves to the thing – a grotesque adaptation. Such a thing is sex, the small physical thing; such an adaptation is the ceremony with which it is decently installed in the opinion.

With sex there seems to be nothing between masturbation (throwing the damned thing out) and romance (grotesque adaptation). Even the scientific attitude is romantic: the implied title of every learned book on sex is *De l'Amour*. The cases in such series as Havelock-Ellis's books on sex belong to romance; they are the scientist's storification of sex. After the reader has grown used to the laboratory manner of the scientist he continues to read from sentiment not science; and the author himself continues, like any romantic author, only from the growing morbid fascination of the subject – a tediously energetic mind unhinged by the baffling triviality of sex. Every psychologist of sex is a psychologist of sex because he suffers from a sex-fixation. He is the principal case of his work.

Masturbation is reckoned disgraceful only because it debases sex to less than what it is; the damned thing is passionately shoved out of sight instead of granted pious functional importance in the household of the mind. There is much less disgust felt toward venereal disease than toward masturbation simply because the former is a large subject, the latter a small one. The campaign against masturbation in homes, boys' schools and sex books is much more intense than the campaign against prostitution. Masturbation cannot be sentimentalized. Prostitution, 'the oldest profession in the world,' has an honoured ritual of obscenity and an equally honoured ritual of commerce.

So great is the importance of accepted sex symbolism – the authorized poetry of sex – that any departure from it is classified as a perversion, as 'erotic' symbolism. 'Normal' symbolism does not even go by its name: it is love. It is not recorded among the cases of erotic symbolism that so-and-so continually wrote of women's lips, or so-and-so of women's breasts. But several pages (fine print) must of course be devoted to a few notorious cases (French) of foot symbolism, and of course to the national case of China, a horrible example to the Western sexual mind of perverse symbolism. Lip-worship and .breast-worship are normal because they are generalizations: the kiss has become so poetically diffuse in meaning that it does not repre-sent the precise local excitement which is its actual sexual rôle, but a vague spiritual lippishness; the breasts, likewise, are officially not part of the sexual apparatus, but the semi-divine sensual equivalent of that heart-bosom-and-chest sentiment into which humanity has glorified mean sex-feeling.

'And up the rosy pathway to her heart
The uncapped pilgrim crept.'

– Byron.

Foot-worship is unnatural because it is local and particular; it connects sex with a physical triviality. It is nearly as disrespectful to romance as if the sexual parts themselves were worshipped.

Sexual energy, if left alone, would adapt itself instead of forcing adaptation, be diffused instead of diffuse. The social mechanism for disposing of sex makes sex as large and complicated as itself, inten-sifies its masculinity. Its femininity reduces merely to an abstract, passive principle of motion in the great moving masculine machine; without separate social personality. The social self is the sexual self, and the sexual self is the male sexual self: the dramatic pleasure which woman feels in sex romance is masculine pleasure; in witnessing sexual embrace on the screen or on the stage she adopts the emotions of the male. Her innate sexual impersonality if not philosophized, would wreck the solemn masculine machine; it is therefore socially interpreted as mechanical receptiveness, metaphysical unconsciousness, social helpfulness. In self-defence woman becomes sentimentally attached to this role: the sexual machine so elaborately concentrated on her confers on her an indignity loaded with prerogatives. Slavish sex modesty is converted into sex vanity. Militant (feministic) woman can do no more than piously emphasize the negative, obstetrical instrumentality of female sex; pretending that motherhood is a rational social end instead of a bigoted natural idiosyncrasy.

This grotesque of socialized sex comes of the stupid attempt of intelligent man to make nature intelligent. Society is the genteel human version of nature. It is based on the assumption that man is a product of the refined integration of nature by time and that it is therefore a superior, evolved nature. A constant forced transference thus takes place from the slums of nature into the respectable terraces and squares of society.

But the very existence of society, of an improved nature, proves rather that man is a product of the refined disintegration of nature by time; that society is in fact a defensive alliance by conscious, contradictory nature against unconscious, consistent nature. And man stands in deformity between them, a creature part social, part natural; but also something else, himself. What is social is unreal. What is natural is unreal. What is himself is also unreal; but unreal intrinsically, not from deformity.

Reproductive sentiment, for example, is an emotional screen to conceal how little we belong to nature. For were we to appreciate this little we should soon appreciate how little we belonged to society. Sex is even more separate from reproductive instincts in human beings than in animal beings. Society therefore strengthens the sympathetic connection between them, this last crucial bond with nature.

But what is this sex that society has raised from a state of nature to a state of respectability among the intelligent passions? A myth in which people half believe to keep up appearances of which they are half ashamed. Only in the private consciousness is it not a fraud; and here, an eccentric mark of physical loneliness, a sort of memory of belonging; when actualized, a momentary extinction of consciousness, as it means momentary consciousness to beasts that belong much to nature. As a public ceremony sex is constantly in need of artificial stimulation; its technique is scarcely more than the technique of costume. It persists through the illusion of numbers, which perform a gross sex-masque, a lascivious fancifying of nature.

Sex is the tribal totem through which society sues Nature for protection and recognition, and through which Nature is ritually flattered. To the Church sex is the essence of flesh. Man is afraid to admit that he lives largely outside of nature, that his body is only a soul, a myth. Instead, he uses the myth to re-establish flesh; God is the authentication of the body.

Sex is the chief religious mystery of man, his most theatrical exhibition of reality. Parents lie in wait for their children, to change their little sexual sillies into portentous symbols. Either they significantly do not 'tell' them but work their transformations by a dark force of silence and suggestion; or they significantly and poetically 'tell' them. Is the child expected not to see that what is perhaps pretty in flowers is rather ridiculous in people, who for the most part have other interests besides seed-making and seed-scattering? Or to treat as religious truth the crazy information that baby comes out of mother? Unprompted, it finds this just a third-rate curiosity. If it hears its mother shrieking in labour it will report without malice but without sentiment that mother squealed like a pig. Naturally without a sexual conscience, it is gradually bullied into superstitiousness, reverence or horror of sex. Shelley, on being read the passage about Geraldine's breast in *Christabel*, saw a vision of a woman with eyes instead of nipples. The child's sight is poetically twisted to see the nipples either so or as sacred knobs of coral. The only way a child can be initiated into socialized sex without deformity of his comic sense is through obscenity, the cynical and painful adult version of the child's sexual insouciance.

Psychology is the modern church of sex, provoking an obscene Tolstoyan piety. Havelock-Ellis says: 'We must, as Bölshe declares, accustom ourselves to gaze on the naked human body exactly as we gaze at a beautiful flower'; and quotes the following account of a totem mystery from Ungewitter's *Die Nacktheit*: 'They made themselves as comfortable as possible, the men laying aside their coats, waistcoats, boots and socks; the women their blouses, skirts, shoes and stockings. Gradually, as the moral conception of nakedness developed in their minds, more and more clothing fell away, until the men wore nothing but bathing drawers and the women only their chemises. In this "costume" games were carried out in common, and a regular camp-life led. The ladies (some of whom were unmarried) would then lie in hammocks and we men on the grass, and the intercourse was delightful [sic]. We felt as members of one family, and behaved accordingly [sic].' And Havelock-Ellis himself again: 'The nose receives the breath of life; the vagina receives the water of life. . . . The swelling breasts are such divinely gracious insignia of womanhood because of the potential child that hangs at them and sucks; the large curves at the hips are so voluptuous because of the potential child they clasp within them.' The juvenile delinquent of the streets reacts to this no more obscenely by singing 'Mother caught her titties in the mangle.'

Lofty reverence of the female sexual organs conceals a fundamental disgust with them. Woman is the symbol to man of the uncleanness of bodily existence, of which he purifies himself by putting her to noble uses. She thus has for a him a double, contradictory significance; she is the subject of his bawdry and the subject of his romance. The sex totem is made in her image and embodies for him the conflict between suicide and immortality. Man himself is unreal. On woman he gets physical reality. She is his nature, the realistic enlargement of his own small sexual apparatus. She is the morphological supplement of his phallus. Through her he can refine, ritualize and vary his monotonous and trivial appendage. She is the means by which he adapts himself to what he is unable to assimilate mentally, to the absurd physical remnant which pursues him in his pilgrimage to extinction and which he appeases by turning aside to reverence. Sex is a perfidious intellectual digression into physical reminiscences.

How does woman play her part as the sacred animal of the sex totem? With ease, since she is quantitatively more sexual than man, more literally sexual; therefore more impersonally sexual. Sex in woman is unemotional, constitutionally well-blended – apart, that is, from the ritualistic education in love that she is subjected to by a masculine society. Sex in man is emotional; it is segregated; it is the last touch of nature in him that haunts and torments him and that he propitiates with pompous and evasive rites. Although, like man, woman is largely not of nature, what nature remains in her satisfies itself without pomp or pathos. That civilized woman is slower than man in arriving at sexual climaxes is due to the fact that her native sexual ease had been perverted by man's tortuous psychology into a self-stupefying philosophical passivity.

Woman, indeed, is so nearly complete in herself, except for the phallus, that it is difficult to see how it happened, if one sex must instrumentalize the other, that she rather than man became the auxiliary apparatus. Phallic worship in man is not pious but politic (unless he is homosexual, which is another matter); an institution for advertising the phallus to woman, hypnotizing her with it, protecting her from the knowledge that she holds the strategical sexual position. It is perhaps fair to say that as a consciousness man is woman's equal. As a physical apparatus he is a clumsily devised gadget. From the point of view of their fertilizing powers there are millions and millions more men alive than necessary. With proper husbanding of sperm (an economy already practised with prize bulls and stallions) one man might conceivably maintain the world-population if a somewhat smaller figure than the present were agreed upon as more reasonable and if birth-control were somewhat relaxed. All propagandist display of physical and mental superiority on man's part, all Rabelaisian gizzard and brain tickling, is an attempt to detract attention from his obviously incidental character as a physical apparatus.

But it is unkind and even irrelevant to over-press the point. What is relevant is that we are in a state of semi-conscious transition between nature and nothing, and the more conscious we grow, the nearer we are to nothing. In this passage sex comes quietly along, obligingly diminishing itself except when man, in panic of annihilation, whips it up and tries to ride himself back to nature upon it. But the passage continues, his hobby-horse is a phantom.

Panic of annihilation, resistance to sexual diminution, is a social emotion. Resistance to sexual enlargement is a personal emotion, the fear of a more brutal kind of annihilation. Sex brings shock; to some rudimentary forms, simple death; to human beings, intricate death, death of self, death of death. Homosexuality is an oblique escape from the violence of this shock. Polygamy and polyandry distribute the frightening physical solidarity of monogamy. Monogamous couples are always hungry for company: to dilute sex. This hunger for dilution is one-half of parenthood; the other half is the regressive hunger for solidarity.

This natural difference between creatures intellectually like is the real perversion. Man is a poetic animal; what is natural in him is pathological. Poetically he is unisexual; when he attempts to make the nature in him poetic he becomes bisexual or homosexual not poetic. It is impossible that through sex nature should approve of man or man of nature. The only way to prevent sex from being a greater source of discomfort than need be is to recognize it as an anomalous hanger-on in man's journey away from nature and to make it reveal its presence by behaving naturally: bringing about a literal diffusion of physical nature in human nature instead of a monstrous hermaphroditism or a monstrous monomania.

§ 3

Sex as a petty eccentricity of the individual can be easily disposed of by the individual. As a social symptom it assumes large metaphysical proportions; it becomes a crux between matter and mind. It demands legal control, giving society an excuse for power; economic control (as a medium of exchange), giving society an excuse for motion; ceremonial control, giving society an excuse for language, manners, communication. That is, it gives society an excuse for society.

Society keeps control of sex by so embroidering it with sentiment that the individual scarcely realizes that he is serving society instead of society him. Every one knows, in the abstract, for instance, that monogamy is an economic expression; yet individuals participating in monogamy would be horrified at the suggestion that they were confirming an economic expression. Marriage is not an economic expression, but a 'sacrament.' Havelock-Ellis says: 'Since marriage is not a mere contract, but a fact of conduct, and even a sacred fact, the free participation of both parties is needed to maintain it. And not only is the economic significance of monogamous marriage concealed by an argument of spiritual significance, but by a biological argument as well. Havelock-Ellis further says: 'Monogamy, in the fundamental biological sense, represents the natural order into which the majority of sexual facts will always naturally fall, because it is the relationship which most adequately corresponds to all the physical and spiritual facts involved.' (Compare Shelley's argument that polygamy was a biological necessity because the noble horse was polygamous.)

There develops, as a counterpart to public sex, not private sex but academic sex, sex the tradition rather than sex the practice. Sex shows itself proudly as an art. It *is* art. And as it is the male not the female who tends to express himself traditionally as *man*, art is male art. It is therefore foolish to point out that there have been very few great women artists: why should one look for women artists at all in male art? Art is to man the academic idea of woman, a private play with her in public. It is therefore foolish to point out that many artists, perhaps the best, are homosexual. They are not homosexual. Art is their wench.

By man's abstractness of mind is meant his personal anonymity; he is a public creature, only mathematically existent. By woman's concreteness of mind is meant the individuality (man calls it 'reality') he recognizes in her and which he attempts under cover of love, to steal. Woman wears clothes, man wears a social uniform. Woman is individual-power (brain); man is mass-power (brawn). Therefore man, though individually a negative force, is as a unit a positive force; defeating woman as a unit, since the fact that she is individually a positive force makes her collectively a negative force. Here is the secret of man's power over woman and of a woman's power over a man.

The mysterious 'reality' of woman is responsible for her mysterious position. The only way to correct this position is for her to make a mystery of man, to flatter, cajole, bully him into individuality. Feminism's great mistake is in concentrating on woman rather than on man. Concentration on woman can only increase the mysteriousness of her position.

The antithesis between intellectual and intuitional faculties is really an antithesis between conventionality and unconventionality. Mrs. Willa Muir, is a short essay on *Woman*, says: 'Unconscious life creates, for example, human beings: conscious life creates, for example, philosophy.' Human beings are not created by woman's intuition (Mrs. Muir should know this), but by the fertilization of the female ovum by the male sperm. What is meant is that philosophy springs from the conventional male mind; but that human beings spring

206

from the unconventional female body; and that the female mind is therefore also unconventional.

The male mind is conventional because the male body is a mere convention. The female body is unconventional because it is individualistic: man gets somewhat socially and vaguely just children, woman gets personally and precisely *a* child. The female mind is therefore unconventional because it is individualistic, that is, because woman is physically an individual to a degree to which man is not. Therefore man is intellectual, woman is intuitional: man is unconquerable monotony, woman conquerable variety. He has a formal, vacant simplicity, she has an informal, experimental complexity. Therefore, since he cannot be entrusted with creating human beings and she can, she must not be entrusted with creating philosophy, which is all he can be entrusted with. She is not good enough to be entrusted with creating philosophy because she is intuitional: she is too good to be entrusted with creating philosophy because she is unconventional.

It is fair to generalize about man because he is a generalization, unfair to generalize about woman because she is not. Man is male, man is 'the sex,' not woman; woman is temperamentally unisexual, a person; for this reason perhaps a mystery. Her sex play is literal, hard, matter-of-fact, truly theatri-

207

cal; the rest is unconventional, a mystery. With man, all is sex; he cannot easily grasp the dualism necessary to any real individual sense. His play is symbolical, realistic; it is 'the reality,' protracted by a tiresome, childish patience that never wears out. Woman, to save herself from boredom, is obliged to enliven the scene with a few gratuitous falsetto turns, which he interprets as co-operation. Even at his boldest man cannot get beyond a conventional anarchism. He cannot see that he is on a stage and therefore he cannot see that it is possible to get off; so that his performance is continuous. And he will perhaps never learn that anarchism is not enough. His fine phallus-proud works-of-art, his pretty masterpieces of literature, painting, sculpture and music, bear down upon woman's maternal indulgence; she is full of admiration, kind but weary. When, she sighs, will man grow up, when will he become woman, when will she have companions instead of children?

LETTER OF ABDICATION

I HAVE done all I could for you, but the only consequence is that you are the same as always. I had the alternative of ordering a general massacre, but I should then have had to go away anyhow. It is simpler to abdicate. It certainly makes no difference to the situation whether I leave you behind dead or alive. Therefore I will leave you behind alive, to afford myself the bitter satisfaction of telling you what I think of you. You will not listen any more than you would if you were dead, but I should not address you if you were dead. Therefore I will leave you behind alive, to afford myself the bitter satisfaction of telling you what I think of you.

You are not gay. You are sticky instead of rubbery. You represent yourself with priggish sincerity instead of mimicking yourself with grotesque accuracy. Because you are photographs you think the photographs are originals. You think seeing is being.

You do not know what you are. I will tell you, though it will not make the least difference to you, since you do not know what you are. You are a conceit. You are what you are not. You are a very fine point of discrimination. But since you do not discriminate, since you are not gay, since you think what you are is what you are, therefore you are not: this indeed is why massacre was unnecessary. You are blind, from seeing; you cannot appreciate the identity of opposites. You are feeble, from a loutish strength of doing; so that you cannot surpass doing, let doing instead of yourselves do; so that you cannot repose. You are cowards, afraid to be more than perfect and more than formal; so that you are only what you are; you have the perfection of mediocrity, not the irregularity of perfection. You are superstitious; you will season the dish with salt, but you will not taste salt itself. You are ignorant; not only do you not know what you are; you do not know what you are not. You are lazy; you will do only one thing at a time; you will act; but you will not act and not act. You are criminal; what you do is all positive, wicked, damaging; you make no retractions, contradictions, proofs of innocence. You are without honour; over-sincere; hypocritical.

I will tell you a story which is in my mind at the moment and may therefore have some bearing on the question. There was once a woman whose mind was as active as her body. And there was once a man who was constituted in the same way. And the combination of them produced a child which was all mind and no body. And no one knew about it. She was, naturally, a woman. Her parents gave her no name but referred to her in a historical manner as 'The Deliverer.' Whenever anything went wrong in any part of the world she put it right because she was all mind. But no one knew about it and so it made no difference. When they became quite hopeless her parents referred to her merely as 'The Angel.' In the end she was plain 'she' to them. At her death she became all body, and her parents, frenzied with disappointment, drove her out. And no one knew about it. Her parents gave her no name but referred to her in a historical manner as 'The Destroyer.' Whenever anything went right in any part of the world she put it wrong again because she was all body. But no one knew about it and so it made no difference. When they became quite hopeless her parents referred to her merely as 'The Beast.' In the end she was plain 'she' to them. At her death she became all mind, and her parents, frenzied with disappointment, took her in again. And no one knew about it.

This is the story which was in my mind and which may have some bearing on the question. The point of it is, I think, that we are all in an impossible position; which you handle by making less, myself more, impossible. For example, it is unlikely that the story that I have just told you would ever have occurred to you. Or if it had, you would have broken down in the middle and called it the end. You stop half-way round the circle in order to spare yourself the humiliation of missing the true end, which is not perceptible in the ordinary way. Indeed if it is not perceived, it makes no difference, the circle goes round and round upon you. On the other hand, it makes no difference even if it is perceived, except the difference of perceiving it, which makes the position, as I have said, more rather than less impossible. So do as you like.

But I shall abdicate if you do, and since you do, I abdicate. You are all asleep, because being awake means being dreamless, and you can only be awake by dreaming to be awake, by dreaming to be dreamless. You turn your back on your own non-existence and are therefore non-existent. When you love, you turn your back on what you love. When you sweep, you turn your back on the dirt. When you think, you turn your back on your mind. Well, keep looking the other way so that I can kick you where you deserve to be kicked. And you will not turn on me but flatter yourselves that you are having spasms of profundity.

Anyway, this is how it is, little wise-bottoms. There is Cleopatra, Rome, Napoleon and so forth on one side, and there is the future on the other side, and there you are in the middle alive. There is that great churning, that continuous tossing up and making of a middle, that bright ferment of centrality; and it is you. My o my o my o, what a thing! But when it was Cleopatra, Rome, Napoleon or any of them of then, or when it will be who it will be, my o my o my o, what a thing. It was not, it will not be you. And what was you and what will you be? You was and you will be dead. And why? Because you are alive now. But come a little closer, darlings, that I may kick you a little harder. Listen: if you was dead and if you will be dead, each of you, then you must be dead now, each of you, you must be dead and alive. Now o now o now o, pumpkins, don't cry. For just think: there is that great big live middle and it is nice and warm and it is you. But it may also be it. And what would become of you then out in the cold if you didn't take yourselves in, if you weren't also you, if you weren't each of you dead as well as alive? And what difference does it make? None whatever, pets, except the difference of a difference that makes no difference.

I will argue further against what I am arguing for. The you which is you is only you, and not only dead but invisible. And you can never be this you unless you see the you which is it and every one hard round the circle to the end, where you can no longer see, and are you alone. And the result, if you do this? You will be so alive that you will be deader than ever; you will have achieved the identity of opposites; you will have brought two counter-processes to rub noses, the you which you are not, which is you alone, and the you which you are, which is it, every one, not you – and much good may it do you, except to make you deader than ever. And the result, if you do not do this? You will save that much life from death, and much good may it do you – enough to wipe your nose on, when it runs with nervousness at the thought that you will have to die anyway.

Yes, I once knew a woman who spent all her time washing her linen, in order to be always fresh and sweet smelling. But as she was always washing dirty linen and thus making the linen she wore dirtier than it might have been if she had washed less, she smelled of nothing but dirty linen. Any why? Because she was over-sincere and a hypocrite. She got stranded in the fact of clean linen instead of moving on to the effect of clean linen, which is the end of the circle. And you are all like that.

And again. Believing it to be you alone and that you are only what you are, think what a small, mean, cosy, curly, pink and puny figure you cut when you set out to be it at a party of it's, naked as in your own bath. Whereas, ladies and gentlemen, if you understood the identity of opposites, your naked-

ness would be an invisibility which you would
have to dress large, from the point of view of
visibility. And to this it-ish rather than you-ish
exterior you would add an even larger and looser-
fitting social skin, a house in most it-ish order, a
most it-ish interior, in fact. But you do not understand. 'Boo-hoo!' you cry. 'What, hide our naked
hearts, paralyse our heroic breasts, sit upon our
grave bottoms, swallow back our great acts?' 'Hush-
a-bye,' I reply, 'there is enough going on for you
forrard without your great acts: drinks free, if you
will only drink, scenery on view, if you will only
look, music keeping step for you if you will only
supply the feet. Instead of spending money on what
you can only get for nothing. Life, lads, is a charity
feed the fun of which is in everybody pretending to
be a swell and everybody treating everybody else like
a swell and everybody knowing everybody is a fraud
and no matter. No matter because of death, in which
each may be rich and proud, and no fooling. And
your great acts? When you are bursting with fraud
and charity and can stand no more, sneak aft and
do your great acts, like private retchings and acts
of death. If they will not come on, repeat to a point
of mechanical conviction some formula of dreary
finality, such as, 'The fathers of our girl friends are
lecherous,' or 'Philosophy is teetotal whisky.'

But you are all sluts, your efforts are not biggish,

and so your fine points are only untidy and trivial. If you would neatly calculate, you must calculate grossly the whole pattern of it, which is the making of the middle; you must conceive first tremendously, then accurately; you must grasp the general initiative which is it not you. From this, if your application be fine enough, the fine points will resolve themselves. But remember you are no fine small point yourself; you are more and less than one; you are the littlishness of biggishness; you are no fine small point but a fine small point of discrimination. My o my o my o, what a thing, poor beastie, to be but dainty when you would be statistical. The best of you are the worst of you: they over-discriminate, put their hand to their chin, stand upon taste, pick the highest and most delicately scorched plum, and then choke over the stone, dying the death of an æsthlete. For what is a single plum, too fine for the eye and not fine enough for the throat?

I might advise you to think; but you are over-eager, all for gain. And thought is just a power of potentiality; as you are of it; as death is of life; without gain. You would make potentiality where there is none, in order to have more thought than is possible; you would turn the future into a bank, as you now do the past, from greed of time.

Or I might say: 'Have shame.' But you would

only expose yourselves a little more outrageously and hang your heads a little lower. You would not understand that only truly abandoned boldness breeds truly abandoned decorum. Your interpretations are ignoble and indecent. You begin with contradictions instead of ending with them; efface them instead of developing them. As, for example, with sex: you seize upon it at the beginning, tease it, worry it, transform it, until you think you have ironed it out thoroughly, whereas you have only ironed yourselves out thoroughly. While if you had not seized upon it, you would have found it at the end of the circle, had you reached the end, an achieved confirmation of the impossibility that makes things possible.

This is one of my favourite subjects; if I were not abdicating I might discuss it elaborately, for your good. Since I am abdicating, I will discuss it simply, for my own good; for it is one of my favourite subjects. The balance of interest in man, I should say, is with the making, with it, with life; in woman, with the breaking of the making into the you which is you alone, into death. Woman is at the end of the circle, she has only to rearrive at herself; man has first to learn that there is an end, before he can set out for it. And the learning he scorns as childish and the setting out as a deathbed rite. Woman he counts passive because she is at the end, and inferior because, being there, she turns round and starts all over again, to rearrive at herself. He adores her when she remains passive, that is his inferior; and despises her when she becomes his equal, that is, his superior. Well, they are worthless, both orders, when they are no more than they are. And when they are more than they are they are of no use to anyone but themselves; which is right but sudden and perhaps too mean for these mean times. For myself, I might confess to you, now that we are parting, that my happiest hours have been spent in the brotherly embrace of a humbug, not from want of womanliness in me or humbuggery in him, but because I was queen and needed repose. Ah me ah me ah me, what is this all about?

And such stickiness. How am I better than the rest of you? Because I have converted stickiness into elasticity and made myself free without wrenching myself free like a wayward pellet of paste. And what of so-and-so, your popular idol and my late consort? He was a strong man, powerfully sticky but not elastic; when he moved, he carried you along with him, he could not have moved otherwise, freely. And so he had great moments but not free moments. He was terribly alive but too terribly, never more than alive. He was merely monstrous, without the littlishness of biggishness. And what of so-and-so, my sometime lover? He was indeed a darling but an insufferable fop, washing away the stickiness till there was nothing left of him. And many others were darlings, of a sticky gracefulness and rhythm. But send me no more candidates, their embraces are either too heavy or too feeble; and I am light, hollow with death, but strong, of a tough, lively, it-ish exterior.

That is the trouble. You have no comprehension of appearance, what it is. Appearance is everything, what you are, what you are not. But your reach is sticky, not elastic; and so you get no further than reality, a pathetic proportion. Appearance is where the circle meets itself, where you live and do not live, where you are and are not dead. Appearance is everything, and nothing; bright and uppermost in a woman, to be sunk darkly inward; dumb, blind, darkly imbedded in a man, to be thrust brutally outward.

No, I am not confused, my blinking intelligences, but understand too clearly, and that is the trouble. I am unnecessary to you and therefore abdicate. Nor do I deny that blinking is sufficient for your purposes, which are sincere rather than statistical. Or that it would be for mine, for that matter – if I had purposes instead of queenliness. Which is my weakness, if you like – the tiresomeness of insisting upon the necessity of what is not necessary. I admit all; I am not wise but insistent, I am an unpaid hack of accuracy. I was queen from tiresomeness, and I abdicate from tiresomeness. I am not enjoying myself.

But perhaps you would like to know a little of my history, before I retire finally. My mother imagined that she suffered from bad eyesight; and to make it worse she wore a stocking round her eyes whenever possible: at home, a white stocking; abroad, a black stocking; and occasionally, to depress circumstances completely, a grey sock of my father's, fastened at the back of her head with a safety-pin. From which, our house was full of small oval rugs made by my mother out of the mates of the stockings which she wore round her eyes and which she was always losing. And these rugs made by my mother were not well made, because she imagined that she suffered from bad eyesight. From which my mother, whose character was all dreariness, acquired in my mind a hateful oddness. From which, I resolved to outdo her in oddness, so that I not only imagined that I suffered from good eyesight: I did actually suffer from it. And with this effect, that by the time I was of age I had no more than one rug, and this was very large and square, and it was well made, and not by me, though I suffered extremely from good eyesight. I lived far away from my mother, having no connection with her except to insist that she live far away from me; and my rug was composed of many small squares; and the pattern of each square was different; and yet the whole harmonious because the stuff was provided by me – the finest silk and velvet rags that I could command from others, and which I sorted and returned to them to be made into squares, a square by each of them. And so each who made a square was my subject. And so I became Queen. Perhaps now you will understand me better. But I am determined to abdicate, however you dissuade me. Before I was in reach of your praise, and liked neither your praise nor lack of it. It would not improve my feelings to put myself in reach of your pity. It was not for this that I told you my story. I told you my story to make my abdication irrevocable.

Yes, even now, it is painful to leave you. Not because I love you but because I am still untired; and after I leave you there will be no more to do. I shall indeed be more untired than ever. For while I was with you I worked hard (as you will not deny) and achieved a certain formal queenly tiredness from being unable to tire myself out no matter how hard I worked. But now concealment will be impossible: my insistence, that before I tried to make pleasant to myself (and to others) by trying to interest it in your affairs, will in the future be plainly horrible, as everything is horrible if sufficiently disinterested, that is, insistent. But the horror of my insistence will not be known to you, because I am abdicating. Nor am I to be dissuaded. The stroke that puts me in reach of your pity puts me out of reach of it as well.

I have said more than enough to satisfy my contempt of you. But I once loved you; and I have not punished myself sufficiently for that. What do I mean when I say that I once loved you? That I knew that being alive for you and me meant being more than alive. But you were afraid to admit it, though I was willing to take all the responsibility upon myself. Then I tried pretending to be just alive, I became for a time a partisan of timidity, in order to show you that being just alive was just pretending to be just alive. But when, aside, I reached for your hand, to press it, you dishonourably misunderstood me, you put me in the loathsome position of flirting with you. Then I tried extorting from you everything by means of which you lived, to show you that when you did not live you still lived. But again you wilfully misunderstood me and over-exerted yourself to supply me with what you thought to be my needs and what you assumed to be yours; and stubbornly refused to not live; and were disappointed when I did not applaud your inexhaustibility. And then once more

I tried. I loaded you with favours in order to show you that nothing made any difference; that the most as well as the least that you could endure by belonged to being just alive; that you were more than alive, dead. But you repulsed me with praise and gratitude; as you would now with pity and ingratitude if I permitted.

Then I said: 'I will leave them alone. I will content myself with being queen. Perhaps if I play my part conscientiously, at no time abandoning my royal manner, they will admit everything of their own accord, like a good, kind, though stupid, timid people.' But my grandeur you interpreted meanly as the grandeur of being just alive, instead of grandly, as the showy meanness of being just alive. You watched me act and admired my performance, but credited me with sincerity rather than talent; you refused to act yourself, paralysed by the emotions of an audience. My challenge, my drastic insistence, made you if anything more timid than you already were. You were hypnotized with admiration, you were, from the vanity you took in watching me, less than just alive. The men behaved more disgracefully than the women because to be a woman requires a strong theatrical sense: requires of one who is more than man to be less than man. For this reason I took many lovers, to humble back as many as possible into activity. And this brought all of us to

223

where we were in the beginning. And so I abdicate, leaving you once more to your heroism. With it you were intolerable to me; without it you were not only intolerable to me, but you would have eventually become intolerable to yourselves, especially after I had left you.

You know only how to be either heroes or cowards. But you do not know how to outwit yourselves by being neither, though seeming to be both. 'What,' you say indignantly, 'would you have us be nothing?' Ah, my dear people, if you could you would all shortly become Queens.

But perhaps it is best that you cannot. For if you became Queens you would in time find it necessary to abdicate, as I have; and you would, like me, be left extremely unhappy, of having succeeded in yourselves but failed in others.

Yes, it is true that I concealed from you the colour of my eyes. But the distance at which I kept you from myself was precisely the distance between being just alive and being more than alive. I was giving you a lesson in space, not a rebuff. Since we are at the end of things, you may come close to me and look well into my eyes ; but since you have not learned your lesson, you will still remain ignorant of their colour. Good-bye. I am going back to my mirror, where I came from.

NOTES ON THE TEXT

Page numbers reference those in the 1928 text. Riding frequently changes the phrasings of her source excerpts; when these changes are substantive, the correct original is included.

Abbreviations

A	*Anarchism Is Not Enough*
ABR	Wyndham Lewis, *The Art of Being Ruled*
CS	*Contemporaries and Snobs*
Enemy	Wyndham Lewis, *The Enemy: A Review of Art and Literature*, 3 Volumes
MM	C. K. Ogden and I. A. Richards, *The Meaning of Meaning*
Principles	I. A. Richards, *Principles of Literary Criticism*
RM	*Rational Meaning*
RR	Herbert Read, *Reason and Romanticism*
TWM	Wyndham Lewis, *Time and Western Man*

THE MYTH

(p. 12) *Words have three historical levels*: these levels presage the linguistic classifications of *Rational Meaning* (Charlottesville: University Press of Virginia, 1997), which Riding was working on in the 1930s under the titles *Dictionary of Exact Meanings* and then *Dictionary of Related Meanings*. In the finished text of *RM*, Riding distinguishes among "word," "term," and "name." We can find some correlation with two of her meanings here: "true words" are akin to what she later called "words" (possessing what *RM* calls "rational distinction") and "logical words" are like what she later subdivided into "names" ("an act of memory," according to *RM*) and "terms" (for *RM*, "not a full rational performance"). The most distinct change is in her later rejection of *A*'s "poetical words": their "supposed suggestive power," their interstitial and penumbral opportunities, opened the language – as she would later see it – to verbal uncertainty, undermining the strength of words even as it seemed to open them up to more opportunities for meaning.

WHAT IS A POEM?

(p. 16) *In Poe the old romanticism ended*: see Riding's strong critique of Poe in "The Facts in the Case of Monsieur Poe" (*CS*, 201–55), e.g., "the spring of imaginative invention in him was not disinterested, accurate curiosity, but a desire to produce a certain kind of effect in a reader estimated as having the mean intelligence of the masses."

MR DOODLE-DOODLE-DOO

(p. 22) *MR. DOODLE-DOODLE-DOO*: (Riding) Jackson reproduced this piece in *RM*, leaving out only the box chart which organizes a set of figures in the original. She also added a note to the end of the second sentence: "The implications of 'get' are somewhat obscure even to me, in this late time. I suggest that it be understood as implying engaging in hunting numbers with fierce scholarly sportsmanship" (504).

Deborah Baker finds "Mr. Doodle-Doodle-Doo" a satirical enactment of Roy Campbell's views of language. Campbell published a critical review of Riding, "A Question of Taste," in *Nation and Atheneum* (March 3, 1928). See *In Extremis: The Life of Laura Riding* (London: Hamish Hamilton, 1993), 164–66.

THE CORPUS

(p. 30) *the catechism instructing children*: from *The Book of Common Prayer: Catechism* (1662). Riding refers again to *The Book of Common Prayer* on p. 31, implicitly comparing the "Corpus" ("the outward and visible sign of a long-extinct grace") to the sacrament, as we see with reference to the *Common Prayer* source: "*Question*. What meanest thou by this word *Sacrament*? Answer. I mean an outward and visible sign of an inward and spiritual grace." Riding's point is that the *repeated* manifestation of a sanctioned (literary) event is the only manifestation the (canonizing) group recognizes.

JOCASTA

(p. 41) *Jocasta*: in Greek mythology, Jocasta is wife of Laius and mother (and then wife) of Oedipus. Riding recorded no comment on the significance of this title (but see *A*, 70, where she writes that "the 'best' prose and the 'best' poetry. . . . is all one: nostalgic, lascivious, masculine, Oedipean embrace of the real mother-body by the unreal son-mind.") In her prose work *Lives of Wives* (1939), Riding turns away from male historical figures to contemplate, in fictionalized accounts, the influence their wives had over them and over events. Naming a "Jocasta" complex may be a similar counter to the famous complex named for Jocasta's son (and husband). See Jocasta's speech in Sophocles, *Oedipus the King*, where she laments that "my words are spent in vain."

(p. 41) *Otto Spengler*: Oswald Spengler's *The Decline of the West*, 2 volumes, translated by Charles Francis Atkinson (New York: Knopf, 1926). Riding may dub Spengler "Otto" because Wyndham Lewis did so: neither she nor Graves knew Spengler personally.

(p. 41) *Wyndham Lewis*: throughout "Jocasta," Riding's principal critical frame of reference is to four volumes by Lewis: *Time and Western Man* (London: Chatto & Windus, 1927), *The Art of Being Ruled* (1926; reprint edited by Reed Way Dasenbrock, Santa Rosa: Black Sparrow, 1989), and *The Enemy. A Review of Art and Literature*, edited by Wyndham Lewis, Vols. 1 and 2 (London: Arthur Press, January and September 1927). Reprints of the latter include all three volumes of the journal, January 1927 to First Quarter 1929 (New York: Kraus Reprint, 1967; Santa Rosa: Black Sparrow, edited by David Peters Corbett). Riding and Graves were personally acquainted with Lewis, as her remark on page 44 suggests. Several letters survive between Riding and Lewis, all but one exchanged between 1927 and 1929, and her remarks about Lewis in an unpublished memoir indicate that she found him intellectually stimulating but ultimately too competitive and success-oriented.

Though he makes little mention of Spengler in *ABR*, Lewis is strongly critical of him in *TWM*. Using his term "the *time-mind*," Lewis says that history, biography, and autobiography are products of obsession with time. The issue begins with an epigraph from *Plutarch's Moralia* on the necessity "that we should hear the truth from our enemies." Riding agrees with Lewis's attacks on Spengler's organizing "historical sense"; she sees a similar time-sense carried out in an artistic context in T. S. Eliot's "Tradition and the Individual Talent."

(p. 42) *to give 'compendious' names*: unidentified. The context suggests that Riding derives the word from Lewis. *Anarchism* includes a handful of quoted single words or phrases, almost all likely to be from Lewis, whose sources could not be certainly identified.

(p. 45) *'I am for the physical world'*: Lewis, *TWM*, 113.

(p. 46, note) *Mr. Lewis does not like Blake*: in *Enemy* 2, Lewis characterizes his literary "enemies" Stein and Joyce as either "frantic" or indirect: "they seem persuaded, with the mystic, Williams Blake, that the 'roads of genius' are 'crooked,' always. . . . [But] [t]he road of genius is usually straight, and what it utters it utters simply" (xi).

(p. 47) *Royal Academy*: Riding refers to the conservative tendencies of the Royal Academy of Arts, founded in 1768 and still headquartered in London. Wyndham Lewis strongly criticized the Royal Academy: see *Wyndham Lewis on Art: Collected Writings 1913–1956*, edited by Walter Michel and C. J. Fox (New York: Funk & Wagnalls, 1969).

(p. 48) *'the unabashed Defoe'*: Alexander Pope, *The Dunciad Variorum* (1729) Book II, line 139: "Earless on high, stood un-abash'd Defoe." See *The Poems of Alexander Pope*, ed. John Butt (New Haven: Yale, 1963), 384.

(p. 48) *E. M. Forster*: Riding's authorized biographer, Elizabeth Friedmann, speculates that Riding's conversation with Forster might well have taken place in January 1926, at a dinner party two days after her arrival in London. She wrote to one of her friends that she "liked him better than any" other literary friends of Robert Graves and his wife Nancy Nicholson; but Friedmann finds no evidence that Riding and Forster developed a friendship.

(p. 54, note 1) *C. K. Ogden's and I. A. Richards' The Meaning of Meaning*: Riding is summarizing a number of their arguments. *The Meaning of Meaning. A Study of the Influence of Language Upon Thought and of the Science of Symbolism* (1923; New York: Harcourt Brace, 1925) was a very successful publication, a kind of popular investigation of the problems of Saussurean linguistics, which went into eight editions by 1948.

NOTES ON THE TEXT

(p. 55) *a novel by Rebecca West*: *The Judge* (New York: Doran, 1922). The passage Riding refers to is as follows:
"She held an egg against the vibrating place in her
throat, and, shaken with silent weeping, thought how
full of delights for the sight and touch was this world
she was going to leave. . . . Even a potato roasted in its
skin, if it was the right floury sort, had an entrancing,
ethereal substance; one could imagine that thus a cirrus cloud might taste in the mouth" (173–74). Also see
Riding's poem "For Rebecca West (On Reading *The
Judge*)" in *First Awakenings* (89). According to Deborah
Baker, Riding read *The Judge* in 1922. West's novel tells
of a penurious young woman, full of grand dreams of
independence, who is swept up into the ultimately ru-
inous arms of a dark and handsome stranger, customer
of the firm where she is employed as a typist. Mothers
and motherhood, it turns out, are the fatal problem
for both heroine and hero, as indeed for more than a
few characters in Riding's work.

(p. 55, note) *'Enchanted Wood of Words'*: Ogden and
Richards, *MM*, 138. The subsequent quotation (*'main
topics of discussion'*) is also from *MM*, 138.

(p. 55, note) *'But in most matters . . . fictitious entities.'*: Ogden and Richards, *MM*, 206.

(p. 56, note) *'In evocative speech the essential considerations is
[sic]'*: Ogden and Richards, *MM*, 239.

(p. 56, note) Textual note: Riding has added an "s" to

the source's use of "consideration," thereby introducing a grammatical error.

(p. 56, note) *I. A. Richards, Science and Poetry*: Riding misquotes slightly. The original is as follows: "An essential peculiarity of poetry as of all the arts is that the full appropriate situation is *not* present." See *Science and Poetry*, second edition (1926; London: Kegan Paul, 1935), 25.

(p. 57, note) *'The transference from the magical view'*: Richards is writing of a change in world view, in "general intellectual background," which is reflected in the poet: "The central dominant change may be described as the *Neutralization of Nature*, the transference from the Magical View of the world to the scientific" (*Science and Poetry*, 52).

(p. 57, note) *'pseudo-statements' of poetry*: see Richards, *Science and Poetry*, 62–74, in which he discusses the gap between scientific truth and poetic pondering of unscientific questions of existence.

(p. 58) *'She looked up over her knitting . . . to meet her lover'*: see *To the Lighthouse*, ed. Susan Dick (Oxford: Blackwell Publishers, 1992), 55–56. In other editions, see part I ("The Window"), section XI. Riding slightly misquotes one of Woolf's sentences: in place of "if one was alone, one leant to inanimate things," Riding puts "if one was alone, one leant to things, inanimate things."

(p. 62) *attacking James Joyce or Sherwood Anderson or D. H. Lawrence*: Riding refers to Lewis, *TWM* (preface and chapter XVI) and *Enemy* 2. Lewis devotes the bulk of the latter to a discussion and critique of matters of race, class, and politics, in part as they are depicted in Anderson's and Lawrence's works. See "Paleface," *Enemy* 2, 3–112, and especially 26 ff. Also see note to p. 78, below.

(p. 63) '*whether we should set out . . . the whole of our datum*': see *TWM*, 112. Lewis's phrasing is as follows: "whether we should set out to transcend our human condition (as formerly Nietzsche and then Bergson claimed that we should); or whether we should translate into human terms the whole of our datum."

(p. 63) *I. A. R. Richards*: Riding is referring to *Principles of Literary Criticism* (1924; rpt. San Diego: Harcourt Brace, 1985), 7 and 16.

(p. 64) '*The means whereby to identify*': Spengler, *Decline*, Vol. I, 4.

(p. 66) *Dr. Whitehead*: Riding refers to Lewis' discussion of Alfred North Whitehead's *Science and the Modern World* (New York: Macmillan, 1925) in *TWM*, 267ff.

(p. 67, note) '*We have a god-like experience*': Lewis, *TWM*, 385. The subsequent reference to Lewis is from *TWM*, 388.

(p. 67, note) *Mr. Eliot*: "the conflict between intuition and intelligence" refers to a characteristic binary in T. S. Eliot's writings—phrased, for example, as the difference between "*poetic*" and "*intellectual* lucidity" in his essay on Dante. For Eliot, "genuine poetry can communicate before it is understood." See his *Selected Essays 1917–1932* (New York: Harcourt Brace, 1932), 200–201.

(p. 68, note) *'Human individuality is best regarded'*: Lewis, *TWM*, 382. The subsequent reference to Lewis is also from 382 (Riding neglects to cite "*alone*" in italics, as Lewis did).

(p. 70, note) *'The Faustian soul looks'*: Spengler, *Decline*, Vol. I, 188. Spengler's full sentence is as follows: "The Faustian soul looks for an immortality to follow the bodily end, a sort of marriage with endless space, and it disembodies the stone in its Gothic thrust-system (contemporary, we may note, with the 'consecutives' in church music) till at last nothing remained visible but the indwelling depth- and height-energy of this self-extension." Spengler's "third-dimensional extension" is simultaneously an architectural and a metaphysical concept, deriving from his analysis of the Egyptian use of stone monuments for the dead.

(p. 71, note) *'somehow we are in nature'*: unidentified. Presumably it occurs in, or paraphrases a passage from, Spengler's *Decline*. The subsequent reference (*'the "I" overwhelms the "Thou"'*) is from Spengler, *Decline*, Vol. I, 192.

(p. 72) *John Middleton Murry*: a prolific journalist and critic whose approaches were romantic, pacifist, and biographical, in contrast to the dominant critical tendencies of modernism. He was a founding editor of *Adelphi* magazine (1923–1948), which was in its heyday in the late 1920s.

(p. 73) *'Logic is a kind of mathematic'*: Spengler, *Decline*, Vol. I, 57. Spengler's sentence reads as follows: "Logic is always a kind of mathematic and vice versa." The subsequent reference (*'Nature is to be handled scientifically, History poetically'*) is also from *Decline*, Vol. I, 96.

(p. 74) *'becoming'* and *'become'*: Riding is reacting to Spengler's distinction between these "two kinds of world-notion": "He who looks at the becoming and fulfilling [in kinds of understanding], experiences History; he who dissects them as become and fulfilled cognizes Nature" (*Decline*, Vol. I, 96–97).

(p. 76) *'Cochran's Revue'*: C. B. Cochran (later Sir Charles Cochran) was an extremely successful theatrical producer, especially of musical revues, at the London Pavilion during the 1920s and 1930s. Riding's official biographer, Elizabeth Friedmann, notes in private correspondence with me that Riding attended at least one of Cochran's London revues, in 1936, to see Graves' daughter Jenny Nicholson perform as a dancer.

(p. 78, note) *'morbid fondness for other races, so severely condemned by Mr. Lewis'*: Lewis discusses the problem of race matters in several parts of *TWM*, *ABR*, and *Enemy*. See for example *TWM*, 220–21, in which Lewis disparages Spengler's pity for Indians and Greeks as a "colonizing" impulse; *TWM*, 277, in which Lewis criticizes Spengler's tendency to attribute generalized characteristics to races and nations; and *TWM* 300–303, in which Lewis is scathing about the colonial brutalities and subsequent cultural paternalism of "the White European." Also see *ABR*, 109.

In "Paleface" (*Enemy* 2, 3–112), Lewis condemns Sherwood Anderson and D. H. Lawrence for being sentimental about "savage" races. Lewis carries out here the sort of racial and cultural generalizing for which he condemns Spengler in *TWM*. Lewis declares his preference for "the average white European" over the average Native American or African, assuming that the first possesses more consciousness, more thinking, than the second (60). To be sure, this preference is meant to counter Anderson and Lawrence; still Riding finds it justly distasteful and unthinking.

While it is impossible to excuse the *language* at the end of Riding's footnote, her praise of the "jazz nigger" is best understood as praise for the perceptual possibilities within what Trotsky called "the privilege of historical backwardness" (in *The Russian Revolution*, edited by F. W. Dupee; [New York: Doubleday, 1959], 3). Her description of the "jazz nigger" as "an individual, unreal, paleface Jew" is another way of putting the paradoxically liberated and perceptive position Riding ascribes to groups deemed inferior according to their race, religion, or gender. See below, second note to page 85.

(p. 81, note) *Bradley's Absolute*: see Lewis, *TWM*, 234–35, 384, 446, 453–54. Lewis refers repeatedly to F. H. Bradley's *Appearance and Reality* (1893), claiming that

Bradley is "discouraged and crushed, himself, by the contradictory, invisible weight of his Absolute. *Nothing* satisfies in his world" (*TWM*, 384). Riding may be responding to both Bradley and Lewis when she writes, elsewhere in *A*, that "[a]ppearances do not deceive if there are enough of them" (19). This allusion might also be a dig at T. S. Eliot, who wrote his thesis on Bradley's idealist philosophy.

(p. 84) *'That the critical spirit . . . in the rarest individuals'*: Herbert Read, *Reason and Romanticism: Essays in Literary Criticism* (rpt. New York, Haskell House, 1974), 15–16. Riding has inserted ellipses, though there are none in Read's text. The subsequent reference to Read is from p. 23.

(pp. 84–85) *'a capacity to receive all knowledge'*: Read, *RR*, 23. Riding leaves out a word; the original ends as follows: "to build up a positive attitude on this clear and serene perceptual basis."

(p. 85) *'poetry is, in short, delectation'*: Read, *RR*, 26. The subsequent reference to Read is also from p. 26.

(p. 85, note) *'"Classical" is for me anything'*: Lewis, *Enemy* 2, 99–100. In *TWM*, 9–10, Lewis discusses oppositions between "romantic" and "classical"; on 282–95, Lewis discusses Spengler's "antithetic 'Classical' and 'Faustian'" vocabulary as well as the idea of the "classical."

The next reference to Lewis (*'we should grow more and more polite'*) is from *Enemy* 2. Lewis is advocating race separateness, and more generally separation between different classes of people (what Riding terms his "courteous prejudice"): "we cannot, in fact, be polite enough to all those other kinds of men that we are called upon to pass our time with upon the face of this globe. We should grow more and more polite; but, if possible, see less and less of those other kinds of men" (101).

The third Lewis reference (*'Mr. Lewis's objections to Bolshevism'*) is also to *Enemy* 2. Lewis damningly compares the emphasis on "*education* and *training*" in Jesuit and Bolshevik doctrine (xxix), and he claims that "the teaching of communism has nothing to do with art or literature, and is the sworn enemy of the intellect" (98). In *TWM*, Lewis also objects to the forces that are encouraging fascism: the Darwinism of Nietzsche's "will to power" and Bergson's "creative evolution" "has brought in its wake all the emotional biology and psychology that has resulted in these values, for which fascismo is the latest political model" (209).

(p. 86) *'the sum total of awareness'*: Read, *RR*, 27. Subsequent references to Read are as follows: *'emotional apprehension of thought'* (55) and *'. . . we find in Donne'* (43), slightly misquoted. The original is as follows: "we find in Donne a mind poised at the exact turn of the course of philosophy—drawing his inspiration right back from scholastic sources, and yet at the same time eagerly surveying the new future promised by the science of Copernicus and Galileo. Chapman, on the other hand, is in a remarkable degree the forerunner of humanist philosophy—of Hume and Spinoza in particular. He is aware, above all things, of 'the consent and sacred harmony of life'."

(p. 87, note) *'to their undoing'*: Lewis, *ABR*, 109.

'Let us rather meet with the slightest smile': Lewis, *Enemy* 2, 110.

Mr Ford admits: Lewis, *ABR*, 43. Riding quotes Lewis directly.

Tacitus, possibly: Lewis discusses Tacitus in *Enemy* 1, 170, and *TWM*, 255–56.

'The Russian workman and peasant': Lewis, *Enemy* 2, 93. Lewis uses a small-case "russian," as in all his uses of nationalized adjectives.

'against human reason, motiveless': Lewis, *Enemy* 2, 93. Lewis states his point somewhat differently: "henceforth all those forms of organized violence must be gone into absolutely against human reason; they are henceforth motiveless, and hence mad."

the 'young catholic student': Lewis, *Enemy* 2, 115. On the first page of the essay "Towards Reintegration," by Henry John, Lewis notes that "This is the third section of a long essay. It is by a young catholic student."

'that some bank-clerk on a holiday': Lewis, *Enemy* 2, 129.

'traverses a wood with complete safety': Lewis, *Enemy* 2, 129.

(p. 87–88) *On Dante and Guido Cavalcanti*: Read, *RR*, 46.

(p. 88) *Mr. Read then quotes*: Read, *RR*, 46. Riding substitutes one word; the original begins: "'The poet was inspired with an overmastering desire . . .'"

(p. 88, note) *Baron von Hugel's definition*: see "Towards Reintegration," by Henry John, in *Enemy* 2, 131–32. John cites von Hugel's *Official Authority and Living Religion* (Essays, 2nd series), presumably referring to Baron Friedrich von Hugel, *Essays and Addresses on the Philosophy of Religion* (London: J. M. Dent, 1931).

Lewis publishes John's essay presumably because it shores up his claims for the usefulness of authority but also because it chimes in against what both writers see as the increasing (and anti-intellectual) "sensationism" of western experience.

(p. 89) *'The true metaphysical poet'*: Read, *RR*, 52. Three subsequent references to Read are as follows: *'Leibnitz* [sic] *has defined'*: *RR*, 53; *'the poet is in a very real sense'*: *RR*, 56; *'to the modern physicists'*: *RR*, 57.

(p. 89) *T. S. Eliot is a serious moralist*: Riding reacted strongly to Eliot's review in the July, 1927 *Criterion*, in which he dismisses Gertrude Stein's work as "barbaric." See Riding's "T. E. Hulme, The New Barbarism, & Gertrude Stein" (*CS*, 123–99), for a lengthy critique of Eliot's attack on Stein.

(p. 90) *Criterion*: *The Criterion* was published from October 1922 until January 1939, with Eliot as its primary editor.

(pp. 91–2) *'By this proposed transfer . . . which apprehends them'*: Lewis, *TWM*, 171. Riding inserts a comma between *"objective"* and *"material."*

(p. 93) *'Mr. Ludovici is engaged'*: T. S. Eliot, *The Monthly Criterion*, v. 6 (July 1927), 69. Eliot is reviewing five books, including Anthony M. Ludovici's *A Defence of Conservatism*. The subsequent references on pp. 93–94 are from the same review (70–71).

(p. 93) Textual note: there should be ellipses inserted in the citation, as follows: "in harmony with Republicanism. . . . The problem of Toryism should be rather"; and "parliamentarians" should be capitalized.

(p. 95) *Mr. Roger Fry*: see *Transformations. Critical and Speculative Essays on Art* (Chatto & Windus, 1927; reprint New York: Books for Libraries, 1968), 3.

(p. 95) *Mr. Richards, we learn*: see *Transformations*, 3–10. Fry is referring to the argument in *Principles of Literary Criticism* that the experience of beauty is a matter of what the observing subject feels rather than of the quality (in Fry's words, "pure" or "impure") of the work of art. This argument permeates Richards' book, but see *Principles*, 20–21, for a sample statement of it.

(p. 95) *what T. E. Hulme called the world of religious and ethical values*: see *Speculations: Essays on Humanism and the Philosophy of Art*, edited by Herbert Read (London: Routledge & Kegan Paul, 1924). Riding refers to the following passage by Hulme: "Let us assume that reality is divided into three regions, separated from one another by absolute divisions, by real discontinuities. (1) The inorganic world, of mathematical and physical science, (2) the organic world, dealt with by biology, psychology and history, and (3) the world of ethical and religious values" (5).

(p. 97) *it is self; not* his *self, but self*: see Appendix II in this edition. See also, for comparison, Lewis' 1925 essay "The Physics of the Not-Self," reprinted in *Collected Poems and Plays of Wyndham Lewis*, edited by Alan Munton (Manchester: Carcanet, 1979), 193–204.

(p. 97) *Mr. Fry describes the reaction to works of art*: see *Transformations*. Fry compares the sense of relation in mathematics, "abstract mental constructions," to the sense of emotional relation in the appreciation of a work of art: "Here I conceive the emotional states due to the apprehension of relations may be extremely similar to those aroused by the esthetic apprehension" (6).

(p. 98) *'the esthetic emotion'*: Fry, *Transformations*, 5. The subsequent reference to Fry (*'In literature there is no immediate sensual pleasure'*) is from p. 4.

(p. 99) *Mr. Fry quotes Dr. Bradley*: Riding slightly misquotes. The original begins: "'For its nature is to be not a part'" (Fry, *Transformations*, 8). Fry is quoting from A. C. Bradley's essay "Poetry for Poetry's Sake," in *Oxford Lectures on Poetry* (London: Macmillan, 1926), 5. Bradley writes about the impossibility of separating form and content and about the nature of "pure poetry." Riding's summary judgment of Bradley's subject as "about romantic humanity" is not far off the mark, when we consider that he believes "pure poetry" is "a spirit. It comes we know not whence. It will not speak at our bidding, nor answer in our language" (27). The first main difference between Riding and Bradley here arises from the fact that Bradley groups poetry with the other arts, finding in their incommensurabilities a like resistance to paraphrase. Riding, on the other hand, finds unique problems and possibilities in the fact that poetry's material is language. The second main difference between Bradley and Riding is the one that Riding expresses in her objection to his idea of a poetic "world": Bradley, like Lewis, posits that "the ultimate nature of Art" is somehow explicable, while Riding begins and ends *Anarchism* in the conviction that the poetic "unreal" is outside of explanatory possibilities.

(p. 101) *Mr. Read blames Mr. George Moore*: Read, *RR*, 61–62.

(p. 102) *'Don Quixote'*: Lewis, *TWM*, 193 (both quotations). Riding inserts two commas (after "Quixote" and "Wadman").

(p. 103) *'the arts are the supreme form'*: Richards, *Principles*, 26. The subsequent reference to Richards (*'systematization of impulses'*) is to p. 51.

(p. 104) *'minute particulars'*: Richards, *Principles*, 61.

(p. 104) *the Revolutionary Simpleton*: see Lewis, *TWM*, chapter VI. Lewis calls Pound an example of this type, "a genuine *naïf*" (38). The subsequent references to Lewis are from *TWM*, 121.

(p. 105) *'world by itself'*: Richards, *Principles*, 74 and 77. The subsequent quotation (*'a copy of the real world'*) is also repeated on those two pages. Richards is quoting from Bradley's *Oxford Lectures on Poetry*, 5 (see note to p. 99, above).

(p. 106) *'has the most great minds'*: Richards, *Principles*, 71.

(p. 107) *'We are our bodies'*: Richards, *Principles*, 83. The subsequent references to Richards are from pp. 83–84 and 88. Riding changes one excerpt; the original is as follows: "To be cognisant of anything, to know it, is to be influenced by it" (*Principles*, 88).

(p. 108) *'Rhythm is that property'*: Read, *RR*, 75. Read is quoting from E.A. Sonnenschein, *What Is Rhythm* (Oxford, 1925). The subsequent references to Read are from p. 87; in one case, Read's phrasing differs substantially: "we must all realize by now that no good artist exists who is not, at every point of his career, firstly a good critic."

(p. 109) Textual note: unclosed parenthetical presumably closes that sentence; i.e., "(Mr. Read's phrase[)]."

(p. 109) *'the narrowness of criticism'*: Read, *RR*, 103. The subsequent references to Read are from *RR*, 90–92.

(p. 110) *'Jung,' Mr. Read says'*: Read, *RR*, 90. The subsequent reference to Read is from p. 106.

(p. 115) *'no adequate literary equivalent in England'*: Read, *RR*, 71.

(p. 122) *'beginning again and again'*: Riding may be para-phrasing Lewis, *TWM*, 347, in which he expresses this notion of self re-beginnings. The subsequent reference (*Mr. Lewis's concrete, 'stable' person*) is to *TWM*, 352.

(p. 125) *'For the former generals'*: unidentified. Riding may be quoting from one of Graves' sources for what became his popular historical novel *I Claudius* (1934). Graves explains that Tacfarinas was a Numidian chief and Roman deserter: "He was for a long time known as the 'Laurel-giver' because three generals . . . had each in turn defeated him and been awarded triumphal or-naments" (300).

(p. 128) *'We are surface-creatures'*: Lewis, *TWM*, 387. The subsequent reference (*'God becomes the supreme symbol of our separation'*) is from *TWM*, 446.

(p. 129) *The novel is a 'spongy tract'*: E .M. Forster, *Aspects of the Novel* (London: Edward Arnold, 1927), reprint edited by Oliver Stallybrass (Middlesex: Penguin, 1976), 25. Forster continues: "it is bounded by two chains of mountains neither of which rises very abruptly – the op-posing ranges of Poetry and of History – and bounded on the third side by a sea" (25). The subsequent refer-ences to Forster are also from *Aspects*, 73–81. See note to pp. 47–48, above.

(p. 130) *'In Dostoevsky the characters'*: Forster, *Aspects*, 122.

245

"Fantasy" and "Pattern and Rhythm" are the titles of Forster's sixth and eighth chapters, respectively. Riding's subsequent quotations from and references to Forster are from pages 130, 134, 135, and 145–46.

(p. 131) *'rhythm is sometimes quite easy'*: Forster, *Aspects*, 146. The subsequent quotation is also from Forster; the original is as follows: "When we isolate the story like this from the nobler aspects through which it moves, and hold it out on the forceps – wriggling and interminable, the naked worm of time – it presents an appearance that is both unlovely and dull" (42).

HOW CAME IT ABOUT?

(p. 134) *There is a woman in this city*: the remainder of this piece (from "How Came It About?") was first published as "Fragment" in *transition* 10 (January 1928), 47–48. "How Came It About?," "Hungry To Hear," "In A Café," and "An Anonymous Book" were reprinted in *Progress of Stories* (1982).

Riding called these late pieces "quasi-fictional." Her official biographer Elizabeth Friedmann posits, in private correspondence with me, that the "woman" of this piece may have been Virginia Woolf, who had little liking for Riding. See Woolf's letter to Ethel Smyth (May 9, 1931) in Volume 4 of *The Letters of Virginia Woolf*, edited by Nigel Nicolson (New York: Harcourt Brace, 1980).

(p. 135) *For if one eat my meat*: John Donne, from Satire 2 ("Sir; though [I thanke God for it] I do hate").

NOTES ON THE TEXT

Donne directs his satire against bad writing, and, in this couplet, against poets who steal others' poetic ideas and pass them off as their own.

HUNGRY TO HEAR

(p. 136) *Hungry to Hear*: first published in *transition* 12 (March 1928), 62.

IN A CAFÉ

(p. 138) *In a Café*: first published in *transition* 7 (October 1927), 31–33. Reprint in *Transition Workshop*, edited by Eugene Jolas (New York: Vanguard Press, 1949), 114–115. Also reprinted in *In transition: A Paris Anthology*, introduced by Noel Riley Fitch (London: Secker & Warburg, 1990), 182–83.

(p. 140) *'Up to the last she retained'*: unidentified. According to Paul O'Prey, "*The Daily Mail* was the only newspaper read regularly by Graves and Riding during these years [late 1920s]; they decided that as all newspapers were awful they might just as well read what they considered to be the worst." See Robert Graves, *In Broken Images: Selected Correspondence*, edited by Paul O'Prey (Mt. Kisco: Moyer Bell, 1982), 362.

AN ANONYMOUS BOOK

(p. 164) *(1) Scientific attentiveness*: Riding adopts and modifies the definition of "curiosity" provided in the 1927 *Webster's New International Dictionary of the English Language*. The first two entries in the *Webster's* definition are as follows: "1. Careful attention; nicety; exactness; fastidiousness. Obs. 2. Careful or artistic workmanship; elaboration; detail. Obs or archaic." Riding effectively injects this definition with science, technology, morality, religion, and ethics.

THE DAMNED THING

(p. 187) *The Damned Thing*: this essay exhibits both agreement with and reaction against Lewis' writings on sex and womanhood. See for example "Romance and the Moralist Mind" in *TWM*, where Lewis asserts that *"Where any sex-nuisance is concerned, the greek indifference is the best specific"* (19). See also "Man and Shaman" in *ABR*, where Lewis' often irksome sexism is the opposite side of the coin from Riding's. For all that "women are equipped and appointed" in new ways, "yet they are not queens"; indeed (according to an unspecified "lady" writer in the *Sunday Express*) "the Girl of the Period is neglected and dethroned" (242–43).

For more on Riding's views of women, see *The Word "Woman" and Other Writings*, edited by Elizabeth Friedmann and Alan J. Clark (New York: Persea, 1993).

(p. 190) *Sex, in the imagery of Stendhal*: Riding refers to *De L'Amour* by way of Havelock Ellis. Ellis refers to Stendhal's claim in chapter XVII that a person who is in love locates the feeling of desire in the physical attributes of the beloved, to the point of idealizing the loved one's physical defects. See Ellis, *Studies in the Psychology of Sex*, vol. II (1906; reprint New York: Random

House, 1936), part I, 9–13. And see Stendhal's *De L'Amour* (1826; Vienne: Manz, 1890) for the source of Riding's reference to the "naked branch" of sex: "par le mécanisme de la branche d'arbre garnie de diamants dans la mine de Salzbourg, tout ce qui est beau et sublime au monde fait partie de la beauté de ce qu'on aime" (29).

Riding makes several subsequent references to Ellis' massive work (she incorrectly hyphenates his name), which is characterized by minute descriptions of case studies in such subjects as sexual abnormality, narcissism, marriage, maternity, prostitution, menstruation, and divorce laws. All of these subjects are introduced and followed by Ellis's deductions about the nature of these cases and the conclusions they suggest about the sexual subjects at hand.

(p. 194) *'erotic' symbolism*: "Erotic Symbolism" is the title of the first section in part I of Ellis, vol. II (1–114). Ellis best defines it as the "tendency to isolate and dissociate any single character from the individual and to concentrate attention upon that character at the expense of the attention bestowed on the individual generally. . . . [I]t may be said that every sexual perversion, even homosexuality, is a form of erotic symbolism, for we shall find that in every case some object or act that for the normal human being has little or no erotic value, has assumed such value in supreme degree; that is to say, it has become a symbol of the normal object of love" (2). Riding's subsequent allusions to "foot symbolism" (195) refer to the second chapter of "Erotic Symbolism," which is mostly on the topic of "[f]oot-fetichism and [s]hoe-fetichism" (15–46).

(p. 195) *'And up the rosy pathway'*: unidentified. Though Riding attributes these lines to Lord Byron, neither scholars nor databases corroborate that attribution.

(p. 199) *Shelley, on being read the passage about Geraldine's breast*: Riding refers to the prefatory material to John Polidori's *The Vampyre*, first published in 1819. The "Extract of a Letter from Geneva, with Anecdotes of Lord Byron, &c.," apparently written by John Mitford, reports on the famous evening in Switzerland when Polidori, Shelley, Mary Shelley, Clair Clairmont and Lord Byron gathered to tell ghost tales to each other. When Byron began reciting the still unpublished "Christabel," "the whole took so strong a hold of Mr. Shelly's [*sic*] mind, that he suddenly started up and ran out of the room. . . . his wild imagination having pictured to him the bosom of one of the ladies with eyes." See The Vampyre *and* Ernestus Berchtold; or, The Modern Oedipus: *Collected Fiction of John William Polidori*, edited by D. L. Macdonald and Kathleen Scherf (Toronto: University of Toronto Press, 1994), 182–83.

(pp. 199–200) *'We must, as Bölshe declares'*: Ellis, vol. II, part III, 112–13. According to his index, Ellis is quoting James Hinton. Though Ellis does not identify the Hinton source, he soon edited and introduced a reprint of Hinton's book *Life In Nature* (London: Elder Smith,

1862; rpt. New York: Dial, 1931). Riding has introduced the two erratum flags ("[*sic*]") into the quotation.

(p. 200) '*The nose receives the breath of life*': Ellis, vol. II, part II, 121.

(p. 204) '*Since marriage is not a mere contract*': Ellis, vol. II, part III, 480.

(p. 204) Textual note: need to insert close quotation mark at end of quoted sentence, as follows in Riding: "Havelock-Ellis says: 'Since marriage is not a mere contract, but a fact of conduct, and even a sacred fact, the free participation of both parties is needed to maintain it.[']"

(p. 205) *Havelock-Ellis further says*: Ellis, vol. II, part III, 494.

(p. 204) *Compare Shelley's argument*: Riding is presumably referring to Shelley's fragmentary "Essay on Marriage." The essay begins "Before the commencement of human society, if such a state can be conceived to have existed, it is probable that men like other animals used promiscuous concubinage." See *Shelley's Prose; or, The Trumpet of a Prophecy*, edited by David Lee Clark (Albuquerque: University of New Mexico Press, 1954), 215.

(p. 206) *Mrs. Willa Muir*: Riding quotes from Muir's short book, *Women: An Inquiry* (New York: Knopf, 1926), 26.

(p. 206) Textual note (errata): "Mrs. Willa Muir, is [*sic*] a short essay on *Woman* [*sic*]"

APPENDIX I

Three Commentaries on
Anarchism Is Not Enough (1974)

Transcribed from the Laura (Riding) Jackson and
Schuyler B. Jackson Collection, Division of Rare
and Manuscript Collections, Carl A. Kroch Library, Cornell University, #4608, Box 94, Fol. 711.
This transcription has been somewhat altered to
accord with a later six-page typescript by (Riding)
Jackson, presently in the private collection of Elizabeth Friedmann.

1974
L. J.

<u>Anarchism Is Not Enough</u> 1928

*<u>The Myth</u>. I begin in this book to try to move
from terrain of literary criticism in which I adopted
what seemed the only posture of honest criticism,
that is, opposition to the reigning critical con-
ventionalities, including those of the prestige-

*A little essay in <u>Anarchism Is Not Enough</u>

unconventionalities, the standardized opposition-criticisms, towards a terrain that would be both personal and have a general validity, including a validity in the area of critical judgement. I endeavor in the first piece, "The Myth," to disestablish as imperative background to considerations of "value" the great screen of cultural historical continuity that all articulate life-effort was assumed to have at its back as an illuminator of its particular significance in its time and its particular place. Away with <u>that</u> screen, I said. And I might be considered to have here made a first declaration of my later theme of the actuality I felt to be the main temporal actuality of my time, that it was a time in which historical time was at exhaustion-point. The end had come of the relevance, the "truth," of what meaning historical light sheds upon human problems of being, knowing, <u>and</u> defining. Poetry is both, there, for me, a life-line of salvation from the historical course of perpetuation of perpetuation, and a factor of the composite cultural doctrine in terms of which every new age is expected to express itself, even if the expression is in dispute with it. It can be seen as I proceed how I am suspicious of the terms of that doctrine, and make my own out [of] the rejection of them, in order to keep clear of speaking a language the words of which overflow with historical implications. I also reject the terms of that doctrine that depict the personal life, and (as I might have said had I used there the language of conventional sophistication) banal conceptions of humane relationship.

In the final paragraph, I hit at the main practical target of all my concern with breaking with historical repetition: the matter of <u>words</u>. I am in that time, of course, as a hitter at targets, acting in the faith of the poet-rôle as the rôle of hope of egress from the historical blind-alley of human destiny. I should be understood, there, in speaking of "true" words, words "of an intrinsic sense," as of a first "historical" level, as meaning a level at the furthest temporal reach from the practicalities of ordinary utterance and the impracticalities of the merely imagined real, expressed as if known in encounter. Each use of a word by one who recognizes the "true word" aspect of words, in their tortured division between the logical use of ordinary practicality and the illogical use of supposition's truth, wrenches it from the distortive clutch of "applied sense," the magnetic hold of the pretended real, and the mere hope of true use excited by recognition of the aspect of words as meaning by the values of truth: free, thus, in a state of utter uninvolvement in the history of its broken-up sense-character, a word can at least start, in use, <u>clean</u>. — This is the intellectual key to the little essay "The Myth."

1974
L. J.

[Further On My Writing On Poetry
in <u>Anarchism</u>, etc. — Incidental Pieces]

I endeavor in that book to extricate the identity of poet from the setting of the collective or synthetic notion of "reality." The "reality" I attack in this book is a reality of what I describe in one passage in it as made of belief. "Reality cannot escape from reality because it is made of belief . . ." My theme, then, is, the poet as one who does not live, think, speak, within the frame of a <u>concept</u> of reality; and it is poetry as of non-conceptual substance; and it is the poem as just itself. That is, I am letting the poetic function meet my sense of an ultimate fullness, perfection, of speaking, an <u>end</u> that words imply, promise, <u>demand</u>. So I say, in that book, in one of the little articles "A poem is nothing." I will not have this <u>pure</u> speaking classified as of the material of collective experience, or reality, subordinated to that as a <u>part</u> of it of a certain kind. I will have it only that the poem does not exist in that synthesis. Or exist by any device of argument that makes it generically a <u>peculiarity</u>.

In my removing poetry to what could only be classified from the point of view of collective reality as <u>nowhere</u>, I attack literature as compromising with conceptual reality in its representations of experience – but allow it relative virtue as accomplishing some purification of experience. I am "against" purposive "creation," purposive happiness-making; I try to bring, precipitate, these antagonisms of "position" into a focus in which their implications will be unmistakable by, as it were, destroying all possibilities of identification of them by comparison. I mean nothing that would fit into the generally governing conceptual differentiations between kinds of doing, experiencing, thinking, putting of thought into words. I try to surround the truth that I am trying to enunciate by nearly surrounding it as nearly communicable: I don't try to surround it as entirety surroundable for complete statement because I am afraid that my terms of statement might be fed by readers back in to the area of conceptual classification – and also afraid that I might myself err enough in the choice of them to nullify some of the point of my evaluating poetry, and being a poet, and poems, as on the side of perfection (the point that there is another side to "reality").

1974
L. J.

Language and Laziness
(a little essay in Anarchism Is Not Enough)

There is evident in this little piece the puzzle-
ment produced for me at that time by the general
state of linguistic expression and the discrepancy
between that and my inward apprehensions of the
potentialities of expression indicated in my own
experience of the potentialities of intelligence. I
see "language" at that time, as I meet it in expressive achievement around me, as an area of compromise between the potential and the actual
(which I do not accept as representative of the
potentialities of expression). Yet I also see language, by my sense of poetry as possibly the realm
of the true actual, i.e., the fulfilled potential, as
comprising the potential that is suppressed or
bartered away in "language as a form of laziness."
I am thinking here more of "intelligence," indeed,
than language[,] I seeing a standardizing of the
sayable in formulas of utterance comparable to
the convenience-notations of mathematics – the
words being as inexpressive, by the measure of a
fully-developed norm of intelligent expression, as
numbers. A number says very little – rather than
saying, it reduces the particular content of expression to an abstraction that squeezes particularity
out of expression.

The prose word is, by my intelligence's discomfort of the time, a stopping-point, a producer of stand-still in expression, intelligence itself. I note here, in autobiographical remark, that until I found a way to speak in poetry, I suffered intensely of consciousness of the poor quality of the speaking around me <u>everywhere</u>. In my reading, which was mainly in prose up to my college years, I took in impressions busily; I read much; but I did not feel that "things" were being "said," in what I read, rather that impressions were being produced by the words.

I think that the account I have given of my early reading experience is applicable to most of our self-education by reading: we are filled with impressions, additions to our direct experience, that our intelligence receives without being directly <u>addressed</u>. Words are little used in actual address from intelligence to intelligence. Even personal communication is hardly a saying from mind to mind, or, to phrase the matter more accurately, from intelligence to intelligence: the words spoken are used to transmit to the hearer's mind mental pictures in the speaker's mind that have not been brought definitively into expressive linguistic form.

In describing poetry as "an attempt to make language do more than express; to make it work," I

was associating "express" with the prevailing talkativeness, spoken and written, that had the blank,
routine quality of numbers. Language was not
working. What was said hung between people, they
took from what they said to one another something
extracted from the words – not the words themselves, in their liveness of <u>meaning</u>. What was generally spoken, or written, I could describe as
mathematics-like because of its inertness: the words
were put down to register something, a certain
something, but just that, and no more – the matter was not finished. Poetry seemed to allow for
<u>finishing</u> what was put down. Remarkably (as it
now seems to me in 1974), forty-six years ago I
both hoped otherwise from poetry, and also anticipated that it must fail in this. "Poetry always faces,
and generally meets with, failure," I wrote.

APPENDIX II

Author to Critic: Laura (Riding) Jackson on "Anarchism Is Not Enough," July 1974

(Extracted from "Comments on a study of my work — a draft, unpublished": TS transcript, Cornell University Library DRMC #4608, Box 95 Fol. 741; carbon MS, private collection Alan J. Clark. Transcribed and adapted by Alan J. Clark.)

Anarchism Is Not Enough begins with a few short pieces, mainly on poetry.... Then, a long solid core called "Jocasta," dealing much with poetry in its course, which in the whole deals with the matter of collective-real, individual real, individual unreal.... Then there are ... miscellaneous pieces, which mainly are treatments in quasi-fictional form with circumstances of a character difficult to identify as "real" or "unreal" — as it were exercises in the endeavor to avoid depicting a false realness.

• • •

This book is concerned with the placing of poetry, the poet, and, centrally & most importantly, the nature of the person who seeks to treat of main things of being, in thought & expression from a position of self-reliance as against reliance upon definitions of things delivered from socially constructed or philosophically systematized frames of authority. The *Anarchism* notion concerns not just "traditional poetics" but the entire social-philosophic collectivist pattern of "reality" and the contesting of that on merely individualistic grounds – and the question, what, if not that, i.e., the collectivist or the individualistic. I in my sense of the difficulty of locating the proper human position, the "real" real position of the human being, invented the term "individual-unreal," but over and over again in that book I point out that the use of this "unreal" is a use forced on me (in my then stage of defining the nature of this and that) by the actual unreality of the makeshift "reality" of social synthesis or philosophical (special intellectual society) synthesis. Not "sovereignty" [of the "unreal"] – just that which was not bogus. . . . What I am trying to get "across" in thus making the "unreal" serve me for identification for a <u>real</u> counter to the conventional-real is a very difficult perception of the inadequacy of existing conceptions of the nature of reality, physical nature, the human actuality, the <u>quality</u> of personal being, the character of the existent (the various existent). <u>If</u> I had, in my effort then, to invent that "unreal," the only hope for an explainer, interpreter, of good service to the reader <u>and</u> me, is to stress what I am trying to do, identify the difficulty.

• • •

I don't make a "dichotomy" of "physical life" and "thought." If I were going to plunge into such an area I would talk of mental life and life as the receptive experience of bodily existence. . . . Don't try to squeeze out of <u>Anarchism</u> a formula to apply to this "period." I deal with certain problems there of identification of what I was trying to do in being a poet and in my thinking and living, the kind of <u>different</u> way that I was endeavoring to pursue. . . . <u>Anarchism</u> deals with the task of knowing the kind of world environment and literary and intellectual atmospheres in it in which you are living <u>your</u> life. And what your values are in difference from what rules or runs in this environ. By the time of this book and of the <u>Love As Love</u> volume I had got myself as to the human world I was marking well-taught in certain things as to <u>it</u>, and I had got myself in my hold of <u>self-knowledge</u>, in relation to my work much increased in concentratedness, or of purpose, concentration upon the mind's will. . . . The title <u>[Love As Love, Death as Death]</u> is taken from a poem in which the poet's

insistence upon dealing with essentialities of experience in words used with strict regard for the essentialities of their meanings is as clear as a
blackboard lesson. . . . Those poems followed no
"definition." There is <u>reflection</u> in all the critical
writing of my way of applying myself to tasks of expressive verbal utterance in poetic form.

• • •

[Editor's note: the following are (Riding) Jackson's
comments on quotations selected by her corre-
spondent]

Man, as he becomes more man, becomes less
nature. He becomes unreal. (p. 64)

The human being, becoming more concentrat-
edly human, more singly human, becomes something not just of nature, but something apart, over
and above, and apart, and thus distinct from what
passes for the embracing reality.

• • •

The material with which an author works is not
reality but what he is able to disentangle from reality: in other words I think the identity is rather
of purity and unreality. An author must first of all
have a sure apprehension of what is self in him,
what is new, fresh, not history, synthesis, reality.
In every person there is the possibility of a small,

> pure, new, unreal portion which is, without refer-
> ence to personality in the popular social sense,
> self. . . . When this self has been *isolated* from all
> that is impression and impurity of contact in an
> individual, then a "thing," a work, occurs, it is dis-
> charged from the individual, it is self, not *his* self,
> but self. (pp. 96–7)

. You could here show the realness implicit in my
"unreal" of this book with that disentangling from
"reality" – reality there is plainly the <u>composite</u>, the
jumble of experience received as impressions. . . .
All you need for explanation or comment [here]
is to point to the insistence on purity of self, the
maintenance of this in the midst of experience,
self kept itself in experience: then there must issue
a pure version of the self's action of experiencing.

• • •

> Words in their pure use, which I assume to be
> their poetic use, are denials rather than affirma-
> tions of reality. The word *hat*, say, does not create
> a real hat: it isolates some element in the real hat
> which is not hat, which is unreal, the hat's self.
> (pp. 98–9)

I am using "reality" there in the entire context
of my discrimination real-unreal. A sympathetic interpreter could point to the reality that, according
to the argument quoted, was evoked with the word,

the realness of "the hat's self" as distinguished from the realness of hat as "thing." I should not <u>now</u> discuss words or things or reality in this way, but I was there carving out something that had never before been carved out by any one, and this was the reality of things as existent to the mind, which knew in terms of words. This is different from the Platonic conception, which involves an endeavor to isolate another reality from the reality of appearance, or things in their jumbled assemblage in numbers. Plato reduced the numbers of things to idea-forms, and synthesized these into his counter-reality to reality — and had thus a purity abstracted from <u>these</u>. My reality counter to the conventional reality, my attempted identification of it of that time, was that which the human self, <u>not</u> extracting its identity from the collective physical or social or any collective intellectual environment, was in itself, as real of itself, thus unreal by the collective modes of definition or identification. ... [Contrast with] "a Platonic form" could be ... helpful by indicating my concern with <u>locating</u> the individual real (under the name of individual-unreal), not of making a counter-reality to conventional, "obvious," reality out of abstraction. ...

[An interpreter of this (pp. 98–9) passage could, further, say that] Miss Riding's feeling about words used purely in poetry is that they convey the essential nature of things, instead of their circumstantial character, deal with them evaluatingly rather descriptively, as they are by a general, not just localized, vision.

SELECTED BIBLIOGRAPHY
OF WORKS BY LAURA RIDING

Editor's note: For a 1976 bibliography of Riding's works, see that compiled by Alan Clark for *Chelsea* 35 (1976), 228–39. Also see Joyce Piell Wexler's 1981 bibliography. For a list of archive materials, see Deborah Baker, *In Extremis: The Life of Laura Riding* (London: Hamish Hamilton, 1993), 425–26.

Americans. Los Angeles: Primavera, 1934.

Anarchism Is Not Enough. London: Cape; New York: Doubleday, 1928.

The Close Chaplet. London: Hogarth; New York: Adelphi, 1926.

Collected Poems. London: Cassell; New York: Random House, 1938.

Contemporaries and Snobs. London: Cape; New York: Doubleday, 1928. Reprint, St. Clair Shores: Scholarly Press, 1971.

Convalescent Conversations. By Madeleine Vara (pseudonym of Laura Riding). Deya: Seizin; London: Constable, 1936.

The Covenant of Literal Morality. London: Seizin, 1938.

Everybody's Letters. London: Barker, 1933.

Experts Are Puzzled. London: Cape, 1930.

Four Unposted Letters to Catherine. Paris: Hours, 1930. Reprint, New York: Persea, 1993.

Laura and Francisca. Deya: Seizin, 1931.

The Life of the Dead. London: Barker, 1933.

Lives of Wives. London: Cassell; New York: Random House, 1939. Reprint, Los Angeles: Sun & Moon, 1995.

Poems: A Joking Word. London: Cape, 1930.

Poet: A Lying Word. London: Barker, 1933.

Progress of Stories. Deya: Seizin; London: Constable, 1935. Reprint, New York: Dial, 1982.

The Second Leaf (broadside). Deya: Seizin, 1935.

Though Gently. Deya: Seizin, 1930.

A Trojan Ending. Deya: Seizin; London: Constable, 1937. Reprint, Manchester: Carcanet, 1984.

Twenty Poems Less. Paris: Hours, 1930.

Voltaire: A Biographical Fantasy. London: Hogarth, 1927.

The World and Ourselves. London: Chatto & Windus, 1938.

Ed., with Robert Graves. *Epilogue* I. Deya: Seizin; London: Constable, 1935.

———. *Epilogue* II. Deya: Seizin; London: Constable, 1936.

———. *Epilogue* III. Deya: Seizin; London: Constable, 1937.

As Laura (Riding) Jackson. "About the Fugitives and Myself." *The Carolina Quarterly* 47.3 (summer 1995): 73–87.

———. "As to a Certain Poem & Poetry" ("Lamenting

the Terms of Modern Praise"). *Chelsea* 47 (1988): 3–5.

———. "Bertrand Russell, and Others: The Idea of the Master-Mind." *Antaeus* 21/22 (spring–summer 1976): 125–35.

———. *Description of Life*. London: Targ; New York: Oliphant, 1980.

———. "Dr. Gove and the Future of English Dictionaries." *Denver Quarterly* 10.1 (spring 1975). Reprinted in *RM*.

———. "Engaging in the Impossible." *Sulfur* 10 (1984): 4–35.

———. *First Awakenings: The Early Poems of Laura Riding*. Manchester: Carcanet; New York: Persea, 1992.

———. "It Has Taken Long – From the Writings of Laura (Riding) Jackson." *Chelsea* 35 (1976): entire issue.

———. "On Ambiguity." *Modern Language Quarterly* 36.1 (March 1975). Reprinted in *RM*.

———. "The Matter of Metaphor." *Chelsea* 35 (1976). Reprinted in *RM*.

———. *The Poems of Laura Riding: A New Edition of the 1938 Collection*. Manchester: Carcanet; New York: Persea, 1980.

———. "The Promise of Words." *London Review of Books*, 7 September 1995: 23–24.

———. *Some Communications of Broad Reference*. Northridge: Lord John, 1983.

———. *The Telling*. London: Athlowe, 1972; New York: Harper & Row, 1973.

WORKS BY LAURA RIDING

————. "What, If Not a Poem, Poems?" *Denver Quarterly* 9.2 (1974): 1–13.

————. *The Word 'Woman' and Other Related Writings.* Edited by Elizabeth Friedmann and Alan J. Clark. New York: Persea, 1993.

Riding, Laura and Robert Graves. *A Pamphlet Against Anthologies.* London: Cape; New York: Doubleday, 1928. Reprint, New York: AMS, 1970.

————. *A Survey of Modernist Poetry.* London: Heinemann, 1927. Reprint, New York: Haskell House, 1969.

Riding, Laura and George Ellidge. *14A.* London: Barker, 1934.

(Riding) Jackson, Laura, and Schuyler B. Jackson. *Rational Meaning: A New Foundation for the Definition of Words.* Edited by William Harmon. Introduction by Charles Bernstein. Charlottesville: University Press of Virginia, 1997. Abbreviated in this bibliography as *RM.*

SELECTED CRITICAL
BIBLIOGRAPHY

Adams, Barbara. *The Enemy Self: Poetry and Criticism of Laura Riding.* Ann Arbor: UMI Research Press, 1990.

Review of *Anarchism Is Not Enough.* *Times Literary Supplement,* 16 August 1928: 590.

Baker, Deborah. *In Extremis: The Life of Laura Riding.* London: Hamish Hamilton, 1993.

Bernstein, Charles. "The Telling." In *Content's Dream: Essays, 1975–1984,* 340–42. Los Angeles: Sun and Moon, 1986.

Ciani, Daniela M. "Laura Riding's Truthfulness to the Word and to the Self." *Revue Française d'Études Américaines* 61 (Août 1994): 301–10.

Clark, Alan. "Riding, Laura." In *Contemporary Poets,* edited by J. Vinson et al., 1278–84. London: St. James, 1975.

Ford, Hugh. "The Seizin Press." In *Published in Paris: American and British Writers, Printers, and Publishers in Paris, 1920–1939,* 385–403. New York: Macmillan, 1975.

Fromm, Harold. "Myths and Mishegaas: Robert Graves and Laura Riding." *The Hudson Review* 44.2 (summer 1991): 189–202.

Graves, Richard Perceval. *Robert Graves: The Years with*

Laura, 1926–1940. London: Weidenfeld and Nicolson, 1990.

Heuving, Jeanne. "Laura (Riding) Jackson's 'Really New' Poems." In *Gendered Modernisms: American Women Poets and Their Readers,* edited by Margaret Dickie and Thomas Travisano, 191–213. Philadelphia: University of Pennsylvania Press, 1996.

Jacobs, Mark, and Alan Clark. "The Question of Bias: Some Treatments of Laura (Riding) Jackson." *Hiroshima Studies in English Language and Literature* 21 (1976): 1–29.

Kirkham, Michael. "Robert Graves's Debt to Laura Riding." *Focus on Robert Graves* 3 (December 1973): 33–44.

McGann, Jerome J. "Laura (Riding) Jackson and the Literal Truth." *Critical Inquiry* 18 (spring 1992): 454–73.

———. "The Challenge of Laura (Riding) Jackson." In *Black Riders: The Visible Language of Modernism,* 124–34. Princeton: Princeton University Press, 1993.

Masopust, Michael A. "Laura Riding's Quarrel with Poetry." *South Central Review* 2.1 (1985): 42–56.

Mathews, Harry. "Queen Story." In *Immeasurable Distances,* 109–133. Venice, California: Lapis, 1991.

Matthews, T. S. *Jacks or Better.* New York: Harper and Row, 1977. Revised as *Under the Influence.* London: Cassell, 1979.

Moran, James. "The Seizin Press of Laura Riding and Robert Graves." In *Printing Presses: History and Development from the Fifteenth Century to Modern Times,* 34–39. Berkeley: University of California Press, 1973.

Norris, Christopher C. "Laura Riding's *The Telling*: Language, Poetry, and Neutral Style." *Language and Style* 11 (summer 1978): 137–45.

Paddon, Seija H. "The Diversity of Performance/Performance as Diversity in the Poetry of Laura (Riding) Jackson and Eavan Boland." *English Studies in Canada* 22.4 (December 1996): 425–39.

Rasula, Jed. "A Renaissance of Women Writers." *Sulfur* 7 (1983): 160–72.

Roberts, Michael. Introduction. *The Faber Book of Modern Verse.* Edited by Michael Roberts. London: Faber, 1936.

Rosenthal, M. L. "Laura Riding's Poetry: A Nice Problem." *Southern Review* 21 (1985): 89–95.

Schultz, Susan M. "Laura Riding's Essentialism and the Absent Muse." *Arizona Quarterly* 48.1 (spring 1992): 1–24.

Temes, Peter S. "Code of Silence: Laura (Riding) Jackson and the Refusal to Speak." *PMLA* 109.1 (January 1994): 87–99.

Vendler, Helen. "The White Goddess!" *The New York Review,* 18 November 1993: 12–18.

Wallace, Jo-Ann. "Laura Riding and the Politics of Decanonization." *American Literature* 64.1 (March 1992): 111–26.

Wexler, Joyce Piell. *Laura Riding's Pursuit of Truth.* Athens: Ohio University Press, 1979.

———. *Laura Riding: A Bibliography.* New York: Garland, 1981.